MW00915311

Cuentos from the House on West Connecticut Avenue

By

Marta A. Lomeli

This book is a work of fiction. Places, events, and situations in this story are purely fictional. Any resemblance to actual persons, living or dead, is coincidental.

© 2002, 2004 by Marta A. Lomeli. All rights reserved.

No part of this book may be reproduced, stored in a retrieval system, or transmitted by any means, electronic, mechanical, photocopying, recording, or otherwise, without written permission from the author.

ISBN: 1-4033-8147-X (e-book)
ISBN: 1-4033-8148-8 (Paperback)
ISBN: 1-4184-1305-4 (Dust Jacket)

Library of Congress Control Number: 2002094895

This book is printed on acid free paper.

Printed in the United States of America
Bloomington, IN

1st Books – rev. 04/15/04

Contents

Introduction

My #2 pencil began to doodle, dancing quietly across the page, forcing images to appear as it continued to define the once blank page. Lines and dots transformed themselves into a railroad track, complete with those nondescript weeds and grasses that often grow with rebellious abandon between the splintery wooden ties.

Others in attendance at that writing workshop may have been following the instructor's directions and actually beginning to write. I was not consciously ignoring them, because that would be rude and rather unfriendly, but still.... there it was, happening only on my page.

A sketchy rectangle mutated into a modest dwelling. A pine tree sprouted from unseen roots there, in the front yard, its long branches shading the front step made of Bricks and I instinctively touched my hair, reaching for that lost pine needle. Then the wooden front door (what color brown?) with a faux brass door knob that began to clickety click in a clockwise direction and within....

The cluttered corners of my thoughts were slowly being emptied. There was the twin bed that I shared with my only sister, Esperanza, and the chest of drawers that smelled of Lemon Pledge and held such things as kitchen towels made out of flour sacks, and clean underwear and handmade doilies woven from family secrets.

The instructor's authoritative voice startled me. I could have sworn that my hand was still down, holding the pencil, but obviously it was not, for now my friends were nodding approvingly in my direction, and the instructor waaay up there in the front of the hall was smiling with great relief, for someone had finally volunteered to share what he or she had written.

I read with great attention to my paragraphs, hoping to avoid the stares of others and just get it over with. I knew that others did not seem to have given themselves to the experience, and I had let it grab me by the wrist. Now that I was actually reading it aloud and hearing my own voice, I liked it. Just as I enjoyed the one time I went skydiving, once the parachute popped open, catching the breath of God.

It was exhilarating, but it was also embarrassing because my eyes had begun to water and my voice became uneven near the end of the page. I could bring back the memories, but not the people in them. During the break, I rushed to the restroom and let the cool tap water restore the usual color to my face.

That's how the first story of this book was born.

As you read these stories, you may recognize some familiar places, especially if you've ever lived in San Diego County, in the southwestern corner of the almost golden state of California. There really *is* a little house on West Connecticut Avenue in Vista, and my family really *did* spend decades in that house. It was our first real house.

We first moved into it in 1954. In those days, the barrio had no sidewalks and the Vista Boys' Club had not even been built yet. The local elementary school was still called Santa Fe Elementary and there were no traffic lights next to it. Mrs. Norwood was still the best kindergarten teacher. If you didn't wake up in time to go to church on Sunday with your parents, you had a long walk ahead of you. I still remember the disappointment and frustration when the price of a Three Musketeers bar went from five to ten cents.

In the early fifties, it was not easy for a Mexican/Chicano/ Hispanic/Latino (pick the label that you feel most comfortable with) family to buy a house out of the barrio.

Little girls with dark brown braids who spoke English with an accent were not encouraged to join the Blue Birds, Brownies, or Girl Scouts.

Some things are made to change, and others stay the same. The little house eventually got that second bathroom, an extra bedroom for the five boys, and a cement driveway. Nowadays, the Girl Scouts do a fantastic job of reaching out to youngsters in a variety of neighborhoods. Through the efforts of many people in the Civil Rights movement, there are now laws that (at least in theory) let people buy a house anywhere they can afford to do so.

Our parents lived in that little house for about forty years. I can still smell the warm, earthy fragrance of fresh, handmade tortillas and nopalitos cooking in the kitchen.

I hope that, as you enjoy these stories, you can imagine what it was like to grow up in those times, in that barrio, on that street, in that little house with the pine tree in front and the carob tree in back.

Dedication

Thank you to my son, Pascual Lomelí Benítez. I wish every parent could have a child as well rounded as you are.

Thanks also to David Miller, my husband and best friend whose comments and support I continue to value. You don't speak much Spanish, and you're not short like most of us, but you're still terrific. *Why didn't I meet you when I was twenty?*

To the family of the late Colonel Wells Miller and his lovely wife, Alice:

Even though our dad had more than one chance to work elsewhere, his respect for your father was deep and their friendship lasted a lifetime.

To my late parents, Jesús and Guadalupe:

Thanks for making us feel special. We miss you both.

A portion of the proceeds from the sale of these stories will be donated to the Lomelí-Miller Scholarship Fund for struggling seniors at Vista High School.

TJ

Our birth is but a sleep and a forgetting:
The Soul that rises with us, our life's Star,
Hath had elsewhere its setting,
And cometh from afar.
From "Intimations of Immortality" by William Wordsworth

There are many things that I could tell you, but I won't.

My sister, Esperanza or *Laly* as I've called her since I could speak, once said that a woman should save a little bit of mystery for herself. "A woman should be mysterious. That way, men will be more interested in her."

Quien sabe. Who really knows? I'm hoping that you'll agree that it makes for more interesting reading, though.

Is everything in here true? Again, not an easy question to answer. The names of persons in my immediate family circle are true:

Jesús the father,

Guadalupe (Lupe, Lupita) the mother,

Eligio (Eddie) the oldest brother,

Refugio (Cuco; Big Jess) the next,

Jesús (Chuy; Little Jesse) the one after that,

Esperanza (Laly), my only sister,

Francisco (Pancho or Quico), the one before me and Rafael (Payo), my little brother and sometimes partner in crime.

The names of our favorite teachers are also true, and the geographic names are as you find them on a Thomas Brothers Map book. I will not vouch for the authenticity of anything else. I sincerely hope that this does not present a problem for you, the reader of this book of treasured and tattered memories. As Alurista, former San Diego State professor, once said, "It's the spirit that counts." There is still plenty of mystery in that one word: spirit.

All things are connected. No matter which dot you point to on a time line, there will always be one before it and one after it. They all have spirit. So it is that, before there could be a little house on West Connecticut Avenue in Vista, there was another house in a town that some have referred to as the Calcutta of the border: Tijuana, México.

***

Sunrise meant the sound of street vendors, hustling to sell fresh bread or baked yams for breakfast to the residents of that crowded border barrio. Organized trash collection being unknown in those days, the residents would burn their garbage along crooked paths that crisscrossed the rocky hillsides like veins. After one of those rare rainy days, the charred and sooty remains of last week's garbage would be washed downhill to the cobblestone street and little tufts of green grass would festively sprout along the margins of the well-traveled paths. The smell of fresh tortillas was quite common in the daytime, and hot chocolate (La Abuelita or Chocolate Ybarra being the top two brands) was the beverage of choice on cold evenings. Somebody's dog was always growling from behind a patchwork fence, the boundaries of its universe.

There, between Calle Juan Escutia and Cañón Johnson, on that somewhat rocky hillside, in the area known as Colonia Miguel Hidalgo, my family moved into a cement block house right around the time my dad became one of those Braceros (foreign guest workers). Mom used to tell me stories about what it was like. There was one light bulb in the middle, hanging from the ceiling. You know the type; you have to yank some little chain to turn the thing on before you bump into something in the dark. There were probably quite a few things to bump into in that one room house. They were mostly human, and I'm referring to my older siblings.

I'm told that I used to run away before I was able to walk. I would crawl out of the crib, crawl out of the tiny house, and crawl over to the neighbor's house, where the two teenage girls, Chayo and Maruca, would happily take care of me until my mom found out that I had escaped again. If Mom hadn't been so careful about counting her children every morning, I might have lived in TJ forever, waking up to barking dogs and street vendors shouting, "Camotes! Come and get your camotes!"

There is nothing else in the world like a steaming hot sweet potato for breakfast. It is delicious, especially with hot Mexican chocolate.

Lobo

... the animal shall not be measured by man. In a world older and more complete than ours they move finished and complete, gifted with extensions of the senses we have lost or never attained, living by voices we shall never hear. They are not brethren, they are not underlings; they are other nations, caught with ourselves in the net of life and time...

from Henry Beston's *The Outermost House*

Chuy, Laly, Mom, and Me

If I cried in the darkness, my only sister would soothe me. When we lived in Tijuana, though, Mom usually had no one to whisper to in the night. Dad was often away for months at a time. The best she could do was surround herself with her half-dozen children, a busy momma duck with her six ducklings quacking all about her.

She could not count on frequent letters, because our father was barely literate, not even able to write his own name when they married, she at 19 and he in his early twenties. Letters from the U.S. usually had just a money order. I'm sure that Mom appreciated, and desperately needed, that money. Sometimes, though, Dad did manage to scribble a sentence on a scrap of paper attached to the money order. The way she would hold the envelope to her heart ever so briefly, turning away from her brood for a second, and then smile for the rest of the day, well... that said it all.

Laly would attend school every morning just as my brothers did, but her afternoons were spent with Mom, taking care of me, washing clothes by hand, and preparing the next day's fresh pot of pinto beans. The males of the tribe were sent out to the urban jungle to hunt for work: selling newspapers, sweeping sidewalks, shining shoes, assisting in a barber shop, or selling Chiclets to crowds of bargain hunting tourists. That's the only way those extra pesos would come to us. Money doesn't walk right up and jump in your pocket. Evenings were devoted to personal hygiene, preparing the next day's school uniform, and doing the necessary homework.

Each student was required to pay for his/her textbooks and all school supplies. Sometimes, you were required to provide your own desk as well. This is still true for many children there, I am told. My siblings juggled school, homework, and part-time jobs, all without being able to brag that their father was waiting for them at home. Mom was always there, cooking and cleaning and praying the rosary, but even most kids whose dads were in prison could say that. We existed then in the little box marked "absent father".

It was in one of Dad's intermissions from working in El Norte that the third eldest boy, Chuy, had allowed the excitement of Dad's latest return to go to his head, producing a kind of euphoria similar to temporary insanity. This clouding of the adolescent mind slows down the messages that the brain sends to the muscles. In some cases, it leaves whole sections of brain matter idling blissfully for hours at a time. Even though he *always* took out the garbage before walking those few miles to school every day, on that particular morning, Chuy's brain was on vacation and did not remind him to attend to this duty before leaving.

Dad would not listen to Mom's pleas for mercy on the lad. "These boys have been softened by your ways, woman, and they need me to teach them what a real man is. It is not such a grand thing that they work after school! That is what they're *supposed* to do! That, and do such little things as take out the garbage before going to sit at a desk with other schoolboys, sharpening pencils and smiling at the girls. They don't know what real work is."

"He will remember when he returns, dear."

"You better believe it. I won't have our home smelling like a pig pen, flies buzzing around our heads as if we had no shame. I will teach him to forget his duties, with the help of God!"

"Remember."

"What?"

"Teach him to remember his duties."

"That's what I said, Lupe. That's what I said."

5

The Loza family (Don Merced, Doña Nacha, Maruca, Chayo), our neighbors, had a large gray German shepherd that would greet my siblings with a wagging tail and woof-woof every afternoon, no matter what the weather. Nobody in our neighborhood had a problem with Lobo, except the occasional midnight wanderer that teetered drunkenly into our yard by mistake. Lobo would bark them in the direction of their own house, and then return to fall asleep in front of the Loza's screen door.

That afternoon, my brothers and sister flew over the cobblestones, eager to be the first to give their daddy a hug. They were greeted, as usual, by Lobo. They bounced right past him and raced to the gaudy lime green door that was already peeling even though Dad had painted it during his last visit. Nobody knew that you were supposed to strip away the old paint before applying three fresh coats. The paint had been discontinued and that's why it was being sold out of the back of somebody's pick-up truck. "Paint is paint," Dad always said.

Breathless and smiling so much that their faces seemed to be in pain, they bubbled over each other, pushing and shoving. "Daddy, we're home!"

Dad was standing by the door, and motioned for everybody to get inside … except Chuy.

"Son, we need to get something settled right now."

The color drained from Chuy's face. His eyebrows formed wide arches over his green eyes as he gasped. "Oh! I just remembered that I forgot to take out the trash! Is that what you wanted to talk to me about?" He gripped his stack of schoolbooks and held them more closely to his sweaty shirt.

"You disobeyed me. You said you would do it and then you went off to play in school, didn't you? You lied to your father." Dad hooked his thumbs over the front of his thick leather belt. His dark brown eyes continued to drill into Chuy, trying to ferret out the truth like tweezers trying to pull out a stubborn sliver of bark, to instill the kind of obedience that his own father must have demanded of him once upon a time, during the days of the Mexican Revolution.

"No, Daddy! I didn't mean to!" Chuy's eyes refused to blink, even though he dearly wanted them to do so. "I thought that I had done it. I just remembered right now!"

"You don't know how much your mother depends on all of you kids. I need for you to be more responsible, son. I'm going to have to teach you a lesson."

Chuy began to cringe, but he did not step back because that would make it worse.

"Please, Daddy, don't." The others were watching, afraid that interfering would bring the belt swinging towards them.

Lobo began to march towards them, unnoticed, his jaw shut, no slobbery pink tongue hanging out, spilling saliva as only Lobo could. His ears became pointed, with an edge to them, like a freshly sharpened kitchen knife, just like the kind that Mom loved to have around the kitchen for slicing red tomatoes and dicing onions.

Nobody noticed this because Dad's deep voice continued lecturing, casting a spell on his wide-eyed son and the rest of his children, a deep, serious, Listen-to-Me-or-You'll-See-Stars voice. A clinging spider web of patriarchal power, even more hypnotic and paralyzing because it was unhindered by the neutralizing presence of Mom, who must have stepped out to buy fresh tortillas at the corner store. My poor brother! Who would be insane enough to intervene???

Lobo's rough feet padded closer and closer to Chuy's side, lifting tiny clouds of TJ dirt. As the thick leather belt was being removed by my father's callused hands, Lobo sat down beside Chuy, resting his haunches next to the boy's shoes. Shoes once so shiny and perfectly black, now having absorbed some of the native color. The edges had softened gradually to resemble the gray of Lobo's paws.

"Let's get this whipping over with, son, so we can go on about our day."

Chuy's voice choked, and Dad began to raise his voice, repeating his earlier words.

Lobo swiftly and silently maneuvered his body between the two, growling his street dog growl. When Dad attempted to raise the belt, Lobo promptly placed his front paws on my father's chest. Right on Dad's collarbones. Staring my father in the eyes, ears rigid, he began to growl, a deep and steady growl, twitching his lip to give glimpses of sharp, yellow fangs. Teeth that could tear apart a whole chicken and not leave a trace of bone or feather in the dust. Strong teeth.

Silence.

"Son?"

Nobody was breathing but Lobo, and he was still looking my dad in the eyes.

"Well, I'll be!" Dad began to chuckle as he lowered the belt and let it hang limply by his side. "And this dog is supposed to belong to the neighbors!"

Lobo returned to his previous place, next to Chuy's shoes. The hairs on his back relaxed to their original position, tail flat on the ground, slightly touching Chuy's school pants.

"Son, you can tell the dog to go now."

Chuy had forgotten to breathe and now he remembered with a short gasp. "Uh… uh, sorry, Dad. Go back, Lobo. Go back now!"

Dad put one hand slowly on Chuy's head. "Let's go inside, son."

"Okay. Are you going to hit me inside?"

Dad laughed. Clean, clear, loud laugh, chin slightly pointed up, eyes closed. "Good God, not any more! If a neighbor's *dog* loves my children like that, then God must be looking out for us! I'm a lucky man, yessirree. A lucky man indeed."

Chuy's shaky hand went out to Dad. "I'll remember next time. I swear that I will."

Dad pinched Chuy's cheek affectionately with his free hand. "Come on inside, kid. Maybe you can tell me what you did in school today."

Good old Lobo.

Your Own Train

A few years ago, at one of our Christmas gatherings, my brother Pancho shared with me his perspective on the transition from Tijuana to Vista, California. That was also when I first heard the real reason why Pancho came willingly to the United States.

Odd, that it had never dawned on me that my siblings might have to be convinced to undergo a major move. I thought that they would be happy enough to be with both parents. I was so young then.

***

When it looked like the Bracero program was going to fizzle out, Dad hustled to find a lasting solution. That must have been when he ran into Mr. Miller, El Patrón, a former colonel during WWII. On one of those days, Dad must have walked up the dirt road of that ranch where the lemon trees were blooming, and knocked on the door of the white house with a green roof.

It couldn't have taken Mr. Miller long to see that he had a good thing in my father. Dad was a plain speaking man who did not believe in coffee breaks and was capable of great loyalty. Mr. Miller needed someone who was willing to learn about managing a ranch and, later, a tree nursery. Through their working relationship, they soon developed a mutual respect and trust. Due to this, Dad was able to go through all of the legal channels to move us into our first real home.

He had convinced Mom that it was a good move. She thought so, too. I was too little to understand the difference between a visit and a permanent move, so I said nothing. The youngest boy, though, had plenty to say.

***

The boy with the brown curly hair and damp eyes sat on the rock and stared at his worn shoes. His hands were in his pockets, making tight little fists.

The man in the khaki pants and straw sombrero walked slowly towards him, and then placed his callused hand on the boy's small shoulder. "It cannot be avoided. Be a man."

A small sob escaped from the boy's throat. He cleared his throat and spit once into the brown dust next to the rock that he was sitting on. His hands remained in his pants. The man placed his other hand on the boy's other shoulder, then gazed at the nearby houses. Very few had anything connecting them to the tall telephone poles that dotted the little urban hillside. Most were patched-together wooden constructions with old nail holes and peeling paint of different colors.

He looked further, at the cobblestone street below them. The vendor's cart was making its clackety-clack noise, worn wheels wobbling slightly as the vendor sweated to push it at a slow but steady pace. "*Paletas! Paleeeetaaaas*! Come and get your fresh *paletaaas*! Mango, coconut, tamarindo, lime, and orange! There are no better in all of Baja California!" The cart had red lettering that said Paletas Dulces = Niños Buenos.

Doors were slammed by little brown hands. From inside the small wooden houses and from behind countless crooked fences, little children emerged and came streaming down the hillside, each one clutching their peso and waving it in the air. Their shouts of, "Don Chucho! Wait!" allowed the vendor to stop and wipe the perspiration from his forehead. Don Chucho didn't believe in bathing, and the perspiration always left a stain on his shirt sleeve.

"Don Jesús! You're back from the other side! Hey, buy a real popsicle from me. Not one of those monstrosities wrapped in plastic! I make mine with my own hands!" The children had already reached Don Chucho and were milling around, trying to place their orders all at once.

Don Jesús shouted down the hillside, "Good to see you, Chucho!"

The boy with curly brown hair and damp eyes stifled a sniffle as he watched the boisterous little crowd of brown bodies bouncing around the ice cream cart. "Why can't it be avoided? Why do we have to go to the other side?"

Don Jesús removed his hands from his son's shoulders. "I have a real job waiting for me in El Norte in a town called Vista." He sighed. "Did you think that we would stay in Tijuana forever?"

"Everybody knows us here. Don Merced and Doña Nacha are like grandparents and Chayo and Maruca are like aunts to us. Lobo thinks he belongs to us, too. Pepe is my best friend and we go to the same school and he lives right there, on the other side of the gutter. That is good luck, to have a best friend so close by!"

Every hillside had a gutter in that part of Tijuana. In the evenings, when the many billboards of Avenida Revolución lit up and blinked Tequila Cuervo and La Rubia Superior all the way into the porches and rickety balconies of Colonia Miguel Hidalgo, small fires were lit in the gutter to burn the garbage of the day. In the morning, housewives in faded aprons would fling the morning's dirty dishwater onto the piles of soot, to erase what had been there the night before. And so it was that when the sun arose, a continuous gray vein began to pulse through those uneven streets, gathering more foam and used motor oil as it flowed silently towards the downtown district. By nightfall, it subsided and the little garbage fires appeared here and there, often with small clusters of people sharing stories around them.

"You need to be a man, my son. Please try to understand that this is not your decision, Pancho."

"Eligio says that a man takes care of his family and I always do what Mamá asks before I go outside to play with Pepe. I give her any extra money that I make selling newspapers near the border. A real man doesn't cry to his Mamá for toys even if he never gets any toys even on his birthday. That makes me a man, doesn't it?"

In Cañón Johnson below, the crowd of children had dispersed. Don Chucho was pushing his cart and ringing his bell as he headed out of their line of sight.

"I found a house for all of us."

"We got one here."

"Yes, but the other one has indoor plumbing. And more than one room."

Silence.

"It has some trees."

Silence.

"On the other side, you won't have to pay for your school books. The libraries will loan you a book any time you want. Even to children! You can read. You should appreciate that."

Don Jesús took his sombrero off, fingered the brim for a moment, then put it back on his head. "Panchito, if you come willingly to the other side with the rest of us, I will get something especially for you. I promise you this, man to man."

Francisco turned to look up at his father's deep brown eyes. "I don't want to forget my friends, and the teachers don't call me Panchito or Quico like you and Mamá do. They call me by my real name. I am somebody here."

He stooped down and picked him up. "You're part of the set, you know? We are not complete without you, the curly haired one! I ..." He pressed his face close to his son's ear. "...I know that you like toys that move, toys that go places, ones that let you use your wonderful mind full of stories and such things. I will get just such a thing for you. I will get a train just for you, Panchito, honest! But you must not tell anyone. Not even your mother."

Francisco hugged his father's neck.

"Now, can we go inside and start packing? We have to move this weekend, son. You are probably the best little packer that I have."

Francisco hugged his father's neck tighter. "I don't want to forget this place. A toy train will help me remember, too."

His father put him back down and took his hand, guiding him back towards the one room house that the family shared. "Your train even makes train sounds, m'ijo. It is in a place that can never be lost, and nobody will ever steal it from you!"

"I will earn the money for the batteries myself. Or does it use electricity? I will work hard and give you the extra money for the electric bill."

His father's mustache began to curl ever so slightly. "You will grow up to be a great man, ... Francisco."

A few days later:

The mother made the sign of the cross. "The Lomelís have arrived! May God bless our new home!"

While his brothers were bouncing around the new house, marveling at such things as the antique heater in the small central hallway and the lock on the bathroom door, Francisco was looking into every nook and cranny, lifting up everything that wasn't nailed down. He did not find what he was looking for, so he went out to the front yard to watch his father take another box out of the truck.

Francisco slowly walked up to his father and motioned for him to lean close. "Papá, I looked everywhere, but don't worry. Nobody else knows what I was looking for."

With a look of chagrin, the father removed his sombrero, wiped his forehead, squinted briefly, and whispered, "I didn't have any money to buy you a toy train. I won't get paid until the end of the month, anyway."

Francisco hugged his father tightly. "Then send me back to Tijuana, please! Don Merced and Doña Nacha said they could take care of me."

The father extricated himself from the tight squeeze. "Wait a minute, there! I think I can still keep my promise. Come with me to the back yard. There is so much more for you to see."

As the mother showed the children how to properly flush their indoor toilet, the father quietly led Francisco around one side of the house, pointing out all of the wonders of their new home. "See this plant? It smells like skunk when you crush its leaves, but your mother knows how to use it as medicine. You already saw the pine tree and that little palm tree in the front yard. If you climb either one, just be careful. Don't let Marta climb alone. She is still too little. Look. Our own cactus plants! And here, in the shade, there are *verdolagas* growing wild. Fresh and free, ready to be boiled and seasoned with cilantro, lemon, diced onion and tomato, just as we all like! There is not much of a fence now in the back yard, but you and your brothers will help me build a new one, a fresh one. You can paint it white, Panchito."

"Francisco."

"This tall grass back here, we can cut down with a machete. I'm sure that Mr. Miller will let me borrow any tool that we need. He is a good man. Not even our relatives working in the ranches in Fallbrook have such a secure job as I do, son. That means something."

Before Francisco could say another word, his father's arms had lifted him up to his shoulders.

"I do not think that I like the view. I see the pretty houses painted pink and blue and yellow, but they are far away. That makes them not so pretty. Pepe lived so close to us in Tijuana that…"

"What's the view like up there?"

Francisco touched his father's hair. It wasn't often that he was above his father, the leader of the Lomelí clan. "You can put me down, now. I won't ask you about my present anymore. Even at the end of the month when you are paid in dollars by El Patrón, Mr. Miller."

"I asked you a question. What do you see? Hurry up and answer, now. My patience is wearing thin, young man."

"I see that the ground goes up and beyond that, a field full of nothing but more rocks and weeds, a black road and those houses that I don't like. They all look the same." The fingers of Francisco's left hand began to twirl a few strands of his father's hair as he sighed. "I won't make you keep your promise anymore. You can put me down now."

And he did.

"I did not lie to you, son. It's just that it's probably a sin to buy shiny new toys when we have so many other more important things to attend to. If you ask your mother, she will say the same and then we'll all have to pray the rosary. If I buy a toy for you, I have to buy one for each of your brothers and sisters."

Silence.

Then, "Did you forget? Because if you did, I will wait until you can afford my train."

With his left hand, the father pointed to the east, maybe half a block away, where four tiny gray duplex apartments stood alone near the remnants of a chain link fence. He placed his right hand on Francisco's curly hair. "I got you the biggest, fastest, strongest train and I will show it to you soon. The wheels are as big as you are, and when it blows that whistle, why, everybody will come to see your train, Panchito!"

Francisco's brows furrowed. Then, he looked back at the house. "I'm not ever getting my own toy, am I?"

"I'm sorry, son, but this is the best I can do. Besides, you know that toys break. Toys get lost. Toys get stolen. Toys always wear out eventually. Then, you don't see them any more except in your dreams. Ha! This train will never give you such headaches. No, señor! Not your train!"

A moment later, the rumbling chugga-chugga, clackety-clack coming from the bend near the gray duplexes announced the arrival of Francisco's train. Within seconds, the rest of the family had appeared and clustered around them to watch it pass. Eligio picked up a pebble and was about to fling it at one of the red cars that had English words painted on its dusty sides, but decided against it when his father poked him in the ribs. "Not now, boy."

When the train had disappeared around the west bend, Refugio asked, "Where does the train come from? Where is it going now?"

"*Sabe Dios.* Only God knows, son. But it will pass by every day, whether you notice it or not."

"Yes, children," added the mother's voice. "Just enjoy the view."

Francisco leaned over and whispered in Laly's ear. "That's my train!"

She nodded and smiled, and the red ribbon in her brown braids bounced in that August breeze of 1954.

The Bottom Drawer

Like my skilled and seasoned colleagues, I often found that caffeinated beverages were indispensable if I expected to stay awake past ten o'clock in the morning during a professional seminar. There were so many factors which increased the weight of your eyelids and pounded you into a coma. Mind-numbing *let's get to know our neighbor* games, pin the post-it-note on the chart, speeches heavily seasoned with the latest buzz words, and all coordinated by tap-dancing bureaucrats who have little intention of ever testing their own theories themselves in a real classroom.

Sometimes, though, you find a nugget of value among the ordinary stones. It was at one required writing seminar that I had an unusual experience. Distracted by my written words, I accidentally lifted my pen up to scratch the side of my head and found that I had volunteered to read what I had written. "Piece of cake!" I thought to myself. "Nobody will be listening anyway."

I thought wrong. The assignment had been to write about your first home. I had written far more than anybody else, but, as I read, the room became so quiet that I felt obligated to read to the end, even if the page was getting a little bit blurry and my throat was feeling heavy. *"Loca!"* I thought to myself. *"It's only words on paper! Get a grip!"*

During the break, I splashed cool water on my eyes and hoped that the world would not notice my craziness.

What follows here is almost exactly what I shared on that day.

***

Renters no more! We had moved out of Tijuana and were finally together in our own home, an affordable little house almost at the end of West Connecticut Avenue, in Vista, California.

Tar paper was still on the walls of the boys' bedroom, a room barely big enough for two twin beds (no closet). Next to their room was the only restroom in the house. In the front yard, a tall pine tree and a scrawny palm stood guard over us.

My four brothers probably thought that they had died and gone to heaven. They had a room with a real door! Two windows! Enough room under the twin bed for four pairs of stinky shoes! Who cared if the walls had cheap black tar paper on them? Not my brothers! They had trees to climb in the front yard, and a door that they could close whenever Mom and Dad let them. It was more privacy than they had ever had before!

My sister shared an even smaller room with me. It had a window looking into the "garage" (more of a car port), one twin bed for the both of us, one closet shared by the whole family, and an old 4-drawer dresser also considered communal property.

Sometimes I would stare at the dresser and imagine the tales it could tell if it could talk. I knew the top drawer would tell stories about picking avocados, lemons, and putting on long sleeved shirts for Sunday Mass. Mom and Dad kept most of their things in the top drawer. The second drawer would probably complain about the challenges of storing underwear for four active boys. The third drawer would be the happiest of all. That's where Laly and I kept our things. The bottom drawer was a quiet place, full of kitchen towels, doilies, and crocheted masterpieces.

One of these drawers was always opened with more patience than the others. In the bottom of this drawer, underneath the embroidered pillowcases and doilies, was one little dress made from a flour sack. It was about the size of a Cabbage patch doll, with a soft green skirt and an off-white top and sleeves with some tiny flowers printed in diagonal rows. It opened a little in the back and it could be closed with a tiny brass snap. Neither Laly nor I had a doll to fit that dress.

"Look, Laly, I found a doll's dress!" I said one day.

She knelt down before the open drawer and gently picked up the little dress in her hands. "This is not a doll's dress."

"It's not?"

Laly sighed as she smoothed the wrinkles out of the tiny dress. "Nobody's ever going to play with this dress."

Great. Just great! One more thing that Mom was saving for "the poor people". Boy, if *we* were poor, she would let *me* play with that little dress.

But I was wrong.

Brushing the hair out of my face, Laly proceeded to tell me about the first Esperanza. "Mom said that she had twinkly brown eyes and a few teeth. Dad said that she wasn't fussy at all, and Eddie remembers that she learned to talk very quickly." She hesitated before continuing. "But, you know, things happen. Things that weren't Mom and Dad's fault at all."

What was that supposed to mean? I demanded more information. A mystery this deep deserved to be probed further. Then, perhaps, we could get on to the important business of playing with that dress. Things were to be used. Mom always said so.

"She started to get sick, really sick, and they didn't have any money for a real doctor."

"Why didn't they borrow some?" How clever of me to think of such a thing! But Laly's eyes didn't light up at my brilliant idea. There must be more.

"The things that happened were … unexpected and ugly things. Dad was a policeman in Aguascalientes then, but the police chief wasn't paying him like he was supposed to. Mom told me that…" She glanced towards the door before continuing.

"Told you what?"

Laly looked straight at me, tilting her head slightly to one side. "Mom told me that a few times, she even had to go to the neighbor's house to ask for food. You know, to feed Eddie and herself."

"And what did Dad eat?"

"Mom never talked about that, but probably day old tortillas and pinto beans or whatever they gave him for free in the restaurants. People then were always trying to be nice to the policemen 'cause they didn't get paid regular like they were supposed to. Anyway, …Mom and Dad tried everything: home remedies, prayer, and long nights spent rocking her to sleep." Laly continued to caress the tiny Cabbage Patch-sized dress. "She would spend silent hours in her crib, leaning on the little wooden rails, until even that was too much for her. That must have been when they called for the priest."

Silently, Laly and I both placed the little dress at the bottom, carefully folding the embroidered pillowcases over it, and layering the nicest doilies on top.

The bottom drawer was indeed a quiet place.

Mom, Dad, and the Other Esperanza

Two Christmas Stories

"Do not handicap your children by making their lives easy."

Robert A. Heinlein, science fiction writer

When I was very young, Christmas was mass after mass and rosary after rosary and long distance calls from relatives in Arandas and Jalostotitlán (Jalisco, México) and a few from Los Angeles. Hand made tamales, hot mugs of champurrado, and, if you were really lucky and especially good, a half cup of Mom's homemade *ponche*: creamy yellow eggnog spiked with real tequila. "Only on holy days, children. Otherwise, it's a sin."

Christmas in the USA meant all of those family traditions that we brought with us and included a few surprises as well. It became an interesting mix. Let me tell you of a few in these two Christmas stories.

A Creesmess Carro

My sister, Laly, and my older brother, Pancho, always buddies, had been picking up English and teaching it to me together. I certainly wanted to be ready for kindergarten, and they did so enjoy boasting of their new knowledge. They taught me to count up to three in English. Maybe they tried to teach me more, but the syllables were difficult to form, and I decided to wait for the other numbers until I entered kindergarten. I wanted to leave a little bit of work for my first teacher, after all. Make her feel useful. I was so considerate at that age.

One cool December afternoon, Laly and Pancho were sitting on the brick step in front of the house, sharing a little blanket, and singing something that I had not heard before.

"What are you singing?" I asked.

"These are Christmas songs in English. Stand over there and listen, *niña.*"

I had no idea what they were singing, this puzzle of sound, odd and beautiful syllables floating up to the sky, merging into the gray clouds! I couldn't get enough of it!

Every time they stopped, I begged to hear more.

"Sing more! Sing the one that goes ha-ha-ha! I like that one!"

That's when Mom appeared out of nowhere, broom in hand. "Go inside right now this minute, Francisco and Esperanza! Into the kitchen!"

In the kitchen, Pancho and Laly were asked about the songs. "Where did you learn language like that? Tell me the truth."

Laly and Pancho cringed in the corner of the kitchen. "Uh, in school. Why?"

"What have I always told you? Huh?" Mom had leaned the broom against the kitchen counter, and her arms were now crossed. I could smell the tortilla dough on her hands.

"We were just singing. Some songs. In English."

"Don't get smart with me, kids. Who taught such language to you?"

I had no idea of what was going on. Laly and Pancho kept looking at each other, stepping back against the wall, stammering and stuttering. "Bu...but our teachers taught us!"

"You expect me to believe that a *teacher* would teach you such trash? What next, you little hoodlums? Are you going to be fighting in the streets like wild animals and trying to pretend that you're Protestant? Are you going to change your last name, too? Ungrateful brats!"

"Mamá, we really *did* learn the songs in school! They are called *Creesmess Carros.*"

"Think you can fool me with those made-up English words?"

Laly added, "The teacher said that the kids sing these songs every December near Christmas time. We think they're Christmas songs."

Mom's hand almost trembled as she reached for the black telephone. As Laly and Panchito cowered in the corner of the kitchen, she slowly announced each letter and number as she turned the dial. "P-A- 4- 3884. Did you know that the P-A stands for 'palace'? Our home is supposed to be our palace, children! We'll see if your story checks out. God help you if you're lying."

Seconds later: "Comadre? Margaret? This is me, Lupe...Fine, thank you... I have a serious question to ask you.... It's about my children... I'm afraid that they might be picking up some bad habits in school, and, because I love them, I must check with someone who knows English before I beat their little brains out...Okay. They were singing some awful things and they say that these things are songs they learned in school,

Christmas songs, but I heard no mention of the Christ child or the Virgin Mary, so naturally I... huh? ... Okay." She turned to Laly and Panchito and motioned for them to approach the telephone receiver. "Sing into the telephone."

They sat there, grabbing each other's sleeves and staring at her.

I must have been too young to understand all of this at the time, but I was riveted to the scene. Amazed. Amazed that *Laly* just might get into trouble for the first time. I tiptoed closer to intervene with my tiny body if necessary. I wouldn't interfere if she whacked Panchito with the broom, but not Laly. She was my only sister, and so had much more value to me.

"Open your mouths NOW. Let's get this over with."

In unison, they managed to squeak out a few words of what we now know as Jingle Bells but this is what it sounded like on that day so long ago: *Chinga bel, chinga bel, chinga va to way.*

For those of you who are not bilingual, the word *chinga* is a cuss word and the word *way* in English sounds exactly like *buey*, which means dumb ox in slang Spanish; it's an almost-cuss word. The word *vato* was considered pachuco or gangster Spanish by Mom and, like the bona fide cuss words, was not allowed to foul the fine air that we breathed. Curiously enough, there also happened to be a very obnoxious boy named Abel who lived down the street, too.

I clearly heard laughter coming from the telephone. Instantaneous and spasmodic. Almost choking. Very brief, but audible even to my little girl ears. Mom made the sign of the cross, whispered a Thank You God to the ceiling, and hurriedly thanked our Aunt Margaret.

After hanging up, she approached Laly and Panchito with her arms outstretched.

"It seems that you have been telling the truth. It is not a song about Abel the dumb ox, children, but about Christmas bells that ring all the way to someplace, with children laughing as they sing. I am so sorry that I did not believe you. Will you forgive me? Laly? Pancho?"

Hugs all around. I got into the act, too.

"We told you we learned it at school, Mom," sniffed Panchito.

"Yes, my sweet curly-haired boy, but you must always be careful when repeating things that you do not understand. That is how trouble is created."

Laly kissed Mom on the cheek.

The last thing that Mom said was, "You see, children," she sighed, "you are representatives of your family and ambassadors of your culture. *Every* little thing that you do, even dropping a crumb of bread in your school cafeteria, or one candy wrapper in the street, *everything*, reflects on all Mexicans. You are not *la plebe,* the common rabble.

You are destined for great things. I believe this and so should you."

In her mind, she was the sculptor and we were her works of art. Like a lump of clay turning on the potter's wheel, spinning, wet from tears or sweat, ignorant from youth and inexperience, we were being shaped by our mother's words. A woman who had never made it past second grade was trying to do to us what Michelangelo did to the Sistine Chapel, but without brushes.

Usually, words were enough.

Our First Christmas Present

My youngest brother, Payo, was born not long after we moved to Vista. I was no longer the baby of the tribe, but at least now I had a partner closer to my age and that could be a comfort at times.

I don't remember exactly when it dawned on us that other children received surprises on December 25. We were rather accustomed to handfuls of candies and sometimes a handmade rosary with shiny prayer beads, but we had to wait until the day of the three wise men, January 6. It was a shock when it dawned on us that other children in the USA received real dolls, miniature trains, or toys from stores. Real gifts. What an awesome tradition!

Maybe it was the Christmas that the boys told Dad that other children in school had Christmas trees in their living rooms. I remember that Dad promptly went outside and chopped down one of the pine trees that formed part of a natural fence between our yard and the Figueroa clan to our east side. It was so tall that it hunched in the corner, jammed uncomfortably, like an unwelcome guest. Laly and Pancho suggested hanging popcorn strings for decoration, which seemed ridiculous to our father. He thought they were going to put a dress on the tree. Eventually, he just sat down to watch all of his children add raggedy pieces of aluminum foil, popcorn, and odd bits of colorful thread here and there. Mom sat next to him on the sofa and an amused expression danced on their faces as they drank their cups of hot chocolate.

On the day of Christmas Eve, Payo and I realized that there were no gifts in the house. No corner of the garage, back yard, or storage shed held any shiny surprises. We spent a few hours digging methodically through the same nooks and crannies a second and even a third time. We scrutinized the inside of each shoe box and peeked inside each paper bag and walked away sadly with nothing more than a few bug bites and angry squeaks from the very big mice that lived in the walls of the house.

We went in birth order, from Eddie to Cuco to Chuy and finally Pancho and Laly, tearfully begging for an explanation. The oldest boys smiled and pushed us away gently, but Panchito and Laly actually listened. They had no answer, of course, other than, "Let's talk to Dad about it when he comes home." This gave us a sliver of hope.

Laly and Pancho kept the wait and see attitude. Payo and I sat on the sofa to think and prepare ourselves. The minutes evaporated into the December air as we wound our thoughts around the possibility that our father might not love us as much as other fathers loved their children.

By the time our poor father came home, it was already dark. We did not greet him with a "Hello Daddy how was your day?" as we usually did. Instead, all seven of his children were in the living room, five standing silently and the two littlest ones sitting on the sofa, clutching each other and crying.

Silently, he frowned and kept trying to remove his hat while Pancho and Laly kept pushing it back on his head. "Hey! What do you think you're doing?"

"Dad," whispered Pancho in his ear, "you forgot to get presents." His whisper was loud enough for us to hear.

Laly kept tugging on his arm, calmly stating, "Papá, in this country the good fathers give the good little kids presents on Christmas."

Mom's voice came from the kitchen. "Don't make me burn the rice, children! Let your father sit down. He's been working all day."

Dad broke free from the leeches and now had both hands on his hat. "Even if I wanted to, there is no money for luxuries. You know that, so why ask? Huh? Many people are sitting down to dinner and resting now."

Eddie, Cuco, and Chuy had been shifting uneasily as they leaned against the walls. One by one, they looked at Dad's callused hands and headed off toward the kitchen. "Dinner ready yet, Mom?" they asked in unison.

Laly impulsively reached for Dad's waist and hugged his grass-stained pants.

"You don't have to buy anything for us, of course, but at least get something for the little ones."

Payo looked at him through big wet eyelashes and hugged me tighter. I used the opportunity to wipe my nose on his little shoulder.

Our father, the mighty oak in the forest.

The mighty tired oak looked at the clock on the wall and grumbled, "I can't promise anything." With that, he went back outside into the cold.

I heard the Jeep's rumble as it pulled out of the driveway and the shhh of its tires as it drove off into the damp darkness of the street, the sound diminishing the farther away the mighty oak was from his forest. To a child, that sound is intriguing and a bit mysterious, but adults are more likely to call it a lonely sound.

When he returned, he had a small brown paper bag, but it couldn't have been from the corner store. It had some numbers and letters printed on the outside, unlike the plain ones that were used for groceries. From that bag, he pulled out a clear package roughly the size of a standard sheet of paper, only thicker. The label had an illustration of a red brick schoolhouse. "I should be saving the money for more important things like food and bills. This is all I could get on such short notice. You two can share it."

Laly and Pancho clapped as Payo tore open the package, tugged on the cellophane wrapper, and dumped it on the floor. I began to run my fingers over the special surprise which our very own father had brought home... the most beautiful little chalkboard I had ever seen.

Smiling, Payo picked up the enclosed sponge, slightly larger than a stamp, and sniffed it. Two pieces of slender white chalk tumbled out of the package. We squealed with glee at the perfect circles and lines that could be drawn on the smooth black surface of the chalkboard and giggled delightedly at how the sponge could undo the work of the chalk. Our father's gift had brought magic right into our living room.

Cobwebs have obscured some of the nooks and crannies in that section of my brain. I wish that I could remember more than what it cost (fifty cents) and what it was.

I can't recall how long our father was gone, or what we did during that time. I tell myself now that I was a child and did not know what it really meant for my father to go out before eating his hot dinner. My crime was more like a misdemeanor, not a felony.

Something that came from childish selfishness and nothing more. That's what I tell myself now.

Chuy and Chuy and Our First Car

On the left, you see my brother Chuy. In the middle, you see our cousin, also nicknamed Chuy. To the right, the pine trees that Dad didn't chop.

Nothing to Fear

When you're number six in a family of seven children, and the youngest of two daughters, you face unique pressures. You're not the oldest, you're not the youngest, and you can't say that you're the middle child. Sometimes you feel ignored, and that can be a good thing. Other times, you feel like you just can't do anything right no matter how hard you try. There is no rule book to tell you what to be afraid of and what to believe in!

Every day, after dinner, it was my job to empty the trash can from the kitchen. I would have to walk into the back yard and dump it on the heap behind the house. Almost daily, we would burn the trash to keep unwelcome little critters away from our property. That way, we could go on believing that only the neighbors had disgusting insects like those black and brown cucarachas and flies with blue black purple wings.

This was, of course, in the days before the town had weekly trash pick-up.

Oh, how I dreaded the winter months when it got dark so soon! I would rarely convince someone to accompany me into the darkness of the back yard. My heart would beat fiercely and I would grip that doorknob for a few seconds, trying to calm my nerves before journeying into that vast unknown inky blackness.

If there was a moon out, the gray outlines of the railroad track behind our house would look as if they were covered with silvery ice. The guava bushes looked like evil trolls, hissing in the bitter night breeze, struggling to reach my shivering body with their leafy arms. Each crunch beneath my tennis shoes reminded me that I was on my own, with nobody to hear my cries if I should fall and break a leg. If a hobo happened to be walking by the railroad tracks, the demonic puffs of steam coming out of his nose would cause me to drop the trash can and fly back inside.

"Mamá, can you make Payo come help me with the trash?"

"No. You can do it all by yourself."

"But Mamá! I already do more work than he does."

"You're bigger."

"How about Pancho? Laly?" I was smaller than them. Surely, she could see that.

"Do my ears deceive me? Is a child of mine afraid of such a simple thing as the darkness?"

I quickly pointed out that it was the darkness *out there* that terrified me. Within the walls of our little mansion with its cute, chipped linoleum floors and one bathroom for nine people, I knew what was and what was not. *Out there*, well, that was a whole different ball park!

She patted me on the head and smiled, "Have you done anything to be guilty of? Aren't you doing well in school? Yes. Have you broken any commandments? No. Well, then, face the night bravely. Remember which family that you belong to, and your guardian angel will be by your side to protect you."

With a smile on her face, she walked away softly humming "La Guadalupana", her favorite song about the Virgin Mary.

Humming the same song loudly like a battle hymn, I marched outside and dumped the trash into the pile. After doing so, I raced back towards the backdoor, my left hand holding the empty trash can and my right outstretched toward the doorknob.

Oh, no! Somebody had locked the door! Somebody had turned the light off in the kitchen *and* in the little hallway to the back yard! My heart pounded within me. Maybe it began to drizzle, because my face felt damp. I could go around to the front of the house, but that would mean being in the darkness for even more time. If I cried out, I would surely be ridiculed by my brothers and Mom would feel that she had failed me.

"If you have done nothing wrong, then you have nothing to be afraid of."

I must have done something wrong! What could it be, what could it be? "Think, think, think! Remember what it was so you won't do it again!" I told myself.

Just then, I heard footsteps in the hallway inside. A few seconds later, Pancho's voice asking, "Iiiis aaaanybody oooouuuut there?"

"Panchito! Is that you? Open the door!"

"Why?"

"Cause I wanna come in, you big stupid!"

The next evening, I felt the same fear return. It seeped into my toes, and went all the way up to my head. My throat felt a little bit tight and my mouth a little bit dry, but I was sure not going to ask Mom for more advice. I couldn't ask Payo for advice; he might use it against me later. Laly would probably give me the same advice as my mother, and tell me the story of the guardian angel who guided the children over the rickety wooden bridge in the darkness again. I wasn't sure if I even had a guardian angel!

Fortunately for me, Mom and Dad had somebody else take the trash out that evening. I was too happy to ask why.

The night after that, however, I was caught off guard when Dad told me to take the trash out. "And make it quick, or you won't be allowed to watch television at all!"

I wandered around the kitchen for a while, hoping to forget and be forgotten. No such luck. Even when the family went into the living room, the trash can was still there in the corner of the kitchen, staring at me, reminding me of my duty to my family. Mom's voice came from the living room, "Hurry up, mija! You can sit next to me!"

Then Pancho popped his head into the kitchen. "Hey, kid, what's takin' so long?"

"Nothing. I can do it by myself."

"Yeah, but you're too slow. You're as slow as a donkey and sometimes not much smarter."

"I'm a little kid."

"You're a slow little kid. What do you think is so scary out there?"

Good question. Where to begin? "Well, sometimes hoboes are walking by the tracks."

"So what? Dad has a shotgun and Mom has a rolling pin, plus you have all of us!"

"Well, yeah, but the plants move around sometimes and, and...it looks like a scary movie."

Pancho grinned. "Wanna hear a story? That might make you feel better and you could take the trash out even faster!"

Oh, I couldn't believe my good fortune! My brother was going to tell me a story, without being forced to do so by either of our parents! He wasn't such a snot after all! "Well, okay, Panchito."

"Well, out there it is dark, that is true. There are trees and bushes, but they're the same ones you see in the day time, right?"

I nodded in agreement, and he continued, "If there is a moon out, well, you've seen it before, right? And nothing happened to you then!"

I felt ready to tackle the job now, but he put his hand on my shoulder. "Only one thing you need to know."

"What's that, Panchito?"

He whispered in my ear, "Watch out for the bad bunnies!"

Wait! This was something new to me! Did everyone older than me know it? Was Mom just protecting me from knowing the scary truth of the night-time creatures?

"Wha —-what are the bad bunnies? Do they look like Bugs Bunny?"

"Yeah," he nodded seriously. "They fight with Bugs at night, and when they can't get him, they go looking for slow little kids and kidnap them."

My eyes must have been bugging out. "Bu—but, but where do they l-l-live a— and wh— where do they take them?" Even in the clutches of fear, I felt that asking questions was a good idea. It kept my legs from buckling under me.

"Well, see, if they get a hold of a kid, they take him into the rabbit hole. It's pretty hard to escape from the rabbit hole. It's like a dark tunnel, but they like it that way."

"Are there any good bunnies?"

"A few. They're so busy rescuing other kids and protecting Bugs Bunny that I wouldn't bet my life on it."

I felt my heart sink within my chest.

He continued, "So, if you hear anything near the ground, run like lightning, okay? Unless you want the bad bunnies to get you!"

Bad bunnies! Something I had not counted on!

Clutching the trash can with both arms, I stepped into the dark night, my eyes frozen open and my short breaths coming out in little puffs of steam.

The night was quite still and the moon was a half-eaten silver tortilla; a cluster of purple clouds seemed to be gnawing at its right side. I noticed that there was a faint wind to rustle the leaves on the guava bushes and make the branches of the carob tree whisper to me. Each footstep carried me farther away from the comforting yellow glow of light coming through the back door's window. My bladder reminded me of the big glass of milk that I had finished at dinnertime.

Maybe if I hummed, or sang! Maybe the evil bunnies would be chased away by my show of bravery! It was worth a try, so I puckered up and got ready to sing a "battle hymn". After a few unsuccessful puckers, finally a sound came out: *"Desde el cielo una alegre mañana..."* (From heaven, one happy morning). I turned the trash can upside down, and slowly turned to face the house.

I knew it was weak start, but it was the best I could do and still be in control of my bladder.

Just then, I heard a rustle in the grass next to my ankles. Not daring to look down and see a bad bunny grabbing a hold of my ankle, I tried to sing louder. No such luck. My vocal chords were experiencing technical difficulties.

When I felt something breathe against my shoe, something damp, something that blended in with the weeds and crabgrass, I dropped the empty trash can and tried to scream but only a pitiful squeak came out.

Who knows how I made it into the house? I don't even remember opening the door, but I must have. The next thing I remember was racing to my room for a fresh pair of underwear, leaving a trail of yellow drops here and there. I must have flown into the restroom and then slammed the door. Only a minute later, when I heard banging on the bathroom door, could I collect my thoughts.

"What the heck is wrong with you?" Dad! It was Dad's voice!

"Sorry, Papá. I was just running away from the ..."

His grumbling footsteps went back into the living room. "A man can't enjoy one lousy television show without interruptions! Darn kids!"

"...Bad Bunnies."

I wasn't sure if he had heard me, but that was my father. He believed that children shouldn't be seen or heard.

When I came out, as quietly as I could, Pancho was waiting for me. "Did the bad bunnies get you?"

I glared at him and hissed, "You'd better stop making fun of me!"

"Oh, like I'm really afraid!" he snickered. "Get outta my way, 'cause I gotta use the bathroom next."

Taking a deep breath, I decided to look through the little window in the back door one last time. If the Bad Bunnies were still there, maybe I could get a good look at one of them. They wouldn't dare come into our house. I felt certain of that. If I did see one, I could call the whole family over and demand an explanation from my parents. They should have told me about them long ago. Kids deserve to be told about such things if they really do exist. I was old enough to know the truth.

Turning off the light in that little hallway and the light in the kitchen, I peered into the blackness of the backyard. Nothing. Nothing moved out there.

"Maybe if I turn on the light for the back yard?" I thought. "Or would that anger the Bad Bunnies? Well, they can't get me when I'm inside, anyway. Here goes nothing!"

I flipped on the switch to light the back yard. Hey, something did seem to move, over there by the clump of weeds and grass, next to the trash can.

Pancho had come out of the restroom and he was curious. "What are you looking for?"

"The Bad Bunnies, like you said, but don't make fun of me."

"You were really scared?"

"Yeah, you big stupid. Why didn't you tell me about them before?"

"I don't think I was supposed to tell you at all. Parents are supposed to do that, so don't tell them that I already told you."

"Okay."

Just then, we both saw a pair of green eyes next to the ground by the trash can. I squeaked again in fear, and Pancho fell down, laughing and clutching his ribs. Fat tears of laughter were rolling down his cheeks.

"Stop it, Pancho. That must be a Bad Bunny!" I felt that my fear had just been justified. We had both seen those sinister green eyes look straight at us!

He rolled over a few times, trying to make the laughter leave his body but there was certainly so much in there. He even put his hands on his head, and kicked his feet out, trying to shake the laughter out.

When he finally stopped writhing in laughter, he got up, clutching his ribs. "Aaah, that was really something. Oh, I can't stand it anymore. Come over here."

"Don't open that door! Don't do it!" I warned.

He didn't listen. Instead, he slowly turned the doorknob and snapped his fingers, tempting the outside forces to approach our backdoor. I marveled at his bravery in the face of danger.

I wondered if the laughing had helped him become so brave.

A second or two later, he was stroking the head of Minino, the neighbor's tabby cat. "Minino, you little rascal! Diggin' around the trash again, huh?" He chuckled.

I turned around and headed for the living room as nonchalantly as I could.

Mom had saved a space for me on the sofa, and the warmth of her shoulder was just what I needed.

First Communion
The little girl waving a holy candle is me.

The Lemon Grove

My early life was shaped by family and work. Work and family. Family and work. Sometimes both at the same time, but that was not so bad. You adapt to it and learn to enjoy it. It becomes imprinted in your very fiber. You're a member of a team.

***

There was a white wooden house on a hill, surrounded by lemon trees. That's the first "ranch" where El Patrón, Mr. Miller, lived with his family in the early 1950's. We weren't really allowed to go near the house (Mom and Dad's orders), but it was sometimes okay to play on the swing set in the lemon grove.

The whole "tribe" would go to pick lemons. Those wooden crates fascinated me and I thought Mom looked so cute and business-like with her apron, canvas bag, and scarf. I wanted to help but I was too little to use the ladders, so my job was usually to watch my younger brother. It wasn't a job I relished, but it was better than nothing. I would amuse myself by teaching him what little I knew of insects. "Look! A spider is crawling up your pants!" For a two-year old, he was surprisingly agile.

The day finally came when I was allowed to participate in the lemon harvest. I didn't use the ladders, but I would hustle about from tree to tree, picking up the good lemons that had hit the dirt and depositing them in the wooden boxes in between the rows of lemon trees. I felt so grown up, perspiring like a *real* worker. I was ready to ask for my own denim work jacket and apron!

One time, El Patrón saw me "working". He smiled and walked over to Dad and they had a short conversation. Maybe he wanted to be sure that Dad was aware of the Child Labor Laws or something. Anyway, he returned at the end of the day to pay my parents. He offered to give Dad fifty cents for my wages. True to form, Dad tried to refuse, saying that kids are supposed to work or they'll turn into lazy-good-for-nothings. El Patrón gave me two quarters anyway.

Since a Three Musketeers bar cost a nickel then, you just know that I dreamed of Candyland *that* night.

Well before I was old enough to work, my little brother Payo and I spent the day stacking empty wooden boxes and flinging rotten lemons at each other. Fresh lemons smell tangy, but once they get those black spots ringed by white and blue mold, they don't smell so lemony fresh. Then, they're just right for Bowling in the Dirt.

It was a cool and cloudy day, and we had spent the entire day bowling, playing catch with old lemons, and building forts. The wind developed a nasty sting to it, but the family was not close by. We had been instructed to not interfere with their important work anyway, so we just shivered and discussed things of interest to us, such as: "Which is bigger, a Milky Way or a Three Musketeers bar?" and, "Why does Mr. Fulano come in by the back door late at night, and why does Mrs. Fulano like rolling pins so much?" Perhaps it was exhaustion, or maybe it was hunger since I had barely nibbled on my chorizo con huevo burrito at lunchtime. Maybe it was a combination of both factors that pressed upon us and led me to what then seemed like a brilliant idea.

"Hey, Payo! Let's see if we can fit into one of these wooden boxes," I suggested.

He twisted his face a bit, stared down the row of tall lemon trees, and then back to me. "Why don't we go see what Dad and Mom are doing? Maybe Laly will let us hold the ladder for her."

Yawning, I said, "Suit yourself. I'm going to curl up in one of these boxes, 'cause it looks like a little house. It's bigger than the drawers at home."

He nodded and a yawn came out. "Okay. Think we can fit into one together? We'll be warmer that way."

I was surprised that such a sensible idea came out of such a little kid.

After crawling into one of those wooden boxes, I felt a raindrop splat on my forehead. With great effort, we pulled another box upside down, on top of us. As the drops gently fell, our breathing slowed down in that quiet little fort, until it matched the rhythm of the natural sounds of the lemon grove.

We awoke to loud voices and the sound of frantic footsteps a few trees away.

"Marta! Payo! Where are you?" Dad shouted, as he stomped around the trees.

"Do you think they went to El Patrón's house to use the restroom?" said our older brothers.

"What if a 'robachicos' got them? Kids have been kidnapped before, haven't they?" wondered Laly, our older sister.

"Payo! Marta! You kids had better come back from wherever you are!" Dad yelled.

"You won't be in trouble! Just come back!" pleaded Mom.

Dad sounded serious as he said, "Sounds like time to get the belt out."

These magic words made our sleepy eyes open wide and my little heart started thumping like a rabbit that smells a fox nearby. Needing no persuasion, Payo helped me to kick at the box above us. We knew that we must reach Mom before Dad got out THE BELT.

After a few frantic kicks, we were able to move the top box over and see the shapes of our loved ones about 20 meters away from us. There was the family, denim jackets pulled over their damp heads, standing in the dirt, in the middle of the lemon grove, as the pace of the falling raindrops quickened. The leaves on the trees were all shiny and dripping, and the powdery brown dirt was sprinkled with big splotches of moisture, more appearing every second.

We sat up in the box, crying, begging forgiveness for having fallen asleep. Laly ran toward us and tried to pick us both up, saying, "They're getting wet, Mom. Dad, I'll help them dry off when we get home."

He grunted and nodded toward the Jeep nearby. "El Patrón let me use the truck. We'd better get going before he changes his mind."

On the ride back, my older brothers teased us about falling asleep. "Ha ha ha! We were going to load the lemon boxes and send you over to the Calavo Packing Plant in Escondido!" One of them added, "Yeah, but they would have tossed you aside. Everybody throws out the rotten lemons 'cause they smell like...."

"Knock it off!" Dad grumbled from the driver's seat. "It won't happen again and ... and *that's all* that needs to be said."

Payo and I squeezed even closer to Laly, there in the back of the red Jeep. Our older brothers then contented themselves with pushing each other and counting the swishes of the windshield wipers as we made our way home.

I felt as if a great weight had been lifted from my little shoulders. The belt stayed where it was, keeping Dad's khaki pants in line instead of us.

My Teacher Can't Speak Right

As you continue to read, you will get to know many characters that added flavor and color to my years on West Connecticut Avenue. Most of them, of course, lived or worked in the barrio. Because they wove themselves into my life, I have included them in this patchwork quilt of words and memories.

The patch with the gold star in the middle is for a woman who gave me my first pink slip.

***

In our barrio, all of the kids went to Santa Fe Elementary School on South Santa Fe Avenue. It had kindergarten through sixth grade, plus one special education trailer that was off in one corner of the playground. There were special drinking fountains for the kindergarteners, and toilets in grades k-2. The playgrounds all had swings and most areas had monkey bars. To us, it was the best school. It was our only school.

Kindergarten was mostly positive. I loved the play kitchens. I loved the piano, even if I couldn't play it yet. I loved the book in the shape of a shoe that had actual shoe laces for you to practice on. Yet, there was something about the teacher that I couldn't quite put my finger on.

Mrs. Norwood had sort of short hair, slightly curly, with some gray here and there. Her glasses went up at the edges, like a movie star. Her sweater was always on her shoulders, held on by a short silver chain that clipped on. She looked like a real teacher.

She let us touch all of the toys, always made sure that we took turns on the slide, and she had a kind voice. She was usually smiling, but ...sometimes, though, she talked in a funny way and repeated herself slowly, very slowly. I knew that you could make a record sound funny if you put it on a slow speed, but that always got me in trouble at home. Why would she, an educated person, talk that way to a little kid on purpose?

Also, I just couldn't understand why she made me lay down on the cold floor every afternoon. Other children had towels to lay down on for their naps. Why would she do this to me? I didn't dare complain. I was afraid that I would be kicked out of school. I didn't want to bring shame to my family. No, señor! Not me! I thought, "Maybe this is how kindergarten is supposed to be. Maybe this is where they decide if they let you go onto first grade or not." If the herd had to be thinned, I was determined to be one of the survivors.

One day, Mrs. Norwood saw Laly waiting in the hallway to walk home with me. "Are you her big sister?"

Laly nodded silently. She would have nodded at anybody, out of respect.

"Come here, please. Come."

I pulled my sweater on and stood next to Mrs. Norwood. "She said come." I waved to Laly with my little hand.

Mrs. Norwood gave her a white envelope, and said, "Please -give -this -to -your -mother -and -father."

Laly cleared her throat and said quietly, "Engleech?"

"Yes, yes it is. It is in English. Give it to your mother and father. Mother and father, okay?"

"Okay."

On the way home, Laly grilled me about what I had done that day. I was near tears, trying to explain my innocence, by the time we got to West Connecticut Avenue. I knew that Mom was home that day, and I dreaded her lecture. I could already see her shake her head. I could already imagine her voice say, "Wait till your father comes home. Do you remember his belt?"

When Mom looked at the words that my teacher had written, she sighed and said, "Well, I do see your name here, Marta. I'm giving you one last chance, young lady. What does this mean? Tell the truth and you may be spared."

Fortunately for me, Lilly was knocking on our front door. She lived next door and could speak more English than anybody on our block then. "Hey, Doña Lupe! Have you seen my kids? They're not back from school yet, those brats."

"We're in the kitchen, Lilly. Maybe you can help me with something. Here, look at this note from Marta's teacher. What did she do?"

Lilly had almost finished high school. Her Spanish was sometimes mangled, but we thought her English was impressive. She held the pink paper and began to smile. Then, she closed her eyes and the smile turned into a grin. Finally, she opened her eyes and told us all to sit down.

"Doña Lupe, do you understand any of this?"

"Well, some. Her name. The teacher's name, too, of course."

"Why don't you let your daughter tell us what she thinks of her teacher?"

Terrified, I began to cover my mouth with my hands. Laly put her arm on my shoulder to give me courage. "Well, she is mostly nice. We play and she lets me color a lot. I think she likes me. She can't talk very well, but..."

Seeing the expression on my mother's face, I tried to explain. "She can't talk right sometimes, but I still like her. She tries."

Lilly let out a giggle and put her hand on my mother's knee. "The teacher just wants to know why Marta takes her nap on the bare cement floor. She's really worried and just wants to know why she doesn't bring a ... what's the word in Spanish? You know, a cloth, like to wipe your hands on."

The three of us looked at her blankly.

"She needs something for her afternoon naps." We had all been speaking in Spanish, of course, but Lilly couldn't think of the word 'toalla' so she used the English word. "She needs a 'towel', you see."

"What is this word, 'towel'? Does it mean pillow?" Mom turned to Laly with a questioning look. Laly just shrugged.

Lilly ran to the bathroom and brought out a towel. "See? This is what your daughter needs to put on the floor for her afternoon naps in school. The teacher is very worried because Marta never brings a towel."

Mom put her arm around my waist. "Why haven't you said something before? Do you think that your father and I want our little girl lying down on a cold cement floor?"

I could feel my eyes getting red. "Mamá, I didn't know why the teacher was making me sleep on the floor. Honest."

Laly patted me on the head. "She wasn't making anybody sleep on the floor. You just didn't understand her. That can happen to anybody."

I buried my face in my mother's shoulder. "I'm sorry, Mamá. Am I still in trouble?"

Years later, when I was a student in Vista High School, I was able to attend a retirement party for Mrs. Norwood. The years had made her hair turn a dignified gray.

She still wore her sweater the same way, over her shoulders, held together at the top with a short silver chain. She had more wrinkles, mostly around her mouth and her bright little eyes (now tired with age). She remembered the good, the bad, and the sad but amusing: the many pictures that I drew to retell the picture stories from the big books, the time I stole her little golden bell and returned it the next day out of guilt, and the time I came to school with alligator tears because Laly had scratched my arm.

Before the party was over, she had taken me aside and told me that she had managed to learn some Spanish over the years. She even asked me what my future plans were.

We talked, we hugged, and then she began to rummage through her pockets for a tissue. She had two and gave one to me.

Mrs. Norwood, wherever you are, thanks.

SANTA FE ELEMENTARY SCHOOL

Kindergarten Photo
We couldn't afford Dippity-Do,
so we made do with beer and curlers.
My hair smelled funny all day.

Little Tony and Doña Lola

In those days, every barrio had many Doña Lolas, women who had already contributed years and years of honest labor to society and family. They tended to walk slowly, wearing those dark cotton dresses like camouflage for their early morning and sunset walks about the neighborhood. On their sagging shoulders, they usually sported hand-knitted *rebozos*. Their gnarled little feet always wore black grandmotherly shoes, the kind that were just a touch too fine for field work and just right for visiting a neighbor. It was a standard look that said, "I don't have to go out to work anymore. I've paid my dues."

Doña Lola lived two houses away from us. Her small arthritic brown hands, accented by big veins and knobby knuckles, were usually puttering around her modest garden, fussing over her rosebushes. Her dark cotton dress stopped below her knees. That's where her beige industrial strength support hose began, and you could always see them rolled up with a striped rubber band, right below the hemline. Whenever Dad or Mom said something funny to her, her little tummy bounced comically up and down, revealing part of her white slip in front, right above those opaque "nylons" that she wore like a uniform. *"No hay que enseñar pierna, Doña Lupe,"* [We shouldn't show too much leg, Doña Lupe].

Her husband had died many years ago, and her only family visitors were her son, his wife, and their child, Antonio, who preferred to be called "Tony". Those visits were quite regular in Tony's preschool days. The older he got, the less frequent the visits became. Before long, the mom stopped coming along. Not long after that, his dad would even leave the engine running as he shouted to Doña Lola, "Mamá, can I leave Little Tony here for a while?"

People were always trying to dump Little Tony on somebody else, and this mystified my mother because all she saw was a little boy who never bothered his grandmother. All she saw was a cute little boy who called her "Doña Lupe" instead of "Lupe". All she saw was a little boy who never slammed our front door, which her own seven children sometimes did without thinking.

I remember a time, in a summer of sweet Navel oranges and ripe watermelons, that I tugged on my mother's apron and begged, "Mamá, can I go with you to Doña Lola's? Please?"

Mom smiled. "Let go of me. You're wrinkling my apron and I just finished ironing it, *muchachita.*"

I pushed my little nose into her waistline. "Mmm! It smells lemony fresh, too! I like the way you starched it."

While one plump hand balanced a fresh pan of corn bread, the other stroked my Pippi Longstocking braids. "*Niña*, you can come, but when Doña Lola and I sit down for some *cafecito* and some of my fresh *pan de maiz*, you get lost. Go play outside, just leave her roses alone, okay?"

"Well, I guess I can play with Little Tony, but I'd rather not."

Unfortunately for me, nobody else was home at that time, there was nothing good on television, and having barely finished first grade, there wasn't much that I could read by myself. I tagged along one more time, following the smell of my mom's cornbread.

Doña Lola and Mom sat inside, sharing fresh corn bread and coffee. I stood outside in the front yard, watching Little Tony pour salt on some slugs that he had found in the garden. He insisted that I watch, and when I refused, he described the torture in minute detail, focusing on the foam and making up wicked cartoon voices for the dying animals. The final straw came when he surprised me by tossing a huge, black, fuzzy caterpillar right at my face.

I ended up getting spanked for screaming and stepping on one of Doña Lola's rosebushes.

A few weeks later, the beginning of a new school year consumed all of my attention.

***

My first day as a second grader had been good so far. Mrs. Teeter, my new teacher, was impressed by my mathematical skill in writing my numbers. Lunch was good, too, because my *torta* had my two favorite ingredients: thick slices of avocado and many fat drops of El Pato hot sauce. In the afternoon, she let us draw whatever we wanted on a fresh white sheet of construction paper.

Near the end of the day, I began to get a little bit worried. Mrs. Teeter hadn't mentioned homework for anybody. I looked at the chalkboard; nothing was written there but her name and a few examples of addition. "That's first grader stuff," I said to myself. "Maybe she will hand out a worksheet as we walk out the door when the bell rings."

The bell rang. My classmates began to file out, hugging my teacher as they went out the door. I stayed at my desk for a moment, remembering what Mom had said so many times before: "The teacher gives homework to the smart kids." I wondered if I *had* convinced Mrs. Teeter that I was worthy of being given homework. I thought that I had been extra careful to erase all stray marks from my math paper, and I had put my complete name on all papers that day. What could I have forgotten? What had gone wrong?

After the last child left the room, I tiptoed up to her and asked if there was any homework.

She smiled in a strange but friendly way. "Well, I am considering it for tomorrow. What did you have in mind, um....?"

"Marta. I sit in the front of row two."

"Oh, yes! There's an empty desk next to you."

"Yeah. I mean yes, ma'am. I just want some homework. Please. Is that okay?"

I stared at her golden curls, nicely combed with pretty streaks of gray that caught the afternoon light in such an artistic way. I liked the little beaded chain that was attached to her silver-framed eyeglasses. I liked those brown freckles on her hands and the way the corners of her mouth were wrinkling.

"Well, I never!" she smiled.

"Never? Never, Mrs. Teeter?"

I resisted the urge to scratch my nose. Nothing says uncool like exploring your nasal passages with your index finger. Especially on the first day of school. It could wait.

"I never had a student ask for homework on the first day, especially not a second grader. However, I am sure that we can, you know, figure something out."

I got to take my spelling book home that day. I marched triumphantly into the living room and plopped down right smack in the middle of the floor, on my stomach, and proceeded to turn each page. I wanted to see how many words I could figure out by myself.

Shortly before dinner, I strolled around our front yard. I could see Little Tony in front of Doña Lola's house, waving at his father's truck as it drove down West Connecticut Street.

"Hey, Tony!" I shouted. "How come you're visiting your grandma today? Don't you know there's school tomorrow?"

Tony turned and snipped, "I can stay with my grandma any time I want. *You* don't even have a grandma, anyway. You don't have anybody to call 'abuela' like me."

He was right. I had never met my grandparents. I wasn't offended, though. I figured that grandparents were an optional item in life. I didn't mind Doña Lola, but, frankly, she didn't impress me as being that interesting. She fussed more over her tiny flower garden and those thick support hose than she did her own grandson. My mom, on the other hand, braided my hair every morning.

"Aw, come on, Tony. How about playing hide-and-go-seek before it gets dark?"

"Nah. My grandma wants to talk to me."

"Okay, I guess. Bye."

I watched Doña Lola open her front screen door and hold it open for the boy. She was saying something to him about eating dinner. When the screen door closed, I sighed and went back to my own little world.

The next morning, I sprinted to school, eager to begin the second day of second grade in Mrs. Teeter's class. I joined the children who were milling around the swings and the monkey bars, and got in some swing time and slide time before the morning bell rang.

After we were all seated, Mrs. Teeter announced that we would be receiving a new student. I hoped that the new kid would be a girl, a smart girl, so we could be friends. I glanced at the empty seat to my left and wished for just that.

About an hour later, I was shocked to see Doña Lola pacing in front of our classroom door, with Little Tony hiding behind her. I crossed two fingers and prayed that Mrs. Teeter would do the sensible thing and sit him next to James, that freckle-faced kid who smelled of room temperature bologna.

I had once complained to my mother about James, but she said that maybe he smelled differently because, maybe, he lived in a part of town where all of the people ate bologna sandwiches made of white bread instead of taquitos made of fresh corn tortillas. I imagined that Tony's nose could not be as sophisticated as mine, and neither boy would suffer much in that arrangement.

As Mrs. Teeter guided him closer and closer to my row, I crossed all of my fingers. Then I crossed my legs. When the edge of her dress brushed a desk two rows away, I even crossed my eyes and stared up at the ceiling.

"Tony, this little girl lives on your same street. Isn't that nice? You can walk home together. Here, sit in this empty desk and say hello to her."

How could she do this to me? Hadn't I been good so far? Why me? Why Little Tony, of all people? He still picked his nose and snacked on the snot when there were no adults about. He thought he was so clever. He would say to us, "It's kinda like makin' your own food!"

For the rest of the day, I did my best to show Mrs. Teeter that she had done me wrong. She was kind of crafty, though. She tricked me into liking her all over again by praising me for every little thing. By dismissal time, I grudgingly accepted her hug.

"See you tomorrow! Remember to do page one in your spelling book!" Her whole face twinkled when she smiled.

"I already did that last night. I'm starting page four."

"Oh, my goodness! I might lose you to Mrs. Dimick if you keep that up."

I beamed and hugged her back. Mrs. Dimick was a third grade teacher. The word on the playground was that she was IT when it came to art projects. Her kids were always painting murals and making the Christmas decorations for the cafeteria and such.

I was walking on air all the way back home. It's so easy to forget about little problems when other things are going so well!

The third day of second grade, however, the storm clouds began to gather. I had been patiently waiting in line for my turn to go down the slide, but Susan Morton kept cutting in front of me. Just as I was starting to climb up the steps of the slide, the bell rang. Not wanting to wait until lunch recess to face the same problem again, I went ahead and slid down. Mrs. Teeter saw it and gave me one minus point for playing after the morning recess bell rang. That afternoon, we worked feverishly on a new math problem. I finished a bit early, and began to draw on the back of my math paper. I got another minus point for drawing during math time. During the reading lesson, I lost one more point for answering when it wasn't my turn.

Although I was chagrined at receiving any minus points at all, I knew that you had to get about five before you were in major trouble in Mrs. Teeter's class. I skipped home with sort of a clear conscience. Since I didn't get detention or a bad note, I knew that Mrs. Teeter would forgive me and I felt certain that my parents would not need to know.

As I came closer to our house, I could hear my mom humming to the Mexican songs on the radio. She liked to do that whenever she was making tortillas. I raced inside, letting the door slam after me. "Mamá! I'm home! I have more homework, too!"

There she was, in the kitchen, one hand on the *comal* and the other flipping a fresh tortilla. "Well, so what did you do in school today?"

I went into lengthy detail about the lessons: reading, math, p.e., and social studies. When I started telling her about a field trip to the zoo for next month, she stopped me.

"Let's get back to what you did today, please. Is there anything that you might have left out? I want to know everything."

I shrugged, and proceeded to say the same things by using different words.

"What about prizes, Marta?"

"Stickers? I might get some tomorrow. Nobody got one today."

"What about points? Can children lose points?"

"Oh, sure, but they have to be really bad to get detention. That's what they call it when you have to stay after school even when you don't want to. I never got detention in first grade, but almost everybody else did at least once."

"Yes, I know, *mija*, but I heard that you got scolded by your teacher today. I just want to understand what is going on."

My little heart began to beat faster.

"Is it true that my little girl almost lost enough points to get detention today? Maybe she would have given you detention if you hadn't asked for homework yesterday. If so, that would be wrong. You have to follow the same rules as everybody else. Remember, you're a Mexican. You represent all of us. Have you... have you forgotten?"

Her blue eyes stared straight at me. I gulped.

"Answer me, little girl."

"Wha…what do you want to know?"

"Don't waste my time. I'm a busy woman. Just tell me what you did to almost get detention. We've got to straighten this out before people point to you in the street and say, 'There's Lupe's daughter, the one who is a turning into a delinquent, the one who pretends to do her homework but is a disgrace to her family at school'. Do you want that to happen? Well?"

My minor infractions didn't seem so minor now. Things got either better or worse in that kitchen. Mom was in all her glory there. The kitchen was her domain. When that stove was on, Mom was all fired up. She ruled that world.

"No, no, Mamá!" I shook my head. Taking a deep breath, I told her exactly how I had come to lose three points that day.

When I had finished, she handed a fresh tortilla to me, put a pat of butter on it, and smiled, "I knew that you would tell the truth without a spanking. You are beginning to grow up. You do know, however, that you are not allowed to break the rules, right?"

I nodded in agreement as I took a healthy bite. As Mom began humming again, I walked out with both hands on that tortilla. The melting butter dripped on my tongue, mixing with the taste of corn. I remember wondering if Mrs. Teeter had ever eaten a tortilla like this one.

As the months passed, Little Tony continued to be a part of Doña Lola's daily life. At first, she would walk him to school almost every day. Before I was aware of it, Little

Tony was racing to catch up with me in the mornings. He would say things like, "My grandma is too slow. Let me walk with you guys!"

One day, Doña Lola was sitting in our living room, having a cup of hot chocolate with my mom while I was in the bathroom. I heard part of their conversation.

"Ay, Doña Lupe, this is not easy for me."

"I can imagine, Doña Lola. Children are full of energy."

"Yes, oh, yes. This Tony, I love him so much. My only grandson, you know."

"He adores you, too."

"Hmm. I'm not so sure anymore, Doña Lupita. I'm an old lady."

I heard Mom chuckle. "Oh, that has nothing to do with it!"

"Well, I can't …you know. Who will teach him to play soccer? I am a woman!"

"Ay, Lolita, don't be so hard on yourself. Let his father and his mother do some things for him."

Silence. All I heard for a few seconds was the clinking of stainless steel teaspoons as they stirred their chocolate.

"Ay, Lolita, you do so many things right. You are a wonderful grandmother. Who was it that enrolled him in Santa Fe School, all by herself? *You* did. Who was it that enrolled him in Saturday catechism class all by herself? *You* did. Why, you're the most important person in his life! He *loves* you!"

"Oh, things are not like when I was a little girl. Things are so different in these modern times. I have trouble enough keeping up with my own concerns, like paying the electric bill and such. Well, at least I think Little Tony is doing well in school."

I stifled a laugh.

"My daughter seems to have a lot of homework from this teacher with the funny name."

"Tony rarely has to bring any work home. My Little Tony finishes his work in school. Don't feel bad if your daughter has to bring her work home to finish, though. Each child is different."

Silence.

"Doña Lupe, is it unusual for a child to bring home a pink paper every Friday?"

"Pink paper? Oh, it might be some kind of, ah…assignment."

"Yes, but it doesn't have any math on it or space for any answers. Just a bunch of words in English. Tony says that his teacher wants to tell me special things about him. Not wanting to make you feel bad, but how many pink papers has your daughter received?"

"Ay, Lolita, as you said, each child is different. Here, have a cookie." (pause) "Lilly, who lives on the other side of our house? She told me about some pink papers once that her Angelina and Donaldo were bringing home almost every Friday. The teacher would send them when something was wrong. That way, they get the parent to sign it. I'm sure she said they were pink."

Doña Lola gasped. "Really? But, how could I have known? What could possibly be wrong? He is okay at home."

Mom cleared her throat. Maybe a crumb had gotten stuck for a moment. "It might help if you talked with your grandson. Talking is good. You find out so much that way."

"Ay, Doña Lupe, for you it is easy. You have two daughters and a husband to talk to your five sons. All you have to worry about is why your daughter doesn't finish her work in school. My Tony, he is a boy. It is different for boys."

I could hear my mother sigh: a long, slow, patient sigh. I imagined her staring at the last few drops of hot chocolate in her cup. I quietly went to the bathroom mirror, curious to see if my face was as red as the anger I felt inside. "The very idea!" I thought to myself." That boy thinks that the letters on M&M candies are W's!"

Second grade was more challenging than first grade. There weren't enough abacuses to go around, and I was having a bit of trouble with three digit addition. So were a few other kids, but I didn't pay attention to that. All I could see was that the clock ticked on and on and I was still on the same page of my math book. "This will just not do," I thought to myself.

Tony leaned over towards my desk. "Psst! What's the answer to number five?"

Number five! I was still on number two! How could that have happened? "Tony, mind your own beeswax. Do your own work."

Mrs. Teeter chose that instant to look in our direction. I lost a point for talking during math time. A minute later, I glanced at Tony's paper and discovered why he seemed to be ahead of me. He had skipped the first four problems! I could see him trying to get answers from the kids in the next row. Too bad Mrs. Teeter wasn't turning around now!

The days were filled with little incidents like that. Little Tony would take cuts in the lunch line, and I was the only one from my class to see him. Little Tony would go down the slide after the bell rang, and nobody noticed but me. Little Tony would pretend to hold the classroom door open for me, and then let it almost hit me in the face. Little Tony would make crude jokes about Mrs. Teeter's name when only I was listening. I seemed to be the only witness to his crimes.

Every time I lost points, however, it was dutifully reported to Doña Lola, who would run to my mother. "Oh, Doña Lupita, I know how you must feel. You have so many children, and two of them daughters. How you must worry when she is in trouble in school! It is so much easier with boys. You don't have to worry about them as much. Don't worry, we don't have to let your husband know. You can straighten her out without his ever knowing. Count on me to keep a secret."

Sometimes I would get angry, and sometimes I would just watch her walk back to her little green wooden house, alone, adjusting her black-rimmed glasses. When her hand touched the doorknob on her flimsy screen door, her voice could be heard asking the eternal question, "Tony? Where are you? What are you doing?" She would always walk in without waiting for an answer.

Tony spent most of his time out of the house, usually playing baseball. He often had grass stains on the knees of his jeans. When he would come back at dinnertime, Doña Lola never asked him about the game. She would clasp her hands together on her chest and say things like, "Oh, *Jesús, José, y Maria*! [Jesus, Mary, and Joseph: a religious way to vent frustration without cursing like a sailor] How you like to make me suffer! Why must you make more work for me? Look at those pants! Now I have to wash them and it isn't even Saturday yet!"

As much as I enjoyed school, I was glad to get out that day. The thorn in my side, also known as the infamous Little Tony, had caused me to lose *four* points that day. Mrs. Teeter had actually frowned at me.

Whenever I wanted to forget my troubles after school, I would take the short cut through the empty lot on Avenida De La Plaza. It had some great weeds growing all over it. My imagination turned the uneven ground into a mountainous region, and the occasional broken beer bottle became mysterious buried treasure. The taller the weeds, the rockier the path, the higher I would jump when I reached the end of the path.

I don't know how Little Tony managed to do it, but he had beaten me to West Connecticut Avenue. There he was, next to the end of the empty lot. I tried to ignore him.

"Race ya to your house!" challenged Tony.

"Well, okay," I answered, cautiously. "Whoever gets to my house first is the winner. Don't you dare cheat, you little brat."

Little Tony spit in the dirt and put his arms on his hips. "Hey, watch your mouth, little girl. I wasn't gonna do it, but I'm glad I did it anyway. I was already at your house and I already told your Mamá that you lost four points."

"What? You didn't!"

"Oh, I did. I really, really did. So there!" He stuck out his tongue and added, "Now you're the rotten egg. I beat you, didn't I?"

"You big stupid, Tony. You cheated."

We went around and around on that matter and I finally walked off in a huff. Battling with Tony would only give Doña Lola more reason to feel sorry for my mom, and I couldn't have that at all. No way.

Later on in the evening, Mom pulled me aside and, instead of scolding me, made me sit while she ironed and told me about her own childhood, going into greater detail this time. "You know, *mi niña*, that I only finished second grade. We became orphans when I was, oh, about five. My madrina would not let me go after I finished second grade because she wanted me to clean the house."

"What about her own kids?"

"They could go, but not me. I wanted very much to go to school. Sometimes, I would cry myself to sleep because I could not go to school. My teacher was like an angel to me."

"Didn't you ever have anybody bother you in school? Even once?"

She paused, holding the iron over Dad's plaid shirt. "Oh, I didn't pay attention to class clowns or rude children. I was so happy to be in school, instead of using that heavy mop to clean the bricks on the kitchen floor or washing all of the dishes by myself. I could barely reach the sink. I would be so tired by the end of the day! A few times, I even dozed off standing up, leaning on that big broom. One time, my madrina caught me and she slapped me for being lazy."

"Why didn't you ever tell your older brother when he came to the ranch to visit you?"

"Even though he was a young man, he still had to find time away from his job to travel to the town that I was in. No social security, no welfare. It wasn't easy for him. He would visit maybe three times a year, whenever he could borrow a horse. He always gave me some of those round, bumpy candies called *colaciones*. Oh, how I would savor those treats! He was so proud of my having learned to read."

"Did your mother know how to read?"

"No. Neither did my father. Neither did your own father, until we got married. No matter how many difficulties you may face in school, just think of what you would be like without school. Think of how lucky you are to have a nice teacher, even if she does have a funny name."

Having finished making a professional looking crease in a pair of pants, she paused to smile down at me. I smiled right back.

The next day was a school day. I left the house a few minutes early, and convinced Payo that today we should take the long way. He protested, but was finally convinced when I told him that, if we didn't, Little Tony would probably follow us to school and call him a kindergarten baby again.

"That kid is a pest, Marta," he frowned.

I put my hand on his shoulder and nodded, "Yeah, and he's not too smart. He lives with his grandma, too. How would like to live with your grandma?"

He gasped. "She's dead!"

"Exactly. Besides, Doña Lola isn't as bad as some of the other ladies in our barrio."

"Well, yeah, I guess. She always invites Mom over for coffee and *pan dulce*. Mom likes that. What I don't get, though, is why she don't see when her Little Tony pulls my hair or when he tattles on you? She's clean, and she's Mom's friend, but it would be better if she watched Little Tony more careful."

"Well…"

"And why she didn't know that the pink papers were bad notes from the teacher 'cause Tony was being bad in school? Our mom would have known something fast. Our mom is the smartest mom, huh?"

"Yeah. She is. She taught Dad how to write his name."

He took a deep breath. "Wow!"

As we quietly walked to school, I noticed the shadows. They were unusually sharp. Looking up at the sky, I noticed that the clouds were absent. "I think it's gonna be a hot day, little Payo." I always used his nickname when I was in a good mood.

"How come you say that?"

"The shadows look like they were painted on with watercolor. They got lines."

"That's what shadows are, right? Lines where the light doesn't go?"

"Uh, yeah, but look at the pinacates, too. Those little stink bugs don't try too hard to lift up their butts into the air when you step near them. See?"

Payo stooped down to nudge the little black body of a stubborn stink bug next to a clump of crab grass. "I guess they're already too tired to care today."

"Well, they better care enough to keep from getting squashed."

That day began pretty much as I had expected.

As usual, Little Tony was acting like himself. During the pledge, he made sure that I saw him place his right hand over his heart. The middle finger was extended. When I waved my hand to bring that to Mrs. Teeter's attention, the whole class told me to be quiet. "Wait until after the Pledge of Allegiance, Marta! You can go to the restroom afterwards. We just came into the classroom, anyway."

I was so embarrassed! What made it worse was that we had a restroom in our classroom. One little girl whispered to me, "Stop acting like a kindergarten baby! We have a bathroom close by, or didn't you know that?"

Later on, I fell for another one of Little Tony's tricks. "Hey, Marta, look! I'm on page 100. This is a story about a family that lives in the olden days in a log house in the forest."

Even though my reading group was the highest, we were only supposed to be on page eighty. "How could he be ahead of me?" I wondered. "He might have skipped a few stories, but...it wouldn't hurt to check out that story ahead of time. Mrs. Teeter is busy writing something on the blackboard. I'll just take a little peek at page 100."

Before I knew it, minutes had passed and Mrs. Teeter was tapping the corner of my desk. "Marta, I've been calling you to your reading group. Don't make me come after you again."

In the reading group, I had to admit that I had not read the assigned story, and instead had skipped ahead without permission. "But, Mrs. Teeter, it was about a little girl with braids! Her mom made butter and her daddy chased away bears in the woods!"

The other kids in my reading group rolled their eyes at me. James, the freckle-faced kid who smelled like bologna, kicked my chair and made it look like an accident. Out of the corner of my eye, I could see Little Tony's donkey grin.

During morning recess, I could see little wisps of hot steam rising out of the blacktop on the playground. I spent most of that time avoiding Little Tony by hiding in the shady spots: the tree near the fence, under the slide, and by the girls' restroom area. He spent most of his break time racing about in a chain of a dozen boys who would chase victims, encircle them, and trip them. At one time, the chain of sweaty boys took possession of the slide, going up and sliding down together, landing in a tangled heap: hollering, hooting, and kicking sand.

Since I had spent some time loitering near the drinking fountain and the girls' restrooms, I was ready to get in line when the bell rang. Little Tony barely made it to the line by the time Mrs. Teeter came to get us. He begged permission to drink water and we had to wait for him.

Back in class, during a social studies lesson, he excused himself to go to the restroom. "Mrs. Teeter, I can't hold it in. Please."

She grudgingly let him get up out of his seat, and scolded him for having to go so soon after coming in from recess.

When lunch time came around, I figured that he would be up to his same tricks.

I was, nevertheless, eager for lunch time to come. Today was fish stick day: fish sticks, smashed potatoes, and green lime Jell-O. I was so happy that Mom had given me permission to eat "gringo" food that day! I knew that, if I asked nicely, the cafeteria ladies would give me seconds. Mmm!

I waited impatiently in that long lunch line. Just as I got near the counter, up comes Little Tony, shoving his way through. He took cuts in front of me, whispering, "Shut up and don't say nothin'. I'll let you have my slime Jell-O."

As we left the cash register lady, he delicately wiped the tip of his nose with his left thumb. Then, he jammed the same thumb into his green Jell-O. "Here. Still want it?"

He laughed at the expression of disappointment and rage in my face. "What did you expect? You think anybody would give their green Jell-O away?"

I sputtered something unintelligible and stood still for a moment, the sea of hungry children walking around me, some trying to push me out of the lane of traffic. As Little Tony danced away, holding his tray above his head, I heard him say, "Aw, I didn't really put my thumb in it. Thanks for letting me take cuts! See ya! Wouldn't wanna be ya!"

The sun was sharp and fierce on the playground. I huddled in the shady spots with a few other kids, venturing out occasionally toward the swings or the slides, but not meeting with much success. Just as I would get near an empty swing, either Little Tony or a bigger child would shout, "My turn! I saw it first!" Back to the shadows. The one time that I managed to get a turn to go down the slide, Tony and his sweaty friends decided to go up the slide, shouting, "Make way for the cavalry! We're here to save you!" Back I went, to the safety and shade of the girls' restroom area.

I would have tried to gather a group of my friends to take over the swings or at least the slide area, but the sand on the playground was hotter than the fish sticks, and they had been fresh from the oven. Even the few bees buzzing around were too tired to sting.

"Well," I told myself, "at least I can drink all the water I want before the bell rings. I'll be one of the first ones in line. Besides, the best part of the day is coming up! Story time!"

Mrs. Teeter's magical voice carried us away to other worlds, worlds where animals could talk, babysitters could fly, and worlds where even little girls got to do exciting things. Last week, she had begun reading *Little House on the Prairie*. I was thrilled to discover that the main character was the same one in that selection in our basal reader, the same little girl with braids.

When Mrs. Teeter read to us, she had our full attention. Nobody would even sniff, scratch, or sneeze. Nobody ever fell asleep during this book, either. We would all beg for her to read more than the allotted fifteen minutes. Whenever she would give in to our pleading, the whole class would erupt into one long cheer. We felt like we were in the story ourselves. The book was alive for us.

When the bell signaling the end of lunch recess rang, many children were already in the shady hallway, patiently waiting for their teachers to come and get them. Little Tony was the last one to run towards the line.

He was red in the face, and his T-shirt was one big perspiration stain.

"Drink all the water you can, Tony. I see Mrs. Teeter coming for us."

"Really? Thanks! Don't tell her I was late or nothin'. If she don't know, it's okay, then." He proceeded to drink and drink and drink, sloppily and hungrily, letting big drops of water land on the tip of his nose.

When she came to the front of the line, she started to count the children, but we were eager to get into the room as quickly as possible. "Hurry up, teacher!" all urged. "Start reading to us, please!"

The line marched briskly towards the classroom. I glanced towards the end, and saw Tony patting his stomach with one hand and wiping his face with the other.

Eventually, Mrs. Teeter inserted her key into the classroom door. We raced to our desks and each assumed the classic listening position: arms crossed over his or her individual wooden desk, head on top of folded arms. If Mrs. Teeter walked towards the windows as she read, all eyes followed her. If she walked towards the back of the room, gesturing for greater effect, each of us would twist to see her body language. If she so much as raised her eyebrows, we would hold our breath for the next turn of the plot. She truly brought that book to life for us.

At the end of that chapter, we refused to let her stop. "No, no, Mrs. Teeter! One more chapter, please!"

I was glad that the class liked the book as much as I did. Looking slightly to my left, I was amazed to see that even Little Tony was sitting attentively. "This is good for the boy," I smiled to myself. "Maybe he'll be halfway nice to me on the way home this time."

A page or two later, I heard a slight squeaking sound to my left. "Don't look," I thought to myself. "He's going to distract you somehow. Don't fall for one of his tricks again."

The squeak happened again. I peeked out of the corner of my eye. Tony was twisting left and right, ever so slightly, even as he kept his head was on top of his hands in the listening position. The boy behind him kicked his chair. "Stop that squeaking or I'll get you after school."

Tony's face looked so innocent. His T-shirt was still wet from perspiration. I wasn't sure if it was the shadow of his desk or if his pants were really extra moist around the waist. Then, as he adjusted his position in his chair, I noticed a damp spot beneath his bottom. "That boy sure does sweat like a pig," I thought. "It's a miracle he doesn't melt like the witch in the Wizard of Oz."

A moment later, I couldn't help myself. I had to see if he was still sweating. Mrs. Teeter was probably getting to the end of the second chapter, anyway. I could afford to peek.

I saw that Little Tony's T-shirt was still sticking slightly to the back of his chair. I saw that his hair still stuck a little bit to his forehead, and that the shadowy circle at his waist level could still be seen. The damp circle under his pants was a little puddle now, and that little puddle was starting to drip over the edge of his seat. Oddly enough, the expression on his face did not match what was going on in the story. In a few seconds, I saw a little yellow drop fall quietly from the edge of his chair.

I listened to Mrs. Teeter read the last few paragraphs of the chapter as I watched Little Tony piddle in his seat. He was so nonchalant! I was amused by his lack of bladder control and, at the same time, I marveled at his ability to maintain his composure in an embarrassing situation.

Little Tony was lucky to have such a forgiving teacher. Instead of pointing out his little accident, she distracted the others by telling us to form four teams for a spelling bee. While my classmates raced to form their favorite groups, she brought her water glass over to Little Tony's desk and pretended to spill it on the floor. Then, she bent over Tony and whispered in his ear. His eyes turned a watery pink. As the other kids jostled for positions in each of the four corners of the classroom, Little Tony sprinted to the restroom.

"Oh, my! I seem to have spilled my glass of water. Will somebody help me to clean it?"

Ten children raced to get tissue paper from the box on her desk. "Hey, you wet Tony. His desk, too!" one boy commented.

"I'll help clean up, too," I added.

When Little Tony emerged from the bathroom, a number of boys patted him on the back and said, "Aw, don't be mad at her. Your pants will dry. Be a man, Tony, and stop sniffling."

When I came home that afternoon, I sat down at the kitchen table. Mom always wanted to know all about the events of the day. She would sigh, laugh, and chuckle at every little detail of the lessons. Occasionally, she would interrupt and offer me some advice on the not-so-glorious parts of my scholastic day. "Hearing about what you learn in school is the highlight of my day. Sometimes you make me feel as if I were in school with you, too."

When I came to the part of Little Tony peeing in class, she was strangely silent. I wanted to giggle and say something like, "What a savage that child is! Doesn't he know that his family will be embarrassed, too? Maybe his family doesn't care."

Mom poured more cherry Kool-Aid into my glass. "You think any of the other children noticed? I mean, besides you? Did you tell anybody besides me?"

I was puzzled. "Not yet. I didn't want to make my teacher look like a liar in front of the whole class, but I know what I saw. Should we go and tell Doña Lola right now?"

"No. Let that be Tony's business. Doña Lola is home right now, and she is his grandmother. She would want to deal with this herself."

The next day was Saturday. I was surprised to see Doña Lola come to our door during breakfast. "Doña Lupe, may I borrow your telephone?"

Mom scooted us into the living room and turned the cartoons on. I gobbled my pan dulce, drank my milk, and watched Popeye on the tube. I was enjoying the cartoons too much to make any sense of the hushed tones of conversation between Doña Lola and Mom. I don't remember hearing anybody dial the phone, but it must have happened.

A while later, Doña Lola walked quietly past us. "Call me when that phone rings, Lupita. Send one of your children to come and get me. I'll be waiting."

It was one of those busy Saturdays when everything is a blur. So many things to clean in the morning, so many tacos to eat at lunchtime, so many games to play in the afternoon. I had forgotten all about Little Tony until I happened to see his dad's pickup truck parked in front of Doña Lola's house.

The man with the new corduroy pants and a sporty mustache must have been his father. He was stuffing a pink paper into a shirt pocket and loading two little suitcases into the back of the truck.

Doña Lola was standing at her doorway, holding open the screen door with her back as she wrung her hands. "Come on, muchacho. You make people wait too much and too much of anything is bad for everybody."

I didn't hear exactly what Little Tony said to her. After all, I was standing by my fence and they lived two houses down from us. After he climbed into the truck, he rolled the window down and, hands gripping the edge of the window, stared at Doña Lola. She was dabbing the edges of her eyes with her embroidered handkerchief. The man who seemed to be his father started up the truck without a word, without even waving at Doña Lola. I wondered why Tony didn't look at him.

As the truck began to rumble away down West Connecticut Avenue, Little Tony turned towards my house. He pressed his face against the rear window and stuck out his tongue. When he stuck his tongue out for the second time, the man's right hand slapped Tony and then yanked Tony's right ear, forcibly turning him to face forward.

Mom had quietly walked out of the house and was now standing next to me. "Mom, did you see that?"

"Yes."

"Doña Lola saw it, too. Why didn't she do something?"

"Can you chase after a truck, even if you wanted to?"

"No, I guess not."

"Mija, bring me some pan dulce. Choose two of the best pieces and bring them to me at Doña Lola's. I feel like sharing some orange blossom tea."

Little Tony never came back.

As time went by, Doña Lola invited me into her kitchen more and more often. "Martita, taste this flan. Is it sweet enough? Take some to your Mamá for me." "Martita, I'll buy you anything you want from the ice cream truck if you rake my yard for me."

Sometimes I would help her for nothing, and I would find out later that she had given something to Mom, saying, "That child of yours won't take money from me. Here, buy her some candy, Lupita."

She would wave to me in the morning as I skipped to school, and she was usually in her garden when I skipped back in the afternoon. Her wrinkled face always gave me a little smile as I passed in front of her house. "Oh, your mother has such strong hands to make such beautiful braids for you. I'm sure you had a nice day in school, too!"

I got used to those little bits of attention. One time, I scraped my knee on my way home. I knew that Mom was working with Dad that day, and I figured that I would have to put a "curita" (band-aid) on my own knee. Doña Lola, however, saw it and insisted that I come into her living room so she could take care of it. "You kids nowadays. You think you can do everything yourselves. I won't have my best friend's daughter bleeding to death before she comes home from work. Sit still."

Would it be okay to bleed to death after Mom and Dad come home? I thanked her when she had finished putting three Band-Aids on my knee. I certainly didn't need three Band-Aids, but I decided to keep my thoughts and opinions to myself. I knew that my parents would ask Doña Lola if they had any questions. That wouldn't be so bad.

I guess that's what it is like to have a grandmother.

I did find out, years later, that Tony did not remain with his father, and even his mother ceased to be a part of his life. Rumor had it that his other grandmother had taken him in, until he disappeared into the foster care system.

Chris Rock, talented comedian, once said, "...If the kid grows up calling his grandma Mom, and his momma Pam, that kid's going to jail!" I certainly hope that Little Tony called his other grandmother "nana".

Anonymous Old Lady

Go Ahead and Hit Me

In the days of the cave men and their little cave kids, it was all black and white. If you could kill a wild animal that fed the whole tribe, you were accorded the status of a grown-up. If you were fast enough, strong enough, and smart enough to do that, what did they care if you were short?

The only wild animals in our barrio were the occasional stray cat or dog. We weren't allowed to hunt them and we were prohibited from feeding them or showing any affection to them, too. We still did it, but not when our parents were looking. Dad would just make the animal disappear by taking it to work with him in the morning and dropping it off at the outskirts of town. "Animals belong in the wild," he would say.

One of the ways that I tried to prove that I was growing up was by working hard at home and at Mr. Miller's ranch. Although that meant perspiring a lot and seeing fewer cartoons on the television, it was usually worth it to see the look of satisfaction on my father's face and hear my mother brag about us to the neighbors. When the whole family went together to pick avocados, lemons, or macadamia nuts, it could actually be quite… unifying.

Those activities were not optional, of course. I still yearned for some unique way to prove that I was on the road to becoming a grown-up. My parents seemed to be trustworthy and strong people. I wanted to prove that I was like that, too.

When the day came that Mom sent me alone to the store, I was ready. I was also so nervous and excited that I got halfway down the block, twice, and realized that my pockets were empty. The third time, however, I made sure that I had the right amount of coins before walking out the door.

"I'm going now for reals, Mom!"

She scowled and muttered something that sounded like, "Finally!" Since I was taking so long to bring the things on her list, she probably threatened me, too. I didn't hear much, though. I was on a cloud of my own and the sun was shining just for me.

We lived almost at the end of our street, where Calle Chapultepec becomes West Connecticut Avenue. From our front porch I headed down past Doña Lola's house and past my Tía Teófila's house to Avenida Benito Juárez. One block. I made sure I was on the south side of the street to avoid the house where the "marijuanos" lived. It smelled funny and the cops were always parked in front there. Three more blocks to go.

Continuing on toward Santa Fe Avenue, I could see the junkyard museum of the barrio, a house near the corner of Calle Independencia. The stucco house had a large front yard, enclosed with a wire fence. Between the fence and the peeling green paint of the front door was an interesting assortment of auto parts and garden tools. The objects in the "museum" were always sprouting weeds and harboring spiders and sometimes small animals that squeaked and breathed in the dark spaces between the crusty chunks of wood and metal. I was in too much of a hurry to stop and peek through the fence. Two blocks down, two to go.

Now, I was almost in front of the Vista Irrigation District office building, the only part of our street that had a sidewalk. Across from the VID was where that mean German shepherd dog lived. El Perro Malo. El Diablo. Sometimes they had that scraggly looking dog tied to a short rope in their front yard, but sometimes he bit through the rope and then, you had to be very careful. That dog didn't want you to even breathe on his side of the street. If you managed to get to the corner of Redlands Street without waking up the old dog, you were usually safe.

Do I have time to wander past the auto repair shop and go down Redlands to look at the sheep penned outside of the slaughter house? Not today. If I hadn't forgotten the money twice, maybe. I could still smell them and hear their bleating. Baa, baa, baa. "Maybe tomorrow, little Bo Peeps," I thought. "Maybe tomorrow I can make a special field trip down to put my hand through the fence and scratch your wooly heads. Maybe tomorrow 'cause my mom's counting on me today."

With great satisfaction, I looked at the street sign that said Redlands and West Connecticut Avenue. Three blocks! All by myself! All I had to do now was cross the street, pass the auto repair shop on the corner, and walk into the Durán Market. The fourth and final block.

"If Laly was here, she would give me a hug for being so brave and coming all by myself," I thought. Laly, of course, was my only sister, and someone whose opinion I valued. I was just beginning to think of that again when the sound of a passing car scattered my small fantasy. Instinctively, my feet scurried faster towards the front of the store.

I stopped briefly at the entrance and took a deep breath. What was on that list? Oh, yeah... Carton of milk. One dozen eggs. Chorizo. Small bag of flour for making flour tortillas. I remembered!

I strolled past the candy display and walked to the refrigerated area at the back. Milk. Whoa! Those plastic containers were pretty heavy! Wait. One carton of milk. That was it! The cartons weren't too heavy for me. Okay.

Carton of milk. One dozen eggs. What kind of eggs? Brown or white? What color were the chickens that laid them? Were the brown eggs laid by chickens who could speak Spanish? No, chickens only spoke chicken. I'll take the white ones. Mom says they call them *blanquillos* in Aguascalientes because huevos can mean something else. Wonder what she meant by that?

Carton of milk. One dozen eggs. Candy. No, no candy. How did that thought get inside my head? Um... uh...what goes with eggs? Chorizo! That's it! What kind? Maybe the one that has the red, white, and green label with the cartoon face of a smiling pig. It looks familiar.

Milk. Eggs. Chorizo. Ice cream? No! Chase those loose thoughts away! Mom said I could get one Bazooka bubble gum if there was any change, but nothing else. Milk. Eggs. Chorizo. What goes with eggs and chorizo? Masa harina for the corn tortillas? I know we don't need any of that. Dad bought some yesterday. What could it be? El Pato hot sauce in those little yellow cans?

This was too much pressure. I felt my stomach beginning to turn.

"Are you okay, Marta? Do you want me to put those things on the counter while you finish getting everything else?" Mr. Durán, the store owner, smiled at me. Even when he smiled, his mustache still covered his upper lip. How could he eat soup without getting yelled at by his mother?

"Oh! No, I can do it by myself."

His head tilted ever so slightly to one side. "Kids grow like weeds in this neighborhood. Taller every day!"

He went on about his business, whistling and dusting the top shelves. I hugged the cold carton of milk with my left arm and gently cradled the gray carton of white eggs in my right arm. "Maybe if I put these on the counter, it will help me remember what else I am supposed to get."

I did that and, for the next couple of minutes, I wandered about the store like a grown-up lady doing the weekly shopping for the family. Whenever another shopper would look my way, I would pretend to become very interested in the price of whatever was in front of me. Just like my mom, I would mutter something like, "Tsk, tsk. That's way too much."

I enjoyed playing the game, but time was running. Fortunately, since there were only four aisles in the whole store, it didn't take me long to get back to the counter. That's where I noticed the bags of flour near the door. Flour tortillas! That's what Mom wanted to make today!

I was done with my shopping. Time to pay and hurry home.

Even though I had to stand on my tiptoes a bit to reach for the change, it felt wonderful to see Mr. Durán count out the coins on my little hands. "Anything else? Do your parents want a pack of Lucky Strike cigarettes?"

"No, thank you, Mr. Durán. They want to quit smoking because it costs too much. I would like one piece of bubble gum, though. Here's the penny."

I didn't unwrap the gum until I was outside and next to the auto repair shop. I leaned against the street sign to look at the comic strip and put the bag of groceries by my feet. This was my treat, and I would make it last all the way home by blowing big pink bubbles that would make the other kids jealous and wish they were me.

I had done it. I had walked all the way to the store by myself, without losing the money. I had bought everything that I was supposed to, without forgetting one single thing. All I had to do now was walk back home with the groceries as I blew fat pink bubbles of joy. I could do that. Left, right, left, right, … I'd be home before I knew it.

The air seemed fresher and the breeze was at my back as I crossed Redlands. I noticed that the German shepherd was tied up and this time, for a change, they had tied him to a shady tree. Even mean dogs need shade.

I had almost gotten to Calle Independencia when I heard a screen door slam. The sound came from the German shepherd's house. His owners were almost as ornery as he was, but they never bothered us. Not usually.

Because of the eggs in the paper bag, I was walking carefully to avoid stones and clumps of crab grass. Maybe that's why I didn't hear the boy running toward me until he was right in front of me.

His jet-black hair almost touched the collar of his once-white T-shirt. "Hey, you got any more gum?"

I shook my head and tried to walk past him, but he blocked the way. "You got any candy?"

"My mom didn't give me any money for candy. All I have is food. I don't have any gum and I don't have any candy."

He crossed his arms and sneered. "You have gum. You're chewing some!"

I shifted the bag to my right side. "I don't have any more. My mom said I could only buy one piece of gum if I got any change."

His eyes got a shifty rat look to them and he started poking the grocery bag with his left index finger. "You got more gum. I know it. How much change you got, little kindergarten baby?"

"I'm not in kindergarten, but you're still bigger than me. Why don't you go pick on somebody your own size?"

He picked up a stick from the gutter and whacked the bag. My heart jumped inside.

"Are you gonna cry or are you gonna give me the money, little kindergarten baby?"

I swallowed hard. I wanted to kick his butt, but I was on a mission. That came first. Besides, I knew that there was no way that I could beat him. I only came up to his shoulders and, even if he had started the whole fight, I would still have to pray endless rosaries at home for breaking the No Fighting Commandment.

My skinny legs became paralyzed. I had grown roots, right into the ground. Like the telephone poles, I just stood there and let him circle me, taunting, teasing, and poking the bag with that dirty stick.

"Say somethin', you little crybaby. I know you wanna cry. Gimme the money and I'll leave you alone."

"Stop hitting the bag! If I come home with cracked eggs, I'll get in trouble!"

No amount of talk would make him stop. I was afraid and at my wit's end.

"Well, what's it gonna be, little *güerita*? You little girl the color of sour cream. Think you're better like *café con leche*, huh? Think you're better 'cause you have green eyes?"

"I was born with them."

"Yeah?" He jabbed my knees and I almost tripped as I struggled to step away. "Wonder what your Daddy did when he saw that!"

My face reddened at the insult. "For your information, you little pachuco, my mamá has blue eyes and it's not her fault."

He continued to circle me as he whacked the bag. I managed to take a step or two, but he was really quite good at mugging little girls with long braids. I was more angry than afraid now, but I kept thinking to myself, "I am on a mission. If I mess up this assignment, I'll never live it down."

Whack! Stab. Ouch!

"Are ya chicken? Why don't you try an' hit me if ya can? Gimme it! Gimme the change!"

I repeatedly told him that I had no gum to give him and that he was not going to get what little change that I had. "We work hard for our money. I work, too." This would only make his eyes get that wild boy look in them and he would smack the bag one more time.

Panic grabbed me by the throat and made my eyes get watery. I might die on the street. Right there, in the gutter, across from the junkyard museum. Flies would be circling my dead body and stray dogs would come by and sniff my shoes. That's where my family would find me. Nobody would be there to pat me on the head before I died. Not today.

My parents would argue over why it had happened. Dad would accuse my mother of being negligent in letting such a young girl go alone to the store. "I told you that she wasn't grown-up enough to handle the job. Why did you have to let her go alone?"

My five brothers would be clutching their stomachs and sobbing, "Why? Why? Why must we go hungry?"

And still, the buzzard circled around me, jabbing the stick at my skinny legs, pulling my braids, and cursing at me in English words that I did not recognize.

Still hugging the bag to protect my family's food, a spasm of my facial muscles squeezed a few more words out of my throat. "Go ahead and hit me, but leave the bag alone."

"What? You're stupid."

His opinion of me wasn't very high, but my words had broken his momentum. He tossed the stick aside and spit on my shoes. "Just you stay away from our yard and our dog. Go on home, little kindergarten baby. I don't wanna play with you anymore."

He sauntered off, laughing wickedly at my fear.

My little feet began to move immediately. I had to get those groceries home pronto! What time was it? No use even wondering. I couldn't tell time and I didn't even own a watch.

The corner of West Connecticut and Calle Independencia! Two more blocks to go. Move, little white shoes, move fast. A police car drove by and made a right turn on Avenida Benito Juárez. Go, little feet, go! Hold onto the grocery bag, little arms, hold on!

The corner where the cop car had stopped. I heard some loud voices and saw a couple of the marijuanos climbing out the back window of their house. Nothing new. One more block to go!

Tía Teófila was watering her front lawn, waving to me. She was always so thin. There's Doña Lola in her garden, with her widow's dark support hose on those old chicken legs and sprinkling water over her roses, humming like always. There's our white picket fence and the tall pine tree behind it.

And there's our screen door, waiting for me!

For dinner that day, we had fat burritos made of nopalitos, scrambled eggs, and chorizo. It never tasted so good.

Second Grade
The sweater was blue and white.
The curl, again, smelled of beer.

Just One Lousy Tortilla

There is no such thing as a perfect childhood even if you are born rich and live in a perfect neighborhood. This is, I believe, because people are imperfect beings. Our reflexes are part of the problem. Our mouths can say whole sentences before our brain weighs the consequences. It is, indeed, a miracle that so many people grow to adulthood without becoming permanently warped.

In this story from West Connecticut Avenue, you will meet the characters that we often spent time with, people that have long since moved away from Vista, California, searching for better ground. You will not find persons with those exact names, but you may recognize fragments of their personality in this person at the grocery store or that person that works in the desk next to yours or the guy driving in the next lane. Or maybe you will see reflections of these characters in your own past.

***

We had all spent the day picking macadamia nuts in the macadamia tree orchard in Oceanside, a day filled with hard work, sweat, and the occasional flinging of a hard nut at an unsuspecting brother. As usual, we sang Mexican songs all the way home in the back of the pickup truck.

Laly always got us singing by putting her arms around me and Payo, the youngest, and yelling, "Come on, everybody!" Then we would go through all of her favorites: "La Delgadina", "Rosita Alvírez", "Los Laureles", and ones we often sang in Saint Francis Church on Sundays such as "De Colores" and "La Guadalupana".

After dinner, we still felt like playing outside, and why not? The weather was just fine and we had worked hard. A few shouts over the fences on either side of our house brought over the neighbor children: Lilly's kids (El Donny and his two sisters, La Angelina and Little Lupita [more about this trio later]), and Little Evie and her big brother, El Eddie.

We played the usual games and laid pennies on the railroad track so the passing train would flatten them and leave them warm to the touch. We made grassy piles of weeds in the back yard and jumped on them. We ate the last guavas on the guava bushes in our yard, and ate the last grapes on the vine in Evie and El Eddie's yard.

Pancho suggested that we toast marshmallows over the burning pile of garbage in our back yard. We even tossed a half dozen plain brown potatoes into the fire. It wasn't a very big fire, but we enjoyed every one of those little marshmallows and, later, shared the baked potatoes without much arguing.

The fun we had was even more delicious because we had worked so hard that whole day. The close feeling of working together with my whole family during the day carried over naturally to the close feeling of playing with my friends in the evening. I fell asleep as soon as my head touched the pillow. Laly's legs may have flopped over me as they always did on the twin bed we shared, but I never felt them. Even my dad's snoring, the kind of snoring that made the thin walls vibrate, didn't wake me up that night. I don't even remember dreaming.

The trouble with having a great day is that the next day doesn't always measure up to it. When you are young, your view of the universe is one-dimensional. You expect things to always go up and never come down. Facing change is like getting a message on your mental screen that says "This does not compute" or "Not enough memory to process this data". The younger you are, the less you are capable of understanding the yin and yang of existence, the fact that all things must balance out.

You really expect to have more fun the next day and even more the day after that. You imagine that fun is just around the next corner. Some people say that this is a way of easing our entry into adulthood. Who would *want* to grow up if they were constantly being told about the very unglamorous aspects of adulthood: personal relationships, aches and pains, fixing the car, income taxes, buying groceries, and life insurance? Children prefer to think that adults have it easy.

"So, what should we do tonight?" asked El Eddie, standing outside of our back door.

Pancho pressed his nose to the screen and answered, "Give us about ten minutes. Go get the other kids while Marta and I finish cleaning the kitchen. We'll think of something!"

Within a short while, we were playing an enthusiastic game of hide-and-go-seek. Pancho usually won. He was the best counter and the most agile of all of us, plus he was the oldest of the bunch. He was known to hide up in a tree or sometimes on the roof of our house. Being smaller than him, we dared not complain.

We tried roasting marshmallows again, until Evie dropped her last marshmallow into the fire.

"That was your fault, Donny!" she yelled, kicking a flaming piece of paper at his sandals.

"Watch it, shrimp," he said, defensively. "You bumped into my elbow."

La Angelina stood protectively next to her brother. "Man, Evie! You get all clumsy and then you get mad at us. I'd give you some of my marshmallows, but you gotta relax first."

Knowing that no good could come of interference, I quietly peeled the black crust off of my roasted marshmallow. Oooh, was that hot! I decided to immediately share the tasty treat with my little brother. "Hey, Payo, wanna marshmallow? Open wide and say, 'Aaah'!"

Of course, he was delighted only up to the moment that the melted marshmallow touched his lips. Instinct made him swallow the smoldering morsel even as his eyes bugged out. He did not thank me for my generosity.

Pancho, though always amused by our antics, had a second sense that told him when it was time to try something new. He knew that, in order for the evening to last, we had to stay together as a group. If we broke off into warring factions, the adults would poke their heads out of the windows and yell at us to come back inside and go to bed. Some form of restriction or punishment would follow, and the next evening's free time would be spent praying the rosary in a corner.

I yawned. "Anybody hungry?"

Payo rubbed his eyes. "Well, but no more potatoes 'cause Mom said we couldn't get any more. Eddie, can you get some from your house?"

"Some *papas*?"

"Well, yeah. From your house."

El Eddie stared into the fire and tossed a few dry sticks into it. "Well, we don't got no potatoes. How about weenies?"

La Angelina and El Donny squealed gleefully. "Yeah! Our parents aren't home, and we got some hot dog bread, the long skinny kind!"

"They call those 'hot dog buns'," Pancho added.

"Whatever," snipped La Angelina. "You wanna eat some or not?"

Payo seemed impressed. "You mean we can cook real hot dogs? Eddie, you really got weenies? Can I get a weenie?"

La Angelina snickered. She was going to say something nasty, but Pancho glared at her and Laly did, too.

I tried to be the voice of reason. "Well, we can cook the weenies but only if you're sure that you won't get in trouble. I mean, if the weenies are for your dinner tomorrow, then we better leave them alone."

Children live in a world of their own. When a child reaches a conclusion, it is usually only half of a complete thought. When a group of children reach a conclusion, it is sometimes less than that. So, it came to be that the "weenies" from the neighbor's refrigerator ended up being roasted on sticks and bent wire hangers instead of being put on a dinner plate.

Our parents were home, so we didn't dare sneak back for more than a few extra marshmallows. We felt justified in eating our share of weenies because, after all, we were the providers of the campfire. We felt that they who hold the Ohio Blue Tip matches should control the direction of the campfire activities.

The next night, Lilly's kids (La Angelina, El Donny, and Little Lupita) stole another dozen hot dog buns from their kitchen. We lit another fire using used brown paper bags from the grocery store. Neither Pancho, Laly, Payo, or I thought to ask again if it was okay with their parents. We knew that their parents lived by different rules, and, besides, we wanted to recapture the fun of toasting the buns and roasting the weenies just as we had the night before.

Eventually, El Eddie and Evie did join us, but without the weenies.

Payo was the first to question them, "Hey, you guys! We have three marshmallows left and lots and lots of hot dog bread and some old tortillas, but where are those weenies? We said we were gonna to do it again tonight. Don't you remember?"

"Yeah!" I added. "It ain't much of a campfire without weenies."

El Eddie distracted us by teaching us his latest game: The Flaming Tortilla Frisbee. He explained the rules and reminded us about fire safety by reciting "Jack be Nimble". Payo and I were both impressed by his classy presentation, and in a few seconds, everybody was standing around the fire in a circle.

"Oh, man, this is gonna be great!" I smiled.

At the count of ten, we each held a corn tortilla, very carefully, into the dancing orange and yellow flames. When all tortillas were flaming on one side, we all began to sing and wiggle around the fire, "One, two, three, la conga! Ha! One, two, three, la conga! Hey!" The object of the game was to hold on as long as possible. When the fire that was consuming your tortilla began to cook your thumbnail, then you would shout and fling it like a Frisbee across the fire to the person directly opposite to you. You scored a point with a direct hit, but the more impressive the hit, the more likely that somebody else's tortilla would hit you in the exact same place.

I don't remember how long we played that game, but we eventually returned to the subject of making hot dogs again. This time, however, we decided to toast the hot dog buns first.

"I gonna do it this time," announced Little Lupita.

She promptly snatched the bag from her sister's hand and tossed it into the fire. Of course, we stood dumbfounded as the plastic melted all over the buns. For a few seconds, we were hypnotized by the drippy, swirling shape of the melting plastic bag and the stinky smoke that it gave out. It made such a pretty blue flame, too! Then, the smell of burning bread forced us to face the sad fact that we had just lost our beautiful golden brown hot dog buns.

I was surprised to see that, for once, La Angelina actually glared at her little sister. El Donny gave Little Lupita's left arm a good pinch and said that if she complained, that there was more where that came from.

That's when the corners of Evie's mouth started to turn down.

Pancho patted her on the head. "It's not so bad, Evie."

"But we don't have no bread anymore."

"Yeah, but we can always roast the weenies!" smiled Payo.

We began to chant, "Weenies! Weenies! Weenies!" but neither El Eddie or Evie were chanting along. As a matter of fact, the corners of Evie's mouth turned down even more.

"Go get the weenies, Eddie."

"Go get the weenies now, Evie."

"Why don't you go get the weenies?"

"Come on, you guys, it's getting late! Go get the weenies so we can roast 'em before the fire dies down and before our parents call us back inside! Hurry!"

As El Eddie pretended to tie his shoe, Evie started to snivel. "Gimme a tortilla, first."

Pancho put his hands on his hips and said sternly, "Ah, knock it off! No tortillas anymore. This calls for weenies! You hear me? I said WEENIES!"

That's when Evie sat down in the dirt and covered her face with her hands.

"You made my sister cry!" shouted El Eddie. "You yelled at her! I'm not gonna play with you guys anymore!"

As he ran over to his own back yard, we all tried to put our arms around Evie.

"Can't you gimme just one tortilla?" pleaded Evie, still covering her face with her hands. We could see tears slowly rolling down her sooty hands.

"But, Evie, we could only play with the old tortillas and we ran out of those. Can't you get some weenies? You and Eddie said you would bring weenies. Why do you say stuff and then not do it?" asked Pancho.

Still holding her hands over her eyes, Evie got up and headed home. Laly lost interest and went back inside our house, but the rest of us followed Evie, gently holding her elbows so that she wouldn't stumble too much. I even held her back door open and helped guide her up the three steps into her kitchen. El Eddie was already inside, locked in the bathroom.

"Eddie, get your butt out here! What's the deal? What's goin' on, anyway?" shouted Pancho. "Make your sister stop cryin' before your parents come home an' before our parents hear her!"

"Come on, El Eddie!" shouted La Angelina and El Donny, as they pounded their fists on the bathroom door. "You're a coward, Eddie Spaghetti!"

"Don't call me that!"

"El Eddie spaghetti, your meatballs are ready!" snickered El Donny.

Evie had made it to her bedroom and was now sobbing. "How come you guys are so mean to me? Why don't you just give me one lousy tortilla?"

We all sat in a circle around her, slightly confused.

"But, Evie," I reminded her, "we told you that we ran out of them. Honest!"

I then tried a new line of questioning, "Evie, come with me to the kitchen, okay? Let's go see what we can use for roasting. We can roast almost anything. Even bologna, if we're careful."

We all walked over to the kitchen. When I looked inside the refrigerator, I quickly slammed it shut.

I felt as if I had swallowed a rock, a heavy rock that was now sitting on the bottom of my stomach. I remembered the delicious *sopa de fideo* and pinto beans that we had gorged ourselves on at dinnertime. It was almost unbearable to stare at the cold little light bulb in their small refrigerator.

"Open it again. I wanna see," demanded Pancho.

Hesitating, Evie opened it again. Everyone else had a good look inside. There was not a weenie in sight. There was, in fact, precious little in their refrigerator: an almost empty carton of milk, a six-pack of beer, and half of a stick of butter.

"Your parents went to the store, I bet," said Payo.

"I dunno," sniffed Evie, wiping her nose on her T-shirt. "My daddy called on the telephone and told my mommy to go to the store, I think. Anyway, she got into the pickup truck in a hurry and said we could feed ourselfs from the refrigerator."

"Didn't you all eat dinner before they left?" questioned El Donny.

"And?" we all asked.

"And we ate some of the butter, but the beer doesn't taste so good to us, so we're still hungry," she sobbed.

In a few minutes, El Eddie had come out of the restroom and we were all huddled together in Evie's room, discussing our situation. We knew that sneaking food out of our house or Lilly's house was out of the question; we had no food to share.

Being children, we felt that it would be senseless to just give up and go to bed! The code of childhood said that no child should go to bed before being forced to do so by a grownup. Every waking moment was supposed to be crammed with as much fun as a child could fit into it. We all firmly believed that to not try to do so was to turn into a grownup before your time. We knew that, once lost, childhood could never be recovered.

"I know what will make us feel better," announced Pancho.

"Just don't say 'weenies', please," groaned El Eddie.

"Well, we're friends, right?"

Everyone nodded in agreement.

"We like to do stuff together, right?"

Again, all heads nodded.

"So, who does more stuff together than a club?"

"What are we gonna call ourselves?" asked Payo.

"The Lions Club!" shouted El Donny.

"Wait, how about the Adelitas Club?" I smiled.

Pancho, El Eddie, and El Donny promptly pushed me off of the bed. "Forget it! That's for girls!"

Little Lupita had gone to sleep in one corner of the bed, so Evie was the youngest one who was still awake, but she had been rubbing her eyes for a while and she began to cry again.

"Let's call ourselves the Tiger Club, because tigers have scary eyes and sharp teeth!" suggested Payo. "Hey, since we don't have a club house, can we still be a club?"

I patted him on the back and added, "Either the Tigers or maybe the Dragons. Something big!"

Pancho agreed with both of us. "Yeah. These are great names. Too good for a club. We'll be a real gang! We'll do stuff together every night until our parents make us come inside!"

We cheered enthusiastically and began to punch each other.

Evie began to sob.

Pancho put his arm around her. "What is it now, Evie? If we're going to be a gang, I don't think that we should be crying, right?"

She sobbed and looked around at all of us. "You all want those names!"

"No," I interrupted, "we haven't decided on the name yet."

Then, Pancho added, "Do you have any ideas? Evie?"

I hadn't expected for him to ask for her opinion. I thought that it would be more appropriate for the oldest ones in the gang to decide on the name. However, I also knew that if she wasn't allowed into our gang, then Little Lupita wasn't going to be in, either. That part, though certainly appealing, also meant that our gang would be way too small to be taken seriously by anybody else in the barrio.

Since Evie didn't answer immediately, the rest of us began deciding on who would be president and vice-president. It was decided that I be the secretary because I liked to play school more than anybody on the block.

As we were deciding on the officers for our new gang, Evie continued to cry quietly.

We began to debate the merits of combining the most impressive names (lions, tigers, dragons, wild dogs, etc.) into one long, bloodthirsty name that would instill fear in the hearts of all others in the barrio.

Evie, however, did not have the courtesy to fall asleep like Little Lupita. Worse yet, she continued to cry and rub her eyes.

"Evie, gang members don't cry," I scolded.

"I can't help it! I'm scared!" she sobbed. "Maybe I don't wanna be in a gang!"

Payo shook her by the shoulders. "Oh, no you don't! You can't quit us! We need everybody and you know it!"

"I'm still scared."

"Of what?" asked Pancho. "This is silly!"

I held Evie's hand and stroked it gently. "Go ahead and tell us what you're scared of. We're a gang now, okay? We just have to make up a gang name, and we can start to be a real official gang. Don't you wanna be in our gang? We all live next to each other, anyway! We need you, Evie, because you live on our block. What are you scared of?"

"The names!" she blurted out, sobbing.

"What?"

"The names! Lions eat little kids and tigers do, too! And wild dogs bite kids in the you-know-what! They don't have to eat weenies 'cause they can eat little kids!"

Ouch! Evie had stirred up a memory that I wanted to forget. I didn't want to be reminded of the evil Dalmatian that lived two blocks from the corner store. That was a most painful and embarrassing incident. Mom had to call Mrs. Quintanilla, the wife of the store owner, and ask for a ride to take me to the doctor's office. Dr. Jansen did, however, soothe my bruised ego by giving me a handful of lollipops and a tiny plastic kazoo... after putting a big bandage on my little pink behind, to cover up the teeth marks.

Pancho leaned his head slightly, and put his arm around Evie's shoulders. "So, if those names scare you, what if we call ourselves The West Connecticut Avenue Gang?"

Nope. Too hard to spell.

"What about something nice and sweet?" suggested Evie.

It was getting late in the evening. Pancho, Payo, and I knew that our parents would soon begin calling us to come home. If we dared to be late, it would be bad news for us.

"Hurry up, Evie! Why not the Lions or the Tigers? How about the Man-eating Bears?"

"I don't like those scary names!"

"Then what?" asked Pancho, still hugging her shoulders. "Tell us what wouldn't scare you because we really wanna have you in our gang. I mean, we don't have the time to get kids from the other blocks. It's got to be just us, so go ahead and say something. Now."

Evie's red eyes turned to Pancho.

"So? Hurry up and say somethin' Evie," urged Payo.

"Yeah, hurry up!" demanded La Angelina.

El Donny crossed his arms impatiently.

"Hey, you guys," I added, "no matter what we call ourselves, we'll still be the only ones who are in a gang. No matter what name we pick, we'll still do stuff together! We're the best kids on the block! I say, let us show everybody that we're gooder than the other kids. We're so much gooder that we can let ..."

"...even the littlest member of our gang choose the name! Yeah!" nodded Pancho. He also wanted to put a quick end to the matter at hand and get to the point.

Evie sniffed. Her nose was beginning to run and it was not a pretty sight. Payo shuddered in disgust when she wiped her nose on her arm, leaving a streak of yellow-green *mocos* from her wrist to her dirty elbow. "Maybe I do like to be in a gang, even if I'm not the biggest one in it. I can choose the name? Really?"

We all shouted loudly, "YES!" and continued to encourage her to speed it up. Already, the little gears in our brains were squeaking as they turned. We began chattering about how to identify ourselves: secret codes, secret handshakes, Halloween pranks, satin jackets with old English lettering, etc.

"I got it," announced Evie, with a smile.

Pancho stopped the chattering with a flourish of his hands and saying, "Laaadeeees and gentlemeeeeen! Reeeememberrrrr this moment for hissstory, this special moment when our gang will officially begin! Reeememberrr this moment for all of your life! And, now, laaadeeees and gentlemen, the official name of our gang is..."

All eyes turned to Evie. It seemed as if the weenie problem would be forgotten forever upon hearing our new name, upon announcing our new identity!

"The Puppies."

That was our first and last gang meeting.

Fritos and Bologna vs. Rice and Beans

Lilly's Kids: A Brief Description
This is not a story, per se. This is the introduction to the characters that pop up in "The Dirt Rock War" and "The Naked Piñata Incident". You will find some of these same characters in "Just One Lousy Tortilla" and they may occasionally emerge in other stories, as well.

First, a little bit about Lilly:
Lilly was a slightly chubby lady who liked to wear bright red lipstick, not that she ever went any place special or anything. Her husband had a thin mustache like that movie star, Errol Flynn, and they both spoke what to us was excellent English. Their Spanish, however, was littered with what Mom called "pochismos", curious blends of English and substandard Spanish which they chose to flavor with vulgar expressions. Since they had almost graduated from high school in the US, they were considered the most educated persons on the block. So, most of us tended to ignore their mangled Spanish.

Lilly was different from Mom when it came to housekeeping. The yellow linoleum kitchen floor in Lilly's house was often sticky, and sometimes *yellow*er than it should have been, if you catch my drift. The roll of toilet paper in their bathroom was usually on the last square, the soap bar was always the size of a quarter, and the hand towels were changed every other week. The oven was cleaned whenever it caught fire.

Other household duties such as grocery shopping and bill paying were attended to sporadically, as well. When Lilly could get her hands on her husband's paycheck, there was food in the house: tortillas, beans, Fritos, chips, lard (for deep frying the breakfast eggs), soda, and bonbons for snacking on during the soap operas in the afternoon...and beer.

We thought it bizarre and shameful that parents who could afford to buy shoes for their children would allow them to run around barefoot outside, for the whole world to see! We weren't used to children yelling back to their parents, and we weren't used to kids being smacked on the head. Mom always said, "Not in the head, Jesús! The head is for thinking." Besides, once we reached a certain age or height, Mom and Dad resorted to restricting privileges instead of resorting to THE BELT. It was a kind of mark that meant we were growing up.

Lilly would talk to Mom now and then and ask for advice. "Doña Lupe, what am I going to do with these kids? They don't want to eat, and then half an hour later, they're begging for Kool-Aid and chips! What do you do when that happens?"

"Well, Lilly, each family is different," Mom would diplomatically nod, thinking of what to say next. "If there are no Fritos or potato chips for them to see, they'll eat the rice and beans that you have prepared for them. You do a very nice job of fixing the bologna sandwiches with white bread, and they like that. Tortillas are good, too."

Lilly would lean on the fence between our two houses, sigh, and say something like, "I don't know, Doña Lupe, I just don't know. Bologna can be expensive sometimes."

Even though we weren't really bothered by Lilly, her children were a whole different story.

La Angelina, the biggest:

The oldest was called Angelina, I think. Sometimes we played together until she got on my nerves with her insatiable thirst for gossip. "Why was your mother yelling last night?" and, "Did your brother get in trouble for wetting his pants in the driveway again? Did they hit him?" and, "I heard that your little brother might flunk second grade." As spoiled as my little brother might have been, I stuck up for him anyway by countering with snappy questions such as, "I heard your dad puking in the back yard last night. Does that mean he spent the grocery money again?"

This crude form of verbal self-defense only allowed for two courses of action for poor Angelina:

    a) stomp away to her own yard, calling me names, and then get her brother to help fling rocks at me, which would precipitate a Hatfields vs. McCoys feud between the children of both families for about two or maybe three days

    b) selective hearing loss syndrome: she would sometimes pretend not to have heard my snappy comeback

When she did choose the latter of the two, I was sort of grateful, but we would both look pretty glum until we hoped the other had forgotten the whole matter.

Unless it was a family thing, she would usually stick with me. "Us girls gotta stick together, Marta. Let the boys try something first, and if they don't get yelled at for it, then we can join whatever it is they're doing, okay?"

Once in a blue moon, she would even ask me for help in controlling her brother. "Hey, Marta, come here! I let Donny lick my popsicle and he ate the whole damn thing. I'll hold him down and you kick him for me, okay?"

Angelina's minuses were many, and her pluses were few, but I still missed her when they moved.

El Donny:

For the life of me, I can't understand why some people, kids and adults alike, make such a big deal out of the color of skin. El Donny was blessed with smooth brown skin, but he got a kick out of teasing the kid down the street, who was not Mexican and had skin the color of night. He snickered whenever he saw us come back from a day working at the ranch.

This is what I mean:

"Heh, heh, heh," he would begin. "Hey, you guys are turning black in the sun."

"What's it to you, Donaldo?" my brother, Pancho, would say as he tried to push Payo and me towards the front door.

"*My* dad doesn't have to work in the field," Donny would say, hanging over the fence that separated his house from ours. "That work is cheap. Man, you're real Mexicans all right!"

"Just ignore the nut," Panchito would say to us.

How could that boy not understand that sometimes it was actually fun to pick avocados with your whole family? Couldn't he imagine how great it felt to lift up that aluminum pole, place the pruning shears right next to the yellow-green stem of that big, fat avocado, and hear it plop into the canvas sack? Didn't he know the joy of an orange and vanilla ice cream bar after a day of laboring in the California sun?

Avoidance was the best policy when dealing with Lilly's kids. Laly was comfortable with it. It was endorsed by our parents wholeheartedly. Unfortunately, they lived right next door to us for a few years. How could we *not* play with them at least sometimes?

Striking fear into the hearts of others only worked for our four older brothers: Eddie, Cuco, Chuy, and Pancho. All they had to do was sneer, flex their muscles like James Dean, and walk away. Who would chase the Lomelí boys, when there were four big ones? Lilly's kids respected power. We had none.

Even sadder still, nobody— even our brothers— was allowed to even think of fighting back! "Fighting is a sin. God will punish you, and if he's busy, thank the Lord that you have a mother and a father!" That mother had a sturdy broom and that father had the world's thickest leather belt. The conclusion is obvious.

Also, every adult in the barrio knew who Doña Lupe and Don Jesús' kids were. A thousand eyes reported our every move. Even if we had been allowed to fight and cuss, there just wasn't much shade to rest in. The big boys in our family could bluff and get away with that, but we felt the squeeze. Payo and I had developed neither the patience nor the muscles that our older siblings possessed. Primitive emotions often furrowed our brows and filled our empty moments. Things were fine when Lilly's kids were halfway decent to us, but how could we protect ourselves when they were so darn sneaky?

Donny gave us a lot to work on!

Mom was standing in the micro-hallway, the space between the living room and the kitchen, with a stern look in her face. A thin film of perspiration covered her skin.

Sighing dramatically, she asked, "Why were you late to catechism? Don't you have two good feet, and two strong legs to get you there on time?"

I watched her fingers twirl and squeeze the gingham kitchen towel in and out, over and under as she wiped every bit of the masa (tortilla dough) from her hands. She could do this without looking down at her hands, and it was beautiful and frightening at the same time.

Mom couldn't speak English, but Spanish would have been her choice anyway for the subject at hand. Her words, the pronunciation, the accompanying body language, that special sigh hinting of impending doom (for the child she was addressing) made for quite a spectacular performance.

I plopped down on the avocado green vinyl sofa and sighed. "Mamá, it was so hot that I didn't want to walk in the sun. I could see steam coming up from the road, and I wanted to walk in the shade of the trees, so I didn't take the shortcut. The long way has more shade."

That excuse sounded lame even to me.

Who had snitched? I made a mental note to investigate that later, if I lived.

"Fine!" she snapped. "You, who have an aunt who is a nun, and a cousin who is a priest in Mexico City, you don't think that catechism classes will do you any good? Do you want to rot in hell? Do you? Answer me!"

I started to get uneasy. Mom rarely raised her voice, and she never cussed.

"Mom, it was hot, okay? The nun ..."

"Oh, no, don't you try to put the blame for your lack of discipline on one who has devoted her life to the Lord! How dare you! Don't you know this is for your own good?"

She wasn't really yelling or shouting, but her voice *was* up a notch or two. They say that you should be thankful for small favors, and I was grateful that it was her and not Dad. He would have gotten out his favorite piece of leather: THE BELT.

It was then that I heard the slap-slap sound of bare feet in our dirt driveway. Who could it be? It was one of those Saturdays when the others had either gone to work with Dad at El Patron's ranch or were doing gardening work somewhere in town.

I turned around to see El Donny pushing his face against our screen door.

I must have been blocking Mom's view of the screen door, because she continued taking me on that guilt trip even if I didn't want to go. She held nothing back. It hurt to hear her say that our own childhood was so easy compared to hers, even if it was true. It really hurt to hear her say that nobody else in the family had ever had this kind of problem, which I then thought was true.

"Mom, I... I'm sorry. I will do the worksheets that the nun gave to us today. I won't wait until the last minute anymore, okay?"

"So! It *is* true, then? You *have* been arriving late and doing little work?" she inquired accusingly. She turned away from me and headed back to the kitchen. "Go and do your work now."

From the kitchen, I soon heard her voice and the usual other sounds. "Young lady, don't speak to me for the rest of the day!" The sizzle of tomato sauce and chopped onion being added to the hot frying pan added an ominous exclamation point at the end.

Moms aren't supposed to shut you out! This had never happened to me before! My heart felt heavy.

From the screen door, the sound of breathing stopped my tears from falling. El Donny!

"Hey, Marta," he asked. "Want to come out and play?"

I sprinted toward the screen door, hoping to push it open quickly and make Donny kiss the ground, so to speak.

No such luck. The little weasel opened the door in a lightning second and I fell on the patch of lawn in front of it.

"You big stupid!" I yelled.

From the kitchen, my mom's voice said, "That had *better* not be a bad word, young lady!"

In Spanish, "stupid" means much worse. I won't distract you now by spelling it out.

"If that was a bad word, you'll be having a little meeting with your father and me when he gets home!"

El Donny snickered as I spit out a bit of grass and brushed the bits of it off of my old tennis shoes. "So, do you want to play with us in our yard or not? I guess you can't play with anybody anyway! Ha!" He then began to stroll away from my reach.

I gave him a "mirada que mata" (stare that could kill). "You big liar! You didn't come over to ask me that. You just heard my mom and you wanted to see what the *chisme* (gossip) was. That's what you live on, *chisme*. You're a chismoso, you're a **boy**, and, and… you're a chismoso!"

My actions were limited by my circumstances. La Angelina, his sister, was somewhere in their yard. Payo was with Dad. If I heaved a rock at El Donny, she'd be over in a flash and it would be two against one. Plus, there was the Mom factor to consider.

Rats! Why do mothers always have to be around?

Having just come from a religion class, I also had that nagging doubt that maybe the powers that be were really watching me. It didn't much matter whether the power was parental or whether it was celestial, it still kept my hands by my sides.

El Donny got away…that time.

Finally, there was the infamous Little Lupita:

Little Lupita was given the wrong name at birth. That was obvious to everyone in our family. The name, Guadalupe, came from the "Virgen de Guadalupe". There were beautiful songs for her, especially "La Guadalupana". Such songs fill churches on Sundays and flow out through the open doors and windows just like the smell of gardenias and jasmine. "La Guadalupana" was Mom's favorite, but I digress.

Nothing about this child resembled gardenias and jasmine. When she was about two and a half years old, Little Lupita would still stroll about in a *diaper* and nothing else except for a baby bottle, filled with Kool-Aid, dangling from her sticky mouth. When Payo and I both yanked hard on it, her cheeks would go in and out as if a plunger was being used to dislodge a slimy hairball, but she wouldn't let it go. That baby bottle was like another limb to her. That child was stubborn.

She had picked up some unpopular habits: coming into our yard without an invitation, playing with our toys without permission, eating whatever we had on our table, and giving our childhood treasures to her brother and sister. Her parents would then believe them when they said, "But, *Maaaammmmmaaaa*! We don't *know* what Doña Lupe's kids are talking about! Little Lupita *found* this!" I can't count the number of little green plastic army men we lost to her grubby paws.

When Little Lupita learned to talk, she wouldn't stop:

"Doña Lupe, Laly was talking to some guy in a car the other day when you were at work."

"Don Jesús, your daughter found a quarter in the street and it was mine 'cause I dropped one there the other day."

"Your kids were yelling at each other yesterday when you weren't home."

"Hey, your kids are telling your dog to growl at us again."

Sometimes, when our older brothers were wrestling on the front lawn, she would waddle over and walk right into their activity, stopping everything. El Donny and La Angelina just watched. I often suspected that they sometimes sent her over on purpose, especially if our parents were home. They knew how our parents felt about telling other people's children what to do.

More than once, Payo and I were scolded by our parents and silently praised by most of our siblings for taking matters into our own hands. When you had to deal with any of Lilly's three kids, you almost had to do it that way. We had our family pride to think of.

The Dirt Rock War

There was no nearby park or recreation center, and the higher the temperature climbed, the more the spirit of the child struggled to find amusement. Spitting watermelon seeds was good for twenty minutes. Playing hide-and-go-seek was good for an hour, but only in the cooler evenings. I liked to play school, but my students were reluctant to return to my "classroom" (garage) because I was known to assign real homework.

The spat began when El Donny, La Angelina, Payo, and I agreed to play war.

"We'll only throw dirt rocks," asserted La Angelina. "You guys better do the same. No steel rocks, okay? Those hurt too much."

"I don't think those are called steel rocks," I interrupted.

"Hey!" snapped El Donny. "You know what we mean anyway, Little Miss Smarty Pants!"

La Angelina was curious, and asked, "What are they called, anyway?"

I wasn't sure, but managed to save face by answering in a casual, yet authoritative, manner: "Well, some people call them minerals, like granola or ignacious rocks. I think that spoons are made of steel. Forks and knives, too. Except the plastic ones."

"So?" they both glared at me now.

Not wanting for them to have the last word, Payo puffed up his little chest and added, "So? *So?*"

La Angelina, anxious to get down to business now, easily ignored his body language and restated her original position. "So we all use only the dirt ones, the ones that go poof when they land on the pavement, and nobody gets hurt."

"Yeah," I added. "Same rules as last time. No hitting on the head, and no fair letting Little Lupita help you 'cause then it means you have more on your team. Ready?"

"Yahooo!" shouted Donny. "We're gonna win!"

"Losers have to stand in front of the corner store and bark like a dog!" yelled La Angelina. "You better practice now, you two."

"Stop it," growled Payo, "or I'll aim for your face with a big dirt grenade!"

El Donny guffawed in the most obnoxious way imaginable. "This is war, dummy! Just stay out of the *sun* so you don't look like your *dad* when he comes home from his cheap work! This war is starting in 30 seconds!"

As we all counted out loud, we used the seconds to gather as many kinds of dirt weapons that we could find. A small, dry piece of dirt with no real rock in it was called a dirt rock. A dirt grenade was also dry, about the size of a fist, and considerably softer. The most colorful dirt weapon was the dirt bomb, a clump of slightly moist soil held together by a very small patch of grass or weeds. Each produced a different effect.

The dirt bombs looked the best flying through the air, and sometimes they would leave a damp patch on a T-shirt which would be hard to wash out. Dirt grenades, being soft and dry chunks of earth, had two uses: making impressive poofing sounds when they landed on a hard surface, and scoring an easy to see point on an opponent. The difficulty with dirt grenades was that the dust could easily be brushed off, leading to arguments about whether or not they had actually touched the body of the intended target.

The preferred weapon was the dirt rock. It didn't have streamers of grass or flowers sticking out of it. It didn't leave a big, powdery, brown circle to prove where it had landed. It wasn't as easy to find or even as big as dirt bombs and dirt grenades. Only dirt rocks, however, had a sting to them that even Lilly's kids could not deny, and that was important because every point that could be proven brought you closer to being declared the winners.

A moment later, the war had begun. The cuffs on my jeans were soon filled with pebbles, dirt, and teeny bits of grass and weeds. Payo's T-shirt had dusty brown spots on the back, where enemy dirt bombs had landed.

When the battle began to migrate to the lot with the abandoned house nearby, things got ugly. El Donny and La Angelina had run out of dirt grenades and dirt rocks. We stayed on the other side of the street, in front of Don Sánchez's corn patch. We had enough standard ammunition to last, and felt confident that this was one war that we would win.

"Payo, look! They're trying to hide behind that pile of wood and rocks," I whispered.

"Donny! You two better get outta there!" he shouted across the street to them.

El Donny and La Angelina popped their heads up for a split second, just long enough to see our exact location.

"We're out of dirt grenades. Let us go into the street and get some that can be used again!" asked La Angelina. "We'll be real fast and you can start firing at the count of ten, okay?"

This seemed fair at the moment.

A couple of minutes later, Payo asked them for the same consideration. He wanted to retrieve a dirt bomb that he had made out of moist earth wrapped around a handful of weeds and geranium stems. It was a good looking bomb, too, with a few pink geranium petals sticking out.

Unfortunately for my brother, the enemy did not care to play fair. El Donny threw a hard rock at Payo's face. It smacked him in the cheek. He stood there, in the middle of the street, too stunned to move. Dirt clods and small pebbles began to rain on my stunned little brother.

"Move outta there, tonto!" I yelled. "You guys are gonna be sorry! You big stupids!"

Having the best aim of all, I soon scored a flurry of points by aiming at La Angelina's behind whenever she squirmed to get out from behind the pile of wood and rocks. Payo forgot the bruise on his cheek when I scored the winning point which sent her tumbling over.

"We won! Ha ha! We won!" I danced around Payo and he began flinging dandelions into the warm summer air. That was his own personal victory tradition.

They went home to eat dinner and sulk, but not before tossing a string of insults at us and our whole family. "You cheaters! You'll be sorry!"

"We won fair and square!" I shouted at them.

"Losers gotta stand in front of the corner store and bark like a dog!" added Payo.

El Donny picked his nose and tried to flick a slimy little something at us as he stated, "Us? We ain't no stinkin' losers. We never hit anybody on the butt, and *you did*, you big cheaters! You wanna see somebody stand in front of the corner store, it probly gonna be your daddy looking for Mexican work, an' if you wanna hear somebody bark like a dog, then you better teach him how yourselfs 'cause he only know one way to talk an' it ain't English!"

Part II of the Dirt Rock War:
The Naked Piñata Incident

The day after our triumph in the dirt war, they completely ignored us. Only near sunset did they even look over the fence in our direction, and that was after their parents drove off.

"Where they goin'?" asked Payo, trying to be friendly.

La Angelina yanked El Donny's sleeve and warned him not to tell us.

When their parents returned, we happened to see them from the kitchen window. La Angelina, El Donny, and Little Lupita were jumping excitedly around them. Their father seemed to have a bag of groceries, and we could barely make out what Lilly was carrying. It had a wire sticking out of it and made rustling sounds. Her arms carried it like a baby, but it was as big as a dog. The kids followed her into their garage and their father carried the bag into the house. That's all we saw.

The following day, we overheard Lilly saying something to them about "cousins coming" and "My, how you have grown this year, my precious little man!"

We put two and two together, and we weren't happy. It being Wednesday, we knew the next few days would be torture. Would La Angelina and El Donny invite us to his birthday party? Would we be forced to listen to the sounds of laughter and children cavorting next door to us, or would we be allowed to join the elite group who got to break the piñata? Would we be able to resist such great temptation?

That night, Payo and I were stewing in anger and jealousy. It just wasn't fair! They were the ones who started to use those darn "steel" rocks! Nobody had told us that El Donny's birthday was so near! We kept going over and over the insults that we had endured, reviewing our behavior to see if we had adequately defended the family honor.

We even discussed the situation with our brother, Pancho. He sympathized with us greatly, but offered no fresh ideas. "That was really a rotten thing they said about Dad, but you know that our parents don't let us fight. Dad has his belt and Mom has her broom. Don't worry, bad luck will find these kids some day."

Payo and I weren't willing to wait for some day. When we were alone, I sighed and wished aloud, "What would serve them right is for something terrible to happen to them. Maybe their garage will catch fire and then the piñata will be gone. No piñata, no party. Boy, if a genie granted me three wishes, that would be the first wish."

That evening, while we were all watching television, Payo excused himself to supposedly get a tortilla to munch on. I was the only one who heard his footsteps leave the kitchen, and the back door slowly open and close.

I chose to say nothing, and instead wandered over to the kitchen myself for one of Mom's famous handmade corn tortillas. I watched the little blue flames of the gas stove warm up the tasty tortilla. I was savoring it when Payo sneaked back in through the back door, tiptoeing, holding two used Ohio Blue Tip wooden matches. One had a tiny wisp of smoke coming out of it.

"What are you doing with that, you nut?" I questioned, in hushed tones.

"Uh...nothin.," he answered, nervously.

"Get rid of that NOW."

"Okay."

Standing there, he reminded me of a rabbit caught in the headlights of a car.

"Gimme that, I'll do it myself," I whispered. "Here, have the rest of this tortilla. I put a little bit of butter on it."

The next morning, Lilly knocked on our door. "Doña Lupe, Doña Lupe! Did you see anybody in our back yard last night? The piñata …"

Mom seemed confused. "Oh, Lilly! My kids hadn't even *mentioned* a birthday party! We'll be sure that they bring a gift, though. Don't you worry about that."

In our barrio, if one child had a birthday party, all children on the block were invited over at least for the piñata. It was considered the proper thing to do.

"What gift? Oh, well, uh...we were thinking of having a little birthday for Donny, you know, but just immediate family, so we didn't invite any of your children, but now the piñata is burned!"

"All of it?" asked my mother, her eyebrows going up slightly.

"Well, most of it," answered Lilly. "It was supposed to be a white bull with cute little paper curls all over the body, and big eyelashes, but it has no eyelashes anymore and the butt is singed! All of the curly-q's on the body have been burned off and it looks …naked!" She looked desperate. "Maybe somebody was trying to steal something, and they wanted to burn the garage as they left. Do your kids know anything about it?"

Mom bristled. "Lilly, your children and mine have been known to have their spats, but this is really beyond that. My children were with us all night. We do not allow our children to leave our yard after dark, not at this tender age."

"Well, you know. Maybe they were playing hide-and-go-seek in the front yard, and accidentally wandered into our back yard."

"Lilly, please! I seriously doubt that. However, in the interest of all, I will ask them. Will you also *please ask your children, too?* Maybe they were simply playing with the piñata and, you know, accidents will happen. It is good that nobody got hurt."

"Oh, Doña Lupe! What if the garage had gone up in flames? What would we have done then? We are only renting this house! I'm going to have to go through everything in the garage to see if anything is missing!"

That seemed to be what was scaring Lilly the most.

When Lilly had returned to her own yard, Mom let us know, in no uncertain terms, that withholding information was a punishable offense.

"Mom, I wasn't in the garage. When we were watching television last night, Payo and I did come into the kitchen once and we shared a tortilla. That wouldn't have given us enough time to sneak out, jump the fence, and do all of what Lilly says before the commercial. I was wearing my yellow blouse, and see? It is still clean. It would have gotten dirty if I had climbed over the fence."

Reassured, Mom went on with her daily chores.

When we finished our indoor chores, we went into the front yard and climbed the pine tree. The branches were slightly sticky, but we were wearing our summer play clothes. After finding our favorite branches, we spent a moment of silence, swinging our legs in the warm summer breeze. We could see rooftops and even a corner of Don Sánchez's garden. It was a glorious feeling.

"Hey, kid!" I whispered to Payo.

"What?"

"We didn't lie."

"We didn't?"

"No, we didn't. Kids don't burn things; matches burn things."

"Saaaaay, you're right! But, still, I'm not going to play with matches ever again."

"Great!" I sighed. After a moment, I sighed again, and nudged him.

"What?"

"You know, sometimes you're *my* hero."

He grinned and continued swinging his little legs and poking a dry, brown pine cone with his free hand.

Payo the Innocent

Learning to Fly

"We are each of us angels with only one wing,
and we can only fly by embracing one another."
                                    Luciano de Crescenzo

Summer was a time of exploration, smelling flowers, collecting popsicle sticks, and climbing trees. Our tribe also spent many days of working together: harvesting macadamia nuts in the orchards of Oceanside and Vista, picking avocados, and working on El Patrón's ranch with its thousand and one things to do. We worked hard and we played hard. My spirit grew wings in the summertime.

On Saturdays, we were a bit more likely to stay home with Mom. Those were the days that I devoted to childhood pursuits with neighboring playmates like La Angelina and her brother, Donny, and Evie and her brother, El Eddie. Sometimes, in the warm summer evenings, even my brother Pancho would join us for a while if there was nothing good on television.

We usually had enough beans, rice, tortillas, and nopales to eat. Sometimes, we even had meat on Sundays. What we really hungered for, however, was entertainment.

***

One fine day, I looked out through the screen door to see Payo, staring at the flowers by the side of the yard. I was curious. What could hold a little boy's attention for that long? If it was something fun, I wanted to be a part of it! So, I went out to investigate.

He told me that he was counting bees. I struggled mightily to keep my facial muscles from twitching into a smile. Instead, I said cheerily but not *too* cheerily,

"Countin' bees, Payito? You must be bored, kid. Why don't you try to catch one, instead?"

I really never expected him to act on my casual suggestion. I certainly never expected him to catch a **bumblebee!** I honestly did not want for him to feel that kind of pain!

Of course, I had to dash into the house and get Mom. She always knew what to do.

His hand was sore for a couple of days, but I knew only one thing could possibly be worse for me. If he ever told our parents about who had put that idea into his tiny brain, I would certainly have to pray a whole rosary on my knees, hands outstretched, all by myself.

After that little incident, I knew that I had to be careful.

About one week later, the people across the street had a new refrigerator delivered. A box the size of a refrigerator was always good for three, maybe four, days of summer fun. Playing monster-in-a-box was the first day's activity for the biggest kids on the block.

"Grrrrr! All you village people will be eaten by ME! Hahaha! Grrreeaaagggh!"

Even though we had all seen rough-and-tough La Angelina get into the cardboard box, it felt wonderful to let the hair stand up on the back of our necks, scream at the top of our lungs, race around the box, then try to knock it down.

The more convincing the growling and heavy breathing was, the louder we screamed and the harder we punched and kicked the giant cardboard box. It became more convincing the longer the "monster" could withstand the abuse of the revolting villagers. If the monster trapped you and managed to land on top of you, you were considered dead and, therefore, out of the game.

"Yeaaaarrrrrgh! I am the monster! This is my yard, and I gotcha!" La Angelina would yell as she landed on a villager. The last villager left "alive" then became the next monster, and the game went on.

It was wonderfully cheap entertainment that demanded total involvement and concentration. The sounds effects alone were worthy of an academy award nomination.

I was just beginning to enjoy my turn as monster when I heard a familiar voice off to one side. "Maaaarta, I waaaannna playyyyy. Can I? Huh? Can I play?"

I got out from the box. "Payo, you're too little. You can watch, though. Just sit over there with Little Lupita."

"Why? She's not playin 'cause she's eatin somethin. I don have anythin' to eat and I wanna play, anyway."

"No."

"Yes."

"NO. Go away."

La Angelina and Evie chimed in, "Yeah, go away. This is for big kids."

He jammed his fists into the pockets of his overalls and pouted. I knew that meant something, but I was so wrapped up in the excitement of playing monster that I failed to remember what it was.

"Come on, villagers!" shouted Evie as she wiped the perspiration from her forehead. "On the count of ten, we attack the monster!"

Just as I was starting to tip the box over and assume the role of the Monster of 346 West Connecticut Avenue, Payo used his secret weapon.

"If you don't let me play, I'm gonna tell Mom on you!"

Visions of angry bumble bees danced in my head!

A hush quieted the villagers in mid-revolt. La Angelina and Evie pulled me aside and whispered, "Do something and do it fast. We're counting on you, Marta!"

Visions of angry bumble bees saying the rosary danced in my head!

I was desperate.

"Let him take my turn as monster. He won't like it, and we can let him quit in a minute, okay?"

Playing by our rules was not easy for Payo. The little monster fell down too often, and preferred to run away from the villagers, a definite no-no in our book! He complained loudly because he couldn't see through the eye holes. We gave up trying to hit the box because every time we kicked or punched it, the voice inside would say, "Hey, you guys! That doesn't feel good! Stop it!"

When the monster-in-a-box wandered into the street, into the path of an oncoming vehicle, we canceled the game in a hurry. The old lady that got out of her car really let us have it!!! "You kids almost gave me a heart attack! Nobody expects to come around a curve and see a box walking into the street! You should be ashamed of yourselves!"

Even though the car stopped in time, Payo started to cry. My peer group had scattered, leaving me to take the heat.

That night, I was made to pray the rosary by myself, kneeling, with my arms outstretched. I thought to myself that things like this could not be allowed to happen again. I knew that I would have to have a plan ready. I wanted to be prepared for the next emergency. "Never again!" I said aloud.

When you're young, "never" doesn't last as long as you think. (sigh)

A week later, we still faced most of the same problems:

Should we go to the store and collect popsicle sticks as we walked along?

No, we should wait until Sunday when we got our allowance and maybe buy a Push-up stick, Sno-ball, or a Three Musketeers bar.

Should we go over to Rayitas's house, knock on his door, and run?

(Rayitas was an old, retired gardener who liked to wear long-sleeved striped shirts and growl at little children who picked his flowers)

No, he would just tell our parents.

Should we go down the block and tease the vicious German shepherd who was usually tied up? Should we put things on the railroad tracks and wait for the train to smash them? Should we this? *No.* Should we that? *Nah.*

Everything seemed to get the same reaction from all of us: Been there, done that, ready for something new.

When somebody suggested that we jump off of the roof of Doña Lola's rickety little garage, it actually sounded brilliant. We began to pull weeds and tall grass to make a fluffy pile to land on.

We chattered about our latest idea. Evie and La Angelina debated how long we would be in the air when we jumped. Donny and I discussed whether we could stay up longer if we flapped our arms really fast. El Eddie, the junior scientist, began to persuade us that we should all point our noses toward the horizon when we jumped. He said, "Paper airplanes stay up longer if you throw them just that way."

Before climbing on top of the garage, we all walked around the big pile of grass and weeds. The ground below the little garage had a few minor hazards. In one spot, it was naturally bumpy, in another it had a rock or two embedded into the dirt, and right next to the wall, there were a just a few bits of broken glass. None of the hazards seemed insurmountable to us. A certain element of danger just made it even more interesting! We were prepared for anything!

When the five of us had climbed up onto Doña Lola's old wooden garage, we peered over the edge to check on the exact location of our huge green pile of grass, dandelions, and assorted backyard weeds. Everything looked perfect for the first flight.

El Eddie was the first to jump. He flapped his arms furiously and tried to keep his nose pointed to the railroad tracks in the near horizon. Poof! He landed in the safety zone, got up, pulled a few stickers off of his Bermuda shorts, and saluted to us from the ground. "Be sure to jump out, instead of down! You land on more grass and farther away from the broken glass that way!"

Evie shrieked in delight. "Me next! Me next!"

She stood at the edge, stared down to the few bits of broken glass, and then to the pile of grass about one meter from the wall. We encouraged her with "You can do it, Evie!" and "Show us your style, Evie!" and, of course, "Keep our eye on the safety zone, Evie!"

She flapped her arms quickly and jumped with her right leg out in front, like a hurdler. Poof! Another near-perfect landing!

She wiped her forehead in triumph. "Hey, you guys! That was *really fun!*"

A few minutes later, we were all lined up again on top of the old wooden garage, ready for our second flight. We were making bets on who could stay in the air the longest and who could "fly" the farthest away from Doña Lola's garage.

Just then, I heard the screen door to our back yard squeak. It was Payo, coming over to see what fun was being had without him. La Angelina grabbed the sleeve of my T-shirt and whispered in my ear, "Do somethin'!"

Almost before I could answer the scowls of my playmates, Payo was next to the garage begging to be lifted up. I climbed down and stared at him.

"Payo," I began, "you dunno what you're askin' for. This isn't for little kids, an that's the truth."

"Why?" he asked, with his arms crossed and a suspicious look on his clean little face.

"Because."

"Why?"

"Tell me why."

Sighing, I led him over to the area where the big pile of grass was. The pile had become slightly flattened from the first round of jumps.

Chunks of dirt and weeds were scattered here and there, evidence of the five triumphant flights already performed.

"See that pile of grass? Well, we're learnin' how to fly and, if we jump out far enough, we land in the pile of grass and weeds and not in the broken glass."

"Why not take the glass out first?" he asked.

"Ay, you're always saying stupid stuff!" I was annoyed by his sudden attention to details.

"Teach me how to fly. You gotta, or I'm gonna tell on you."

I remembered the bumblebee incident and the time we let him be the monster. This time, I was ready. "What will you tell, Payo?"

He smiled confidently. "You know. I'll tell Dad that you don't wanna let me play with you guys. I can tell Mom, too."

Even more confidently, I smiled back. "No, you don hafta do that anymore. I'm not gonna say you can't learn to fly with us, an I'm not gonna say you can."

He tilted his head slightly. "What? Just tell me how you guys do it!"

That I readily did, showing him how to bend at the knees slightly, how to flap his arms out to the side while pointing his nose to the railroad tracks, and how to land correctly in the safety zone.

"Hey, kids!" I yelled at the group waiting on the rooftop of the small garage. "You're my witnesses, okay? I never told him to join us and I never told him he *could* fly!"

Donny and El Eddie looked confused but Evie and La Angelina smiled. They were the ones who helped Payo up onto the flight deck. "You know, Payo," they told him, "that this is kinda dangerous. Marta told you not to do it, but we know that you're gonna do it anyway. So, do not, we say again, do not land on the broken glass."

"I won't. I'm gonna jump and fly and land way over on the grass pile."

"If you hurt yourself, we're gonna tell your daddy that Marta didn't want you to jump."

"Okay." He peered over the edge to the ground below, and put the tips of his tennis shoes next to the edge of the rooftop. "Sounds fair."

Donny and El Eddie added, "Ladeeees and gentlemennnnn!!! Captain Payo reeeeeadddyyy for his first flyyyyyinnnng lessssooonnnn! Flap your arms real fast, boy!"

"I'm gonna fly! This is gooder than anythin' I ever done!" he said, breathlessly. "I'm really gonna fly!"

They placed their hands on his shoulders. "You sure are!" they said. "One, two, three—-JUMP!"

He jumped just fine. For the second that he was in the air, the look on his face was pure childhood pleasure, pure fun! For that second, the world was his!

It's where he landed that was a problem.

The over-used grass pile was next to his feet. He had managed to land on his bottom, and just out of the safety zone.

He smiled a little crooked smile. "I almost landed on it, huh?"

I hurriedly jumped down to ground level to put my arm around him and help him up. "Yeah. Almost."

"I was really flyin' for a minute, wasn't I?"

"Yeah."

"Ya think I shoulda flapped my arms more?"

"Oh yeah. No doubt."

From the rooftop, the other kids were shouting at me to come and take my turn. "Don't ya wanna fly anymore?"

I didn't even bother to answer them because I was bunching up a corner of my

T-shirt to wipe the tears from my brother's eyes. I didn't want anybody else to see. "Maybe I'll be back later. You guys go ahead and fly without me. Keep an eye out for Doña Lola!"

Donny shouted, "Suit yourself!"

As we walked to our own backyard, I flicked bits of brown glass off of the seat of his pants and removed a few fluffs of dandelion that were still in his hair. "You okay?"

He nodded bravely.

"Wanna try out those new Band-Aids with the cartoons on em? They're real nice."

He nodded bravely again, and this time he spoke, but in a hesitant voice, "You gonna tell on me?"

"Nah! What for? You're my brother!"

Taking a deep breath, he smiled at me and said, "Thanks for letting me play with you guys. Maybe, when I get as big as you, I can fly longer and gooder than I did today, right?"

I groaned and looked up at the sky.

And Then Came Eloisa

Over the many years that we lived in that little house near the end of West Connecticut Avenue, we had many guests. Some were Mom's relatives:

Tía Elena: a nun who devoted her life to taking care of oldsters that nobody wanted; Tía Nacha: also a large woman, devoted her life to eating (not cooking, but eating)

When these three sisters were together, we called them Large, Extra Large, and Not In Stock.

Some were our father's relatives from Jalostitlán, Jalisco:

Tía Trina: a very kind aunt; a wonderful lady who treated our mother like a sister, only better; Tío Miguel: her husband, who always wore a sombrero just like Dad, because "a real man always wears a hat"

Some were people that our mother had grown up with in her godmother's house. They were the ones that had been allowed to finish grade school, while Mom was kept home to clean their house once she finished second grade. As the years went by and especially after their own mom (my mother's godmother) passed away, they all grew closer.

Occasionally, we would have cousins our age stay with us for a summer so that Mom could feed them castor oil and "fatten them up before sending them back home". I enjoyed those times the best of all because I had somebody else to play with.

Although they each came to see us, many were also coming to see if the streets really were paved with gold. Dad had a steady job and we were buying our house, not renting. We had indoor plumbing! We had a black and white television that got three channels! We could buy anything that we wanted in the stores: milk in cartons, soup in cans, and popsicles packaged in plastic. We had found the land of milk and honey.

Mom had just finished putting the letter into her apron pocket. "So, what do you think, Jesús? Can she come to visit?"

Dad toyed with the toothpick in his mouth. "Hmm. She's not family."

Mom sat down beside him. "Yes, but she is from Arandas, my home town. I would gladly welcome any friend of yours from Jalostotitlán, even if I'm not from there."

He poked her elbow with his toothpick and smiled. "Yeah, I know, but why us?"

Mom shrugged and gave a little sigh. "We do live in the United States. She's never been out of the homeland. The only people that she considers family are the priests that she works for, and she only works for room and board. Besides, she knows what it is like to be an orphan."

"She is a grown woman, Lupita. Anyway, how can she afford to fly up here?"

"Well, I guess they're paying her way because she hasn't had a real vacation."

Dad put the toothpick back into his mouth. "Of course, she hasn't had a real job, either. I understand that she can't even type."

"Ay, Jesús!" She gently chided him. "Neither one of us finished grade school, remember?"

My father continued to sit at the kitchen table, patting his stomach with one hand and playing with the toothpick with the other. "Hmm. Only a few weeks?"

"Yes. Three weeks. I swear."

"I guess it's okay, but…"

"I know. I entertain her. You don't want to be bothered."

"I guess it would be kind of nice to hear what's been happening in the old homeland. Write back to her and ask her to contact my sister Trina. Trina is sure to send something to me. I sure miss her."

Near the end of August, Eloisa arrived with six suitcases. Dad's eyebrows drew close together. "Where the #@$% are we supposed to fit all this?" he whispered into Mom's ear.

When she first came into our living room, she headed straight for Dad's favorite chair.

Dad, pointing to the sofa, said, "Go ahead and sit anywhere you like, Eloisa. We have a nice, soft sofa over there."

"Oh, no, but thank you. You can put my little suitcases on the sofa."

I was going to ask Mom if we were supposed to sit on the carpet, but she motioned for me to help my brothers move the suitcases into the boys' bedroom.

Payo panicked. "Marta, where am I supposed to sleep? The only other place is the garage."

Cuco, our second to the oldest brother, put his arm around Payo and whispered in his ear. "Payo, us guys will camp out in the living room, just like in the days of long ago. Remember, we're the men of the house."

Laly and I silently smiled, as we heaved one of the suitcases on top of a twin bed. I wondered if the little bed could support her suitcases. We all wondered if the other twin bed could support Eloisa.

Since it was almost time for lunch, she begged for Campbell's soup. "I would really like to try some of that canned American food. Isn't it amazing how they put the little vegetables in there? How do they cut the carrots into such perfect squares? Oh, this country is so..."

"Expensive?" Dad grinned sarcastically.

"So advanced! Jesús, you are such a clown! You married a man with a sense of humor, Lupita."

"Yes, and as you can see, he is a good provider, too. We aren't renting. We're buying this house."

"Ah, but who lives in that little house in the back? If you don't have the right neighbors, it doesn't matter if you own or rent, you know. A good provider should take these matters into account."

I had positioned myself next to my father's boots, on the floor in the living room. I looked straight at her and put in my own two cents. "It's not a house, it's a storage shed. That's where my daddy stores all of his tools. He knows how to do a lot of things."

Eloisa gave a hearty laugh and motioned for me to approach her. "My, my! Such beautiful braids! Come here, child." She gave me a nice big hug and then pinched both of my cheeks, shaking my head left and right while she did so. "I live in a room not much bigger than that storage shed. You're so lucky to have your own house."

My cheeks were glad that Mom interrupted her. "Come on into my kitchen, Eloisa! Let me show you our gas stove!"

Eloisa expressed her approval. The stove didn't burn wood, the refrigerator had its own freezer section, and there was room in the cupboards for all of the traditional kitchen tools such as the tortilla press. Even the telephone gave her something to talk about. "Lupita! You have so many numbers on it! Why, back home, the mayor has a telephone. The hospital has one, and the old folks' home has one, and of course, the priests have one. I'm in charge of that, as you know. I don't know what they'd do without me. But, look at this! Yours is right in your kitchen. 'Palace 4-3884' it says. So elegant, in my opinion! Sounds like royalty."

Mom now had somebody her own age to talk to her all day. Eloisa spent hours telling her everything that she had heard from the homeland, and always putting her own secret blend of herbs and spices into each morsel of news:

Lola and Lupe are still single. God only knows why! They come to church constantly to pray for boyfriends. I hope they find a job or a man soon.

Doña Maria is still in good health. That pair of support hose that you sent worked like magic! It makes her look older, but she's married anyway, so she doesn't care.

Armandito, the storekeeper's teenaged son, is still retarded. Must have something to do with the fact that the boy drinks nothing but Coca-Cola all day long.

While our mother enjoyed the conversation she craved, my brothers adjusted to sleeping on the sofa bed. In the mornings, you could see the comical arrangement of human bodies. Heads would often be wedged between big feet, and arms would often be wedged into the crack between the lumpy mattress and the worn edges of the avocado green sofa.

Since Mom wouldn't hear of having Eloisa join us to work on the ranch, Laly and I had to go help out more often. When we returned, Mom would be ironing and Eloisa would be sipping Kool-Aid and munching on Twinkies, telling her about the latest hometown miracle of San Martín de Porres.

Even our weekly ritual of shopping for groceries was altered to accommodate our guest. Dad found it necessary to take an extra trip in the middle of the week, and Mom sent us almost daily to fulfill Eloisa's last-minute requests.

At the end of one particularly grueling workday, we returned from Mr. Miller's ranch to find Eloisa, sitting on our picnic bench, drinking Coca-Cola, and fanning herself. "Ah, Don Jesús! You're back from work!"

Dad got out of the Jeep and wiped the perspiration from his forehead on his long khaki sleeve. "Well, how has your day been, Eloisa? Hey, I thought that you didn't like Coca-Cola!"

"Oh, you know that it tastes different up here in El Norte. It's not the same kind that Armandito drinks. Here, come and have some! Oh, my! Look at those dirty hands of yours! Tsk, tsk. I never see hands like that on the priests. Well, they're men of God. You, on the other hand, are getting richer each day, but you know what it says in the good book. It's easier for a camel to pass through the eye of a needle than for a rich man to enter the gates of heaven."

Dad looked up to the sky and took a deep breath.

I could see the Jell-O of her arms wag as she kept fanning herself. I shuddered and thought, "Oh, God! Please don't ever let me grow up to be like that!"

Now, sitting on the other bench in the shade, our father smiled tiredly at her. "No, thanks. Seven Up is the drink for me. Hey, kids, go get me a Seven. Put some ice cubes in it."

Eddie, Cuco, Chuy, Pancho, and Laly were already inside, fighting over who got to use the shower first. Payo and I both ran to the door at the same time, but I got through first.

In the kitchen, a few pots were bubbling. I could see my mother ironing in her bedroom, with the window propped open to let the faint breeze wander in when it could. "Mamá! We're home! Want some Seven? I'm getting some for Dad."

"There isn't any Seven Up." She sprayed starch on a long sleeved shirt.

"What do I do, then?"

The iron hissed as it made contact with the damp sleeve. "Get him a Coca. Put lots of ice on it."

A minute later, I handed the glass of soda to Payo. "Hey, Payo, you get to take this to Dad."

He smiled, "You sure it's okay? I get to do it?"

"Sure. I don't want to get all the credit."

I watched from behind the screen door of the living room. Dad was rubbing his eyes as Eloisa repeated the details of her last contact with his sister, our Tía Trina. When Payo tugged on his sleeve, Dad looked down and frowned. "You must be mistaken, son."

Eloisa grabbed the cold glass of Coca-Cola and pinched my little brother's cheek hard. "What a sweet young man! Oh, I would have married if I knew I could have children as sweet as this!"

Dad glared at him. "Get this straight. I want a Seven Up. Bring me the whole bottle. I can finish it myself and eat the ice cubes on the side. Hurry!"

Payo was rubbing his red cheek as he came inside. "Ow! Now what?"

Eventually, our father resigned himself to ice water.

That night, after dinner, we all went into the living room to watch television. Just as Dad was about to sit in his old recliner, Eloisa grabbed his elbow and led him to the couch. "Now, you two lovebirds should sit together. I don't mind sitting by myself over here. I'm just a guest. I don't want to keep you two apart. You've been slaving away all day, and you haven't had a chance to sit next to your wife. Go. Go on and sit next to her. Put your arm around her."

Mom smiled a little, but Dad cleared his throat and headed for the television instead.

"Martita, would you please put it on channel twelve for your father? I'm sure he wants to watch a movie in Spanish instead."

"Eloisa, we always watch the Rifleman after dinner," said Laly and Pancho.

Eloisa clasped her chubby hands together. "Oh, but this is a special movie. This is one with lots of singing in it, and in Spanish!" As she plopped down into the recliner, it groaned sadly.

Dad must have stayed silent because he hoped that the singing would at least be done by the likes of Pedro Infante or Jorge Negrete, in full charro costume. Unfortunately, it wasn't even a cowboy movie. It was an Elvis Presley movie dubbed in Spanish. "Look, how disgusting!" Dad would point to the screen and say things like, "Those girls have skirts with poodles on them! What kind of mother would let her teenaged daughter dress up with pictures of circus dogs?" and, "What's wrong with that boy's lip, anyway?"

Not long after that, Eloisa invited some of our relatives from Hemet to come on down for a Sunday lunch. "You don't mind, do you, Lupita? I haven't met everybody, and..."

Dad happened to be passing through the kitchen at that moment. Instead of harrumphing about feeding a large crowd, he smiled. "Eloisa, have you heard of the giant watermelons that her nephew, Nacho, grows in Hemet? They are the juiciest you have ever tasted. Oh, and has Lupe told you about the apricots? They're bigger than peaches sometimes."

Eloisa's eyes got big. Watermelons and apricots were hard to come by, at least for her. "Oh, is Nacho the one that has his own farm? Here in El Norte?"

Dad nodded. "You bet. He's one smart fellow. He found the right kind of boss, kind of like my patrón, Mr. Miller. Not long ago, his boss needed to sell off some of his farm land, and, well, I guess the rest is family history."

"Who helps him run his business? Surely, his wife must be busy caring for the children. He does have a family, doesn't he? A man without a family is a sad thing to see."

"You may not believe it, Eloisa, but Nacho learned English and went to school at night to learn how to do the math. He pays his income tax by himself. He doesn't need to go to anybody else for that. He's my Lupita's nephew, and he is such a nice man. His wife, Paz, is a real gem, too."

Mom turned to Dad and said, "Call Nacho and Paz. See if you can get them to bring a few watermelons or apricots with them, the ones that are already ripe enough and can't be sent to market."

When our relatives from Hemet came, they brought a pickup truck full of huge watermelons and four bags of apricots. When they left, they had three of Eloisa's suitcases in the back.

"Looks like our cousins got a raw deal," whispered Panchito. "Will she stay three weeks or three months with them?"

"Hush! Somebody might hear you!" said Laly.

Payo and I started to chuckle as we all waved goodbye to Eloisa. She rolled the window down and blew kisses at us, much to our disgust. "Don't worry, kids! I'll be back in about two weeks!"

Well, she did return two weeks later, on the day before school began.

I usually experienced a feeling of euphoria at the start of a new school year. I looked forward to a new teacher because they were usually so nice and most of them knew our family. I yearned to see what my new school books would be like. What kind of new stories would I get to read this year? Who would my new best friend be? I even liked the smell of chalk dust.

Now, I dreaded the mornings because Eloisa always wanted to help out by getting us ready herself while breakfast was being prepared. She had a fondness for tight braids, and by the end of

September, I was looking Chinese. My new classmates began calling me Fortune Cookie.

Poor Payo! His situation was even more terrible. She insisted on tucking his shirt in tightly every morning. With her plump hands yanking his underwear up and then jamming the shirt tail into his buns, my poor little brother always had a devil of a time just walking to school. He would scowl and grumble about how starched shirts gave him a rash, but the more he protested and the more stiffly he walked, the more she would clap her fat hands together and praise our mother for having raised such a fine little soldier, a real "little man".

Even Laly was trying to find reasons to stay away from the house. After school, we would try to spend time with the Hernández girls because they lived even closer to school than we did. When we couldn't get permission to go there, we would sneak down the street to study in Tita and Lupe's house. Mom never got too upset about that, being that they were our cousins and that she could count on their mother to send us home by dinnertime.

It dawned on us that the original three weeks had come and passed. When we asked Laly about Eloisa's departure, she had no new information. So, we went up the chain of command and finally got to Eddie, the oldest. His advice was to quit whining. "If Dad can take a few more weeks, we can too. Remember, we Lomelí's stick together."

One Saturday morning, while pulling weeds on a hillside at the Miller ranch, we finally got the nerve up to ask Dad about Eloisa's extended stay with us. Eddie tried to shush us, saying that it was no business of ours, but Cuco and Chuy didn't try to stop us from asking. Pancho, Laly, Payo, and I begged for answers.

"Well, kids, it's like this. She's not family, but she has some things in common with your mother, things that none of us can understand…"

Chuy and Pancho tried to stifle a snicker as they whispered something to Laly about Eloisa's dress size, but Laly gave them the look, and their faces ended up with twisted smiles.

Our father had continued talking: "…which have something to do with not growing up with any parents. Personally, I think this is given way too much importance, having grown up with my parents and wishing otherwise at times. Maybe it's different for a man."

Eddie nodded.

Dad frowned for a second, unsure how to interpret that.

"Anyway, as I was saying, your mother and I had a little talk about this not long ago."

"And what happened?" asked Laly.

"And she's still here. Eloisa. Not your mother. Well, your mother is still here. I want her to be here, of course. Your mother. Not Eloisa. I mean…"

"That's okay, Dad," said Panchito, putting his hand on our father's shoulder.

"Yeah, Dad, we can sleep in the living room a while longer," added Cuco and Chuy.

October was halfway over. I would usually be looking forward to my birthday and Halloween, but not this year. This year, the last two weeks of October would be quite different. Eloisa had gotten Mom's permission to call up all of our relatives that lived within driving distance. I got nauseous every time I heard her on the phone: "We're going to have a party for Martita! Lupita has been so wonderful to me, that I just couldn't let this auspicious occasion go by without the proper celebration. I'm going to make my best delicacies, so Lupita can rest on that day. I'll be making chicken soup using the whole chicken and *tacos de sesos* (cow's brain). Oh, and lots of fresh green beans. I'm even making a piñata myself, and stuffing it with lots of delicious treats for the kids."

At first, our playmates in the barrio were excited for me, until they heard what would be on the menu. El Donny expressed his concern by asking, "Eww! Brain tacos! What if you eat the brains of a stupid cow? Will you turn into my big sister?"

Little Tony wanted me to find out what would be in the piñata. Tita and Lupe, our cousins who lived down the street, offered to get their mother to find out for us. "Our mom is real good at asking questions and getting answers."

We all nodded in agreement. Their mom, my Tía Teófila, could be counted on to infiltrate the circle of adults and report back to us. We crossed our fingers and hoped for good news.

Sadly, we soon found out that, to Eloisa, "delicious treats for kids" meant walnuts, macadamia nuts, oranges, green apples, and tangerines. These were things that we could get for free from Mr. Miller every time we went to his ranch! I mean, we liked them… but not in a piñata.

"Mamá, can I ask you something?" I hugged her around the waist while she was trying to make corn tortillas.

"Of course, my daughter. Would you like a fresh tortilla? You can put some butter on it."

"We're out of butter, remember? Eloisa finished it this morning. You said that Dad would buy some more when he got home from work today."

"Well, a little bit of lard and a sprinkling of salt, and it tastes about the same. I'll fix it for you. After you finish your homework, I'll fix you another one, if you want."

"Mamacita, can I skip my birthday this year?"

"Heavens, no! What are you talking about, silly? When you were born, you made many people happy. We wanted another daughter. Esperanza wanted a little sister. You don't remember, but when you were learning to talk, you couldn't say her name, so you gave her a new one. You called her Laly. I remember like it was yesterday…"

"Mamá, please! At least put some real treats in the piñata. Fruit doesn't go into a piñata. Everybody knows that. Maybe you can get somebody to invite Eloisa to their house for a few weeks? She likes to travel."

She dipped a spoon into a small carton of lard. "You know that we can't afford everything in the stores, but we can afford a lot more than some people."

"Brain tacos? They are slimy. At least, you could make them out of beef tongue. I like that meat."

"Eloisa is going to prepare everything, though. I suppose I could suggest a slight change. Maybe, maybe. You see, my daughter, it all depends on which meat she can get for free from the butcher. In the stores where few Mexicans shop, we can get those kinds of meat for free because the gringos usually just throw it away."

"But the piñata? Why put fruit and nuts into it? Why not some real toys or candy?"

"Who do you think is going to pay for it? She spent practically her life's savings just to come over and visit us, and she wants to take care of the preparations all by herself. She is trying to show her appreciation." She finished dabbing lard on the handmade tortilla, sprinkled salt lightly over it, and handed it to me. "Now, go and finish your homework and please let the adults be in charge of arrangements for adult guests. You're just a little girl. Go."

It was the week before Halloween, and time for the birthday get-together. On that morning, Eloisa woke me up early by singing in her imitation opera voice. "Marrrtaaaa, little chapelll of ro-o-o-ses! You are a go-o-odess, flowwwer of myyyyy lo-o-o-oo-vvve!" The words were from an old fashioned romantic song of the forties.

I would rather have been awakened by her fingernails on a chalkboard, but what could I do? Even when I tried to pull the blankets over my head, Eloisa would laugh playfully, thinking that I was joking around.

Life can be so cruel when you're a child.

Mom tried to comb my braids after breakfast, but Eloisa would have none of it. "No, no, dear Lupita! Today you rest. You gave birth to this precious child. You enjoy the day. I will comb her beautiful long hair."

She made my braids so tight that I could barely blink. Later on, when she wasn't looking, I had Mom and Laly help me loosen them a bit. I didn't want to have a headache all day.

The relatives began pouring in way before the appointed time. I wasn't at all surprised to see Eloisa end up sitting in the living room (watching television and drinking coffee) with my mother, while the other women were in the kitchen chopping, boiling, seasoning, and following Eloisa's directions to the letter.

The adults were so absorbed in chatting and such that they almost forgot about the piñata after lunch. It was Eloisa that made the grand announcement. "And now, ladies and gentlemen," she said, with a sweeping gesture that made her flabby arm jiggle, "it is time for the piñata. I want all of the men to find a rope, a big stick, and a handkerchief. Ladies, let's move these chairs and picnic benches to one side. The men can handle it."

The batting order when it comes to breaking a piñata is this: smaller and younger first, taller and older kids last. I knew that I would be near the end of the list, but I didn't mind. Some traditions make a lot of sense.

Then, Eloisa made an announcement that brought squeals from all of the kids. "I've mixed in some American treats with the traditional piñata fillings. I used my last American dollars so the children would remember this piñata for a long time!"

Like Pavlov's dogs, I began to salivate in anticipation. What could she have added? Party favors? Bazooka bubble gum? Pez candy?

Fizzies? Green army men? I tried to not get excited, but who can avoid the feeling when you're talking about a piñata, especially after an announcement such as that?

There must have been about 15 children lined up to smack the piñata: cousins, neighbors, and friends of the family included. They gave it a good battering, but I could tell that the men in control of the piñata were making sure that the killing blow would be struck by me, the birthday girl.

When it was finally my turn, I hurriedly put the blindfold on by myself. As I gripped the stick hopefully, I took a deep breath and forced all negative thoughts out of my mind, placing each unpleasant thought on its own shelf. One shelf was for all of the times that I wanted seconds on beans or tortillas but couldn't have more because Eloisa had eaten the last of the food. Another shelf was for all of the times that she had braided my hair too tightly, given my little brother wedgies to make him walk like a "little man", and all of the nights that my five brothers had to share the lumpy sofa bed in the living room. The last shelf was for how she teased my father about coming home with dirty hands.

I tried to focus in on the piñata. I wanted to hear the slightly rough sound of the rope as it was pulled over the branch of the pine tree. I wanted to hear the swishing sound that meant the piñata was swinging in a new direction. Mostly, I wanted to hear the thwack of the stick on the piñata itself.

It all happened so fast. I don't remember how many times I hit it, but when I heard the sound of breaking pottery and tearing paper, a shout came up from the crowd. I knew the piñata was dead.

I yanked off the blindfold and tossed the stick aside. All of the kids old enough to walk were piling on top of each other, searching for the goodies. It was a mass of laughing faces and wiggling, pushing, and grabbing hands. I waited for a gap before diving in. When I did, I went past the green apples, tangerines and oranges. Most of them had footprints on them, anyway. Here and there was a walnut or a macadamia nut. These I grabbed quickly, but my eyes kept searching for something shiny, something with paper, something that was store bought, something that would make this feel like a real birthday piñata.

Finally, amid the scrambling, I heard the sound of a plastic wrapper. One of the boys had something dark brown in his hand,

something that had a white squiggly line on top of it. A cupcake! A
Hostess cup cake! This find started a cupcake frenzy.

By the time the pile of children had thinned out, I had a grand
total of five macadamia nuts, six walnuts, one orange that was only
slightly bruised, and three chocolate cupcakes that were more or less
intact.

Laly and I moved aside to share. Payo joined us, bringing with
him three more cupcakes.

Nearby, I could hear all of the women patting Eloisa on the back.
"Oh, Eloisa! What a wonderful party you have made!" "Oh, Lupita!
We never had little cakes like that when we were growing up! This is
so expensive, but the kids deserve it, don't you think?" "Oh, Don
Jesús! Isn't it wonderful how Eloisa spent her last cent to do this for
one of the children?"

Each individually wrapped cupcake had a small orange sticker on
it and a big X on the label. "Where did these come from?" I asked
Laly.

"I know where they came from," answered Pancho, who had just
joined us. "They came from way over on West Vista Way. There's a
store there that sells nothing but bread things. I think that they're
cheaper over there because they're closing down the store."

"Hey, look at this." Payo had already opened one of the cupcake
packages. "The chocolate isn't dark-dark brown. Looks dry."

"What's that on the side?" I pointed to what looked like very tiny
coconut sprinkles on one side of his cupcake.

Pancho and Laly leaned over to get a closer look. "Hmm. Don't
eat that one."

We inspected all of our cupcakes, and each one of them had
visible signs of "coconut sprinkles" that wiggled by themselves.

Other children were gorging themselves without a care in the
world. "Wonder what they're going to be feeling tonight, when
they're at home?" sighed Pancho.

I hung my head down low. Laly, Pancho, and Payo all clustered
around me, trying to cheer me up. They volunteered to pool their
allowances next Sunday and buy fresh cupcakes from the corner store.

For the next hour, we hid in Dad's storage shed. When we had
heard the last pickup truck leave, we felt it safe to come out. Just as
we were turning the knob, we heard Dad's footsteps approaching. "I
know you kids must be in there. Get yourselves out right now. You

have some explaining to do. Acting like you were raised in the hills by wolves, I am so…"

Laly stepped out first and grabbed his arm, hugging it tight. "Papá! Don't get mad before you let us explain!"

Pancho held out a cupcake that been broken in half. "See, Dad? That's not all cream filling."

I could feel my eyes getting misty and mumbled, "You should have let me skip my birthday."

Dad's eyes had a sad and far away look to them. "Cupcakes for my daughter on her birthday." Sighing, he continued, "I should have gone with them. Your mother is so easily distracted sometimes. She probably saw the prices and was well, swept away, just swept away by the …Well, what can I say? Throw them away. It seems such a sin to throw away food, but this time, there's nothing more to do. Dump it before your mother sees it. I never thought we would be throwing away food." He put his hands in his pockets and looked at the back door of the house.

"Don't you want to tell her?" questioned Payo, the only one of us who could get away with asking him that particular question.

I could extend the story by going over the events of the disastrous Halloween a week later. Eloisa wanted to dress me up like a blonde princess and ended up dressing me up like a boy because I rebelled. I could tell you that she also ate all of our Halloween candies while we were at school, but details such as those would merely serve to make the story longer than necessary.

What I will share with you is that, in the next two weeks after the get-together, both Mom and Dad made many phone calls and visited local relatives more often than usual. Two or three times, I saw them both in the kitchen, talking with Eloisa. Both of those times, she would be staring at her cup of hot chocolate and pan dulce while my parents talked with her in soft voices.

It seemed to me that Mom was even sitting closer to Dad than before, but I couldn't be sure. Whenever one of us tried to loiter in a corner of the kitchen, we would be scooted out by our mother before our father had a chance to even look at us.

Early one Saturday morning in November, Dad woke us all up early to load Eloisa's suitcases into the Jeep. After a simple breakfast, we all gathered in the front yard as Mom, Dad, and Eloisa stood next to Mr. Miller's Jeep. "We're taking her to Mexicali to catch the train to Guadalajara. Say your goodbyes, children."

Mom stood quietly by Dad's side, her arm in his. She looked like she was ready for Sunday mass: scarf on her curly hair, lightly powdered face, a touch of lipstick. The only thing missing was her Sunday morning smile.

One by one, we voluntarily gave Eloisa a light hug. She seemed surprised. When I hugged her, she put a hand up to my cheek. This time, there was no pinch. Just a quiet touch and a pat on the head.

As they pulled out of the driveway, our mother blew us a kiss and said the usual, "Be good!"

We continued waving until we could see the Jeep turn the corner to go south on Santa Fe Avenue. Then, our curiosity finally got the better of us. "Eddie, where did she get the money for her ticket back?"

He began to lead us back inside the house. He held the door open with one hand and snapped his fingers with the other. "Didn't you notice all those phone calls and visits these last two weeks? When family sticks together, they can do almost anything."

The Famous Hemet Watermelons

Left: Tia Elena, the nun
Right: Mom

Ranger

Fighting is for hoods. Hooligans. Pachucos. *Chusma. La plebe.* Low-class people that give Mexicans a bad name. That's why the Lomelís don't do it. Ever. Under no circumstances.

Your father is always right. (Dad made this one up)

Never fight, lest ye be mistaken for a child belonging to others.

Never waste food. There are poor people starving in Mexico.

Take a shower at least every Saturday, whether you need it or not.

Always wear shoes, even in summer.

Never bring animals into the house, unless they are to be eaten.

Other children were not subject to extra commandments. They could confidently tell you off, waving a menacing fist in the air, but not us. No way.

"Turn the other cheek, like our Lord." Mom was such a comedian.

"Turn both cheeks and run!" That was what we usually did. Fortunately, our barrio wasn't that big. There weren't even any sidewalks. The Durán Market was only four blocks away. Santa Fe Elementary was only about two or three blocks away. That wasn't so bad when you have to sprint home in a hurry. Sometimes, I hardly missed the little bit of pride that was chipped off when I had to make a fast getaway. It wasn't so bad.

Mom had told us many stories of the effects of violence. "Your father used to be a police officer. He was one of the few honest cops in Aguascalientes. He could stop a fight without even using his gun. The true mark of a civilized person is avoiding the fight. Let the riffraff scuffle and scream bad words. They are the responsibility of the police. You show the world who you really are." In our mother's peculiar little world, everybody in our family was close to sainthood, we were the smartest kids in the barrio, and all of the cockroaches and flies came from the neighbors.

I suppose that most of the bad influences in the neighborhood avoided us because they tired of the sport. Why wouldn't they give up? We wouldn't stick around long enough to let the disagreement become interesting! Instead, we would turn both cheeks and sprint home. Perhaps that's why most of my brothers did so well in the cross country team in high school.

There was one time that was different, however. It is worth mentioning. It was the time Eddie refused to fight Tomás, a boy with a knife. Mom wouldn't believe it, and refused to condone any violence even in self defense. Dad, however, arched his eyebrows and yanked him outside to where my mother couldn't hear. "Listen to me, young man. Don't you ever let anybody pull a knife on you and walk away, because you may not live a second time. Remember this. Those who are sneaky enough to pull a knife on you in an honest fight are cowardly enough to stab you in the back. I don't like fighting any more than your mother does. However, if that son of a bitch pulls a knife on any child of mine again, you give him the beating of his life. If you don't, you'll have to face me. You hear that? Now, you be prepared for next time. I'll take care of your mother. You just do what has to be done."

It was no more than two days later that Tomás surprised Eddie in our front yard, a minute after our parents had gone to the Durán Market for groceries. He ignored Eddie's warning and began to pummel him with his thick fists, shouting and grunting unknown but vulgar-sounding words in English. He was quite proud of his bilingualism, that's for sure. Eddie, though, was filled with the Holy Spirit of Our Father of the Leather Belt with the Brass Buckle. It was a short and humiliating defeat for Tomás and a somewhat satisfying experience for our oldest brother. He had done what he had to do.

The reign of terror began the day after the big fight, when Tomás gave his dog the freedom to roam.

That German shepherd had no name. On good days when the sun was covered by gray clouds, he existed in a comatose state, a two-meter length of rope holding him to an old tire in the dirt driveway. On bad days when the sun was out in all of its glory, the poor animal would be too hot to sleep. He would just watch the dirty water in his dish evaporate, leaving a green film behind. Nobody in that dull blue house with the dusty windows had thought it important to provide a name or proper shelter for his tired bones.

Because he had nothing else and because he was a creature of instinct, there was only one thing that dog took great pride in: protecting his turf. When he was tied to that crusty tire with its nest of black widow spiders, we would walk on the other side of the street, not wanting to disturb him in any way. As an added precaution, we would avoid looking into his fierce eyes for fear that he would chew through the rope and eat us alive. When he was loose, we would literally fly past that house, sometimes barely reaching the auto repair shop (on the next corner) in time. The mechanics would always wave a screwdriver to scare him off. The frantic bleating and mooing from the slaughterhouse next to the auto repair shop would be heard long after he had returned to his own front yard.

"Why doesn't that dog just run away to find a nice family?" some would wonder aloud.

Would you stay if the only time somebody talked to you was to yell at you, kick you, or tell you to go bite somebody?

Where else would he run to? He was a German shepherd, a dog. His legs were short for his breed. Big yellow fang teeth. Claws that could gouge out the eyes of an Alaskan wolf. That Tommy boy, that Tomás El Tonto, was the only one who paid attention to him. Nobody else in that house remembered he existed unless he woke them up with his barking, which only served to direct curses in his direction. Tomás didn't play with him or feed him a whole lot, but he was the only living creature who even took his existence into account. That's why he stayed.

Yeah, that dog was a king in his own yard. A king without a crown.

We congregated on the corner of Calle Chapultepec and West Connecticut to make sense of it all. There we gathered, sitting in the dirt, leaning against the street sign, licking a Big Stick popsicle or chewing Bazooka bubble gum. Everybody would get a chance to put in their own two cents' worth. There was big talk of walking in teams of three and riding our bicycles in groups as well, with the fastest person in charge of distracting the dog from the others in the pack. We hashed and rehashed our little plans, schemed our little schemes, like stockbrokers trying to survive a market downturn.

Whose fault is it when such things happen?

We didn't really hold Eddie responsible. It was common knowledge that Little Tommy Tonto had really been begging for it for some time. It just happened that he picked on my oldest brother. Anybody would have done the same.

Was the dog the root of this evil? He had a chestnut color, with a dark chocolate back. His legs were shorter than most dogs of that kind. Yellow teeth. Tail that would smack a fly senseless when he was in a snapping mood. Nasty breath. Bald spots on his body, where he regularly gnawed on the itchy spots. He wasn't a thing of beauty, but that wasn't what made him mean.

More than one mother knocked on the door of that faded blue house, demanding that The Beast From Hell be tied up with a new cord. Sometimes the mom's boyfriend du jour would answer the door, wearing a sleeveless T-shirt, holding a cold can of beer in one hand. "If he bites you, then we have a problem. Until then, or until all the dogs in the barrio are tied up, you have no case. You come back with nothing but empty complaints, and I call a cop or the immigration office, maybe both. Adiós."

The fastest boys in the barrio soon made a sport out of running away from the furious beast. The Figueroa boys and my brothers were usually the winners. The spectators, of course, would cheer noisily from behind the safety of somebody's picket fence. Spain has the running of the bulls in Pamplona, and Vista had the running of El Perro Malo on West Connecticut Avenue.

Tomasito didn't care for it, but that's how it was. His poor beast had become a terror to the many that he didn't care for and almost a sport to those that he wanted to dominate.

Things continued in this way for many months, until the day that something unexpected followed Chuy home.

It was almost time for dinner. A faint breeze gently wandered through the open kitchen windows and out the rusty screen doors, gossiping of sopa de arroz and pinto beans again. The fathers of West Connecticut Avenue were in their back yards doing "manly" things: tinkering, fixing, or sipping cold drinks and sharing tall tales of their free-and-easy days.

Mamá had sent me out of the kitchen to bring my siblings in to wash their hands before dinner. I was in the front yard, calling their names. Eddie, Cuco, Chuy, Pancho, Laly, Payo! Irene Sánchez, from two houses down, was running towards me at a pretty good clip.

"Hey, Irene! What's up?"

Her dark brown skin was shiny from the sweat. "Look down there! Isn't that Chuy coming up the street on a bicycle? You better call your Dad!"

There was Chuy, pedaling like his legs were on fire, with a dog right behind him. My heart rate doubled almost immediately.

"Do you think that El Perro Malo will knock him off the bike?" I could see the brown blur racing closely behind my brother's aged Schwinn bike.

"Don't wait to find out, *mensa*! Do the smart thing and go get your Dad or at least your Mom! I'll go inside with you."

We bumped into each other as we flew to the front door.

My mother was on a long distance telephone call from México. "One more minute, dear."

Dad was sitting on his throne and refused to be disturbed. "Bang on the door one more time, and I bang on your head when I get out! Let me finish my magazine!"

We dashed back to the front door, ready to leap out and save Chuy's sorry bones and become heroines and living legends. The newspaper would take our picture and the caption would read "Two Girls Save Foolish Teenaged Boy from the Jaws of Death". News at eleven.

It only took a few seconds. Chuy was already in the driveway, dismounting the bike and motioning for us to come out. "Look what followed me home!"

Behind him stood a beautiful, golden brown dog with a pug nose, two pointed ears, and stub for a tail. His eyes were riveted on Chuy.

We approached cautiously, clinging to each other, watching the dog's big pink tongue hanging out, watching the drool drip from his teeth.

Chuy put his hand up for us to stop. "Watch this, muchachas!" He then put his bike down and took three steps away from it and the dog. Then, he said, "Come on, boy!"

I was hypnotized by the beauty of the strange dog, but Irene gasped in fear.

The dog came and stood beside him, drooling and panting, but watching Chuy's face and hands at all times.

"Sit, boy! Sit!"

And the dog sat.

"Speak, boy!"

The dog barked once.

I ran back inside and snatched a tortilla from the stove. "Try it with this. If he runs away with it, then that means he belongs to somebody else."

Chuy quietly turned the tortilla over as he blew on it to cool it off. The dog sat patiently, observing every flick of the finger, every twist of his wrist. Finally, he held the tortilla in front of the dog's wet nose. The dog stared at it and continued to drool and pant.

"Hungry, boy?"

Nada.

"Here, boy! Eat!"

Finally! The dog took the tortilla in his mouth and devoured it quickly.

We were astonished. Irene wiped her forehead with the back of her right hand. "Wow! This dog must belong to some rich guy and when he finds out, you're going to be in trouble for stealing his dog."

Chuy frowned. "He followed me home. Really. Didn't you, boy?"

The dog licked Chuy's open hand.

Irene turned to me. "I'm going home. If you see a cop car, hide your brother just in case. If they ask about the dog, just pretend you don't speak English. It might work, okay?"

Chuy shook his head at her. "Irene, you're scaring the dog. Go home."

With a shrug of her shoulders, she strolled towards her house, two doors down the street. Every few steps, she would casually turn her head towards us and the chrome barrette in her hair would snatch a piece of departing sunlight and fling it back in our direction.

Never bring animals into the house, unless they are to be eaten.

Never waste food. There are poor people starving in Mexico.

What could my brother be thinking, bringing a dog home? Dogs can't earn money. If they did, we'd have lots of dogs. We couldn't afford to buy special food for a nonhuman creature, no matter how beautiful and well-behaved he was! We could barely afford to eat meat once a week, and then only the cheapest cuts.

And yet... the animal was gorgeous to behold. Such brawny legs and back. Such alert eyes. Pointed ears. White paws, like elegant socks on a refined gentleman. Pug face with wrinkles. So much more obedient and intelligent looking than any cousin of ours.

Why would an animal such as this be loose, following teenaged boys into the barrio? The dogs that belonged here never ate canned or dry dog food. They got table scraps: crusty old tortillas, chorizo con huevo that had accidentally spilled onto a linoleum floor, odd chicken parts. On West Connecticut Avenue, a dog would be lucky to get a soup bone with the marrow still in it.

I waited with the dog while Chuy called everybody outside and dragged our father out by the shirtsleeve. Dad must have been in the kitchen then, because we could hear him voicing his strong objections all the way: from the kitchen, through the tiny hallway, the living room, and then… and then the gruff complaints stopped as the front door creaked open.

Chuy motioned to the dog to come closer. Nada.

My brother snapped his fingers. "Come on, boy! Here, boy!" The dog approached and sat beside him, panting and staring up at the beaming teenager.

Dad scratched his chin in thought as his eyes inspected every centimeter of the animal. "He looks healthier than any of my boys." The left side of his lip twitched. Then the right side.

The only other animal that our father had ever respected was the late Lobo, the gray German shepherd that had protected us in Tijuana while Dad was a Bracero in the USA. Lobo had once growled menacingly at Dad to stop him from using the belt on one of the boys. "Well, I'll be!" our father had exclaimed with some surprise. He then replaced his belt slowly, chuckling, as the hairs on Lobo's back gradually went down to a relaxed position. "And this dog is supposed to belong to the neighbors!" Animals like that become legends to the people that loved them.

Lobo was used to sucking the last bit of taste out of corn on the cob. He could crack bones and suck the last drop of marrow out of them. Lobo had always been one of us. But this dog with the pug nose and pointed ears, this dog with the clean teeth, must have been raised on real dog food. Wouldn't he tire of simple cuisine?

Sit, boy. Jump, boy. Roll over, boy. Come, boy. Everyone applauded. Mom put her hand on Dad's shoulder and casually commented that she could make an extra effort to obtain scraps from Mr. Durán's meat counter.

Payo clung to Dad's waist and squeezed. "Papá, this dog could go to work with us."

By the time Monday morning came around, we had named the dog "Ranger" because his pug face resembled Teddy Roosevelt, former president and Texas Ranger. Perhaps some teacher had once extolled the glorious achievements of the man and his administration, but we knew little of that. All we knew was that our father admired Pancho Villa, a general in the Mexican Revolution, a man who, like Mr. Roosevelt, liked hats and big mustaches.

We almost named the dog "Pancho", but there were two objections. First, Pancho predictably objected because it was one of his nicknames. Second, our mother pointed out that it was a human name and that the Catholic church might have some rule against that. Nobody wanted the Pope to crown us with his scepter for being foolish or disrespectful!

On most Monday mornings of summer vacation, our parents had a devil of a time getting all of us up and ready to go work on the ranch with them. That Monday was different. We were eager to see if Ranger would pass the on-the-job test.

If Ranger did nothing more than amuse us, he would be left by the side of the road on the outskirts of Vista and we would cry all the way home. It had happened before with other animals that we found, mostly kittens and puppies. We knew that Ranger had to prove his worth to the man we called papá.

M & N Tropical Tree Nursery was a part of Mr. and Mrs. Miller's ranch on the outskirts of Vista. They lived at the top of the hill, the tree nursery was in the middle, and the orchards went all the way down to the edge of Ormsby Street. It was a lot of responsibility for a man who was barely literate and bilingual only when it came to cuss words, but Mr. Miller trusted him to get the job done.

The most troublesome problem for Mr. Miller's ranch was that of controlling the squirrel population. These cute little woodland creatures were getting fat from gnawing on the many varieties of avocados. They were almost impossible to trap and were known to invite other more ravenous pests like possums that climbed avocado trees. If that happened, then the bubonic plague rats were sure to follow and civilization as we knew it would end. At least, that's what Dad always said.

We poured out of the Jeep, chattering and rushing to get started. Ranger's nostrils were flaring and his stubby tail twitched uncontrollably. "Let's see what this dog can do. Come on, family, let's walk through the avocado orchard and pick up all of the avocados that fell over the weekend."

Cuco, Chuy, and Pancho ran to bring two dingy canvas sacks and one large brown paper bag. One for the throw aways, one for those not ripe yet, and one for those too ripe. Too many soft, black spots or a rodent's teeth marks doomed an avocado to the sack that would eventually be emptied into the big trash can. If it had only a few imperfections or if it gave a little to the touch, it would be deposited into the big paper bag that we could take home with us. Those avocados that would ripen soon ended up in the other gray canvas sack, destined to end up in some fancy produce department.

As soon as we stepped into the emerald shade of the avocado jungle, our eyes went to the ground, carefully scanning the leaf-strewn floor for fallen fruit or small leafy bumps that might conceal an avocado or two. Ranger, in the meantime, proceeded to mark as many trees as his bladder could manage, sniffing the air and circling around us as if we were his responsibility.

Somebody saw a little furry something dash away from one tree. Cuco shouted, "Sick 'em, boy!" and pointed in the direction of the squirrel that was sprinting away from us.

Ranger bolted towards the animal and snatched it before it could climb to the protective branches of the leafy canopy. He held it firmly without chewing and came towards Cuco, who had moved and was now standing next to our father. If the squirrel squeaked or wriggled, the sharp teeth would squeeze it a bit more and shake it left and right until it stopped its feeble protests.

"Ranger!" The rest of us were watching in silent amazement, but Dad called him again. "Ranger!"

We crowded together and watched in awe as the dog dropped the squirrel in front of our father. There was a touch of squirrel blood on Ranger's lips and saliva was beginning to drip from his quivering lower lip. He stared intently at the moribund squirrel, his nostrils flaring more with each spasm of the furry animal's body.

"Good Ranger. Good Ranger." I had never seen our father pat an animal on the head before, unless he was going to wring its neck, pluck its feathers, and hand it to Mom for making our dinner. There he was, though, alternately scratching his head, adjusting his straw sombrero, and patting the dog on the head. "El Perro Bueno! Good Ranger. Good Ranger!"

Mom brought us back to reality by pointing out the fact that there was a near-dead squirrel next to Dad's boots. "What are we going to do with that?"

Dad pointed to the mortally wounded squirrel. "Eat. Good Ranger. Eat."

Ranger went to work with our father every day after that. Dinnertime conversation began with the Ranger Report, where Dad would tell us of the dog's exploits. "Today, he climbed almost halfway up that gnarled avocado tree on the west side and caught a possum that had ruined the fruit of two other trees." "Today, he caught two squirrels." "Today, Mr. Miller came down to check on the potting of the Macadamia seedlings and Ranger chased away a fat snake that was ready to bite him."

Ranger responded eagerly to affection: hugs, scratches behind the ears, and pats on the head. He would fetch sticks, tennis balls, anything that we threw. Always, the object would be returned and laid at our feet.

Never waste food. There are poor people starving in Mexico.

There were so many fruit trees at the M & N Tree Nursery that not all of the fruit could possibly make it to the supermarket. We were allowed to take some home almost every day: macadamia nuts, lemons, passion fruit, oranges, avocados, cherimoyas, sapotes, you name it. Mr. Miller's ranch had a little bit of everything.

Because fruits were in season, we had more to give to Ranger: beans, old tortillas, some milk, chicken bones, soup bones, or scraps of cow's abdomen from Mom's latest batch of menudo. Every belly is full when the weather is good.

One Sunday, Felipe and Silvina (relatives from Fallbrook) came to visit. Felipe was a tall man with a thin mustache and a hearty laugh. Silvina was his petite wife who added color to all family gatherings with her hearty *grito* whenever we all broke out into song.

"Our house is your house," Dad would say, like a wise elder of a growing tribe.

"Tell me that when you're rich, Jesusito!" Felipe would answer, slapping him on the back. Then everyone would clink their bottles of beer or Kool-Aid midst great laughter.

While the adults watched a boxing match on the black and white television set, the younger crowd split into two groups. Pancho, Cuco, and Chuy had decided to hike along the railroad track, towards the west. That also happened to be where the roller skating rink was, but our parents did not know that yet. As they began to march along the tracks, Ranger trotted behind them, sniffing for trap door spiders in the gray dirt. The younger group, including our cousins Imelda and Esteban, decided to pool their Sunday allowances and undertake the perilous journey to the Durán Market, past the pale blue house where the notorious Tomás still lived.

We walked close together, chattering childish gossip about other cousins and fingering the coins in our pockets as we kept our eyes and ears open for El Perro Malo. Much to our delight, this time the poor beast was tied up. Tomás, however, was not.

"Get away from my house!" he shouted, standing next to his snarling animal.

Esteban puffed out his chest. "We're not even in front of your house yet. We're at the corner, see? We'll just go around."

We circled his block, intending to cross on Redlands. "We've got plenty of time anyway," Esteban reminded us. We all agreed. What were a few more minutes if it made that other strange boy happy and saved our skinny hides from who knows what? It was an acceptable compromise.

Almost at the end of Avenida De La Plaza, Tomás surprised us by jumping out from behind a bush. He must have jumped over his back fence, because there he was: jutting jaw, rock in his left hand, and right hand curled up into a tight fist.

Here we go again! "Come on, everybody, let's walk back home," I said with a sigh. "We can try again later."

Tomás dropped the rock and walked after us to make sure that we left his block swiftly. "A little bit faster, if you please!" A few seconds later, he was almost next to us, staring at Esteban. "Where you from?"

"Fallbrook."

"Rancherito! You're a country boy! I bet you have an outhouse. Maybe two."

Keka and Imelda pulled their brother along, shushing him. "Just ignore him. It's not worth it."

"But I'm a man!" said Esteban.

"Me, too!" stated Payo.

Tomás had heard it all. "You two little vatos? You're in what, second? First grade, maybe? Double ha. Ooh, I'm scared!" Then he spit on Esteban.

Just as our eyes began to water from anger and fear, I heard a low growl. For a split second, I thought El Perro Malo had come loose and was ready to devour us and crack our bones with his yellow fangs, sucking out the marrow with great enjoyment. There would be little left to bury. That dog was always so hungry and we weren't very big.

From the corner of Avenida Benito Juárez and Avenida De La Plaza came Ranger, trotting briskly toward us.

I took a deep breath and held Payo's hand. "Tomás, leave us alone or you'll be sorry."

"Why? I bet I could even slap you and you'd still get in trouble. If you socked me on the nose, it wouldn't even hurt me but you'd have to pray another rosary. Ha!"

That was the last straw. I pointed a shaky finger at the troublemaker. "Ranger! Sick 'em, Ranger!" It worked with squirrels, and I prayed that the command would work on Tomás.

I had never noticed how flat Ranger's back became when he ran at top speed. His little white paws became a blur. The stubby tail pointed straight up. The two ears pointed forward, marking the intended target like sights on a rifle. The lips curled in a promise of pain to come, baring the white fangs that seemed capable of puncturing the tires of an eighteen wheeler. That dog meant business. Bless his loyal little heart!

Tomás turned tail and set a new record for the 100 meter Barrio Dash: over parked cars, over trash cans, and through bushes. When he got to his back fence, Ranger was able to grab a hold of his tennis shoe.

There was the big boy crying big boy tears, the wooden fence digging splinters into his stomach and hands as he struggled to get his sorry foot out of the shoe held firmly by Ranger's fangs.

Not wanting to stifle the dog's creative urges, we let Ranger shake the boy's leg once or twice just enough to get the point across. We were disappointed to see that there was no blood in Ranger's mouth, but we all agreed it was for the best. Tomás needed to be shaken, not stirred, in order to learn his lesson. Nobody wanted to involve the police or our parents.

During the next few weeks, Ranger's skills were tested a few more times. First, we would wait for darkness until some borracho or hobo would be stumbling on the railroad tracks in the quiet moonlight. We hated the way they left broken beer bottles on our railroad tracks and odd little scraps of torn aluminum or small plastic packages in the weeds. Those that were drunk or high often got a little nip in the pants, but never to the point of bleeding. We were always able to call him back in time.

Then, we tried it on the very annoying Abel, the thief of the neighborhood. *Chinga Abel, chinga Abel, chinga el vato buey.* This was the Christmas Carol of West Connecticut Avenue, sung secretly by the many victims of his petty crimes. Abel of the snotty nose and shifty eyes. Abel, the disgusting little criminal who liked to peek into little girls' windows. He was more annoying than El Donny and almost as tall as Tomás.

Abel never sneaked around our windows again. Long lost items mysteriously reappeared in our garage. When playing baseball with my brothers, he argued less and tried harder. In fact, he became downright tolerable.

The cats in the neighborhood wisely maintained their distance, but the dogs were another story. All it took was a "Sick 'em, boy!" and Ranger would go for it: snarl, snap, shake, and toss. The invader would soon beat a hasty retreat into the horizon, a few puncture wounds in the neck as the unfriendly reminder to stay away from us.

Scrawny kids have always been an easy target for big, rude dogs. With Ranger on the scene, the safety of our friends was guaranteed. "Bring your dog with us to play baseball" or "Come to the store with us and bring your dog" they would say.

Strange dogs learned to avoid West Connecticut Avenue.

He was showered with hugs. The best leftovers were saved for him, the dog that looked like Teddy Roosevelt and Pancho Villa. Ranger was our guardian angel. No wings, but good, strong fangs and a loyal heart.

The only dark cloud that remained was El Perro Malo, the most dangerous dog we had ever known. El Perro Malo had kept his distance from us ever since Ranger's arrival, but would he be wild enough to attack Ranger alone? Ranger fought with discipline and honor, stopping before too much blood was lost, but what about that other raggedy dog? That dog without a name? He had nothing to lose and yet he was still there. Did he dare to face Ranger paw to paw, just the two of them? If he was able to hurt Ranger, we knew it could be serious. Dad would never pay for a veterinarian.

"Everybody, run! Dog fight! Hurry!" Irene was screaming at the top of her lungs one October morning, hysterically waving and jumping in the middle of the street.

Television sets were turned off in mid-cartoon. Screen doors swung open and were slammed shut in the haste to reach the commotion before it all became old news. Children streamed into the street: La Angelina, El Donny, Little Lupita, Evie, El Eddie, Carmen, Marilú, the Filipino kids next door, the Chavez girls, the Figueroas, crazy Irma, Abel, and many more. The crowd headed east, down West Connecticut Street.

"Where's Ranger?" I wondered aloud.

Irene's frantic shouts and waving arms answered my question. She had been dashing up and down the street, gathering her crowd and was now leading us towards the pale blue house, where the short-legged and short-tempered German shepherd was attempting to bury his yellow fangs into Ranger's sinewy neck.

Trembling, Payo and I stepped toward the snarling animals to halt the madness but the rest of the motley crew pulled us back. "Aw, let them settle it. Besides, if it doesn't go the way we want, we can all get Tomás."

Carmen, La Angelina, and Marilú threw rocks at the front door, continually yelling "Tomás, get your butt out here!" and, "We know you're in there!"

Crimson drops were being scattered violently in that dirt driveway, blending fat drops of canine sweat and saliva with the oil stains that never went away. Ranger got in a few good bites, but that other dog was fighting with just as much passion. Nobody dared get closer.

La Angelina nudged me with her bony elbow. "RanGER, RanGER, RanGER..." She worked the crowd into a frenzy, waving her fist rhythmically in the air until we were all chanting with her.

Now fully aware of our presence, Ranger reared up like a stallion and, holding his front paws up like a boxer, forced a gap in the German shepherd's line of attack. We all cheered when Ranger's teeth sank firmly into the other dog's neck.

Perhaps he had been waiting for a sign giving permission to do what had to be done. A few bloody seconds later, Tomás silently appeared with a garden hose and sprayed both dogs. We exchanged a few dirty looks and led Ranger away to our front yard to cleanse his wounds and feed him a hero's banquet of scrambled eggs, tortillas, and liver scraps.

There were no more challenges to the throne.

He had rid Mr. Miller's ranch of the squirrels, chased away vagrants, and defended us on more than one occasion. This should have been the point where he settled down to live a long and happy life without a care.

As seasons change, so do circumstances. The avocados, oranges, and lemons that we had enjoyed would not appear again until warmer winds returned. Some fruits could still be bought at big supermarkets like Safeway, but at scandalous prices. Much to our dismay, the butchers began charging more than a token few cents for what we had gotten for free before: liver, heart, kidneys, stomach, tongue, intestines.

The nights got colder and Ranger got thinner. "Let him stay inside at night" we would whine. Dad finally allowed him sleep in front of the heater at night, but that didn't last long. In a family of seven children, there is always somebody who has to get up at night to urinate. All it took was one sleepy child to be frightened at the sight of red eyes in the shadows and the poor dog was tossed out into the open garage to sleep on the cold cement floor. No blanket. No dog house. Nobody to hug him and say, "Good dog."

"He's just a dog, after all," Dad would remind us.

"It might be a sin to worry more over an animal, who has no soul, than over your father. Or me," Mom would add.

Homework and the holiday season distracted us, so nobody could be sure when they first noticed his absence.

Did someone forget to feed the dog? Nobody knew, but we never had a real dog dish for him anyway. "Dogs are dogs," repeated our mother. "It's not a tragedy."

"We should have tied him up again," harrumphed our father, but some of us weren't so sure that would have made him want to stay. Butterflies and brave boxers should be allowed to enjoy their freedom.

Where was Ranger? Did he return to the people that must have trained him and fed him so well? Chuy said no, because animals have pride, too. "He left them and came to live with us. He would never go back there."

Maybe he had found a new family by venturing west towards Melrose Avenue. Over there, on the other side of the railroad tracks there were many middle-class families, each with lots of dog food, a nice little yard, and a garage with real walls. We drove by there sometimes on our way to Saint Francis. "Keep your eyes open for Ranger," Laly would say, her nose pressed to the window of the rumbling truck.

No luck. No luck at all.

In the gray shadows of slumber, I would see him walking east on the railroad tracks, carefully picking his way around patches of broken beer bottles, his stubby tail wagging no more, his proud ears pointing down. I imagined that he would stop and lick a scab until the pink scar remained, and then get up and continue trudging on, ignoring the dust of the gray dirt. Those were sad dreams.

"He was never really ours to begin with," Mom would comment, hoping to ease our minds. "Besides, dogs have no soul."

We had seen his dark brown eyes smile at us as we scratched behind his ears. We had felt his wet tongue lick our forehead whenever we hugged him. We were there when he rallied to our cheers and battled with El Perro Malo, ending forever that vicious dog's reign of terror. Ranger most certainly did have a soul.

On warm, quiet nights, we would sometimes hear a bark or a growl in the street and somebody's cat would hiss and run up the pine tree for safety. On cold or rainy nights, the melancholy sound of the train clackety-clacking on the rusty rails would mingle with a distant howl of somebody else's dog talking to the moon.

The years passed and other memories filled our heads, but the spirit of Ranger lingered. It is hard to forget someone with that much soul.

> His friends he loved. His direst earthly foes —
> Cats— I believe he did but feign to hate.
> My hand will miss the insinuated nose,
> Mine eyes the tail that wagg'd contempt at Fate.

"Epitaph" by Sir William Watson (1858-1935), British
poet

The Carob Tree and the Cactus

Carob Tree with Pancho in the Way

In the southeast corner of the comfortable back yard, there was a carob tree, just like the many carob trees on El Patrón's second ranch, the one they moved into sometime in the late 1950's. His carob trees had a little white wooden sign that identified them: "Carob trees, also called Saint John's Bread." In finer print, you could read all about how Saint John supposedly made bread out of ground carobs and how wholesome and nutritious carobs were. It even said that carob fruit could substitute for chocolate.

Our carob tree was a tree of many uses. It was a safe haven for Minino, one neighbor's tabby cat, whenever Chavela, the other neighbor's Chihuahua, was not tied up. On a lazy summer afternoon, after chores were taken care of, it was a very good tree to climb or use as a goal post. Mostly, we used it as a shade tree while we prepared nopales (cactus) for cooking.

There were a few cactus plants on our east side, and a few near our back yard. Nopales are tough little plants. They are vegetables that grow with little care and even less water. They are not so bad to use as fences, since unwanted visitors (2-legged and 4-legged) avoid the pointy needles, which we called stickers. Even in small towns, nopales had more than one use.

Mom or Dad would grab a large brown paper bag, the biggest knife in the house, and a pair of leather gloves. Then, they would cut the tender, bright green nopales that had grown from the tough pencas (older branches of the plant) and drop them into the paper bag, until no more bright green, tender nopales were to be found on that big cactus plant.

It was on one of those hot summer days that we began to prepare nopales. Before too long, Dad and my older brothers disappeared to do something more interesting, and Mom and Laly headed for the kitchen to rinse the first potful of nopalitos for lunch. This left me and Payo, to finish cutting up the nopales that hot summer day.

I was nice enough to show him how to protect his fingers from the evil stickers by using a piece of folded paper bag to hold the nopal down on the cookie tin. This allowed the left hand to have a firm hold of the nopal while the right hand sliced off the stickers, one by one. Then, shifting the torn piece of paper to the base, the right hand could cut vertical lines in the nopal. After that, it was easy to slice the nopal into evenly sized chunks by cutting horizontally. These bite-sized chunks could then be dropped into the pot on the picnic table, ready to be rinsed and boiled in the kitchen. Then, voila! Another free meal compliments of Mother Nature!

My idea was to impress Mom and Laly by having this second pot full before lunch was ready. I knew that we could do it. We had everything we needed: fresh glasses of Kool-Aid with ice cubes in them, paper bags to tear up or use as trash bags, good knives, and very tender nopales.

Payo, however, did not share my vision. "I gotta go do #2," he would announce. Then he'd be gone for about 30 minutes. Later, "I gotta go do #1," he'd say. When he *did* return, he would usually have one hand in one pocket and the other hand on his face, brushing off the crumbs of whatever he had nabbed from the kitchen.

One time, he said, "I gotta go ask Dad a question. Be right back."

"Yeah, I wonder how long 'right back' is," I remarked.

He skipped away without even looking back once!

The hot sun seemed to mock me as I slaved away, alone, slicing off the stickers from the young nopales. Sweat trickled down my forehead as I focused on the task I was left to finish. I couldn't quit! These nopalitos would be the main course for today, tomorrow, and probably most of the coming week.

Our top four faaaavorite nopal dishes were:

a. *boiled nopalitos (onion, cilantro, chunks of fresh
    tomatoes, a dash of chile powder, and lemon)*

b. *nopalito omelette (onion, cilantro, tomatoes, and
    El Pato hot sauce)*

c. *nopalito tortilla omelet (crunchy pieces of old
    tortillas, onion, cilantro, tomatoes, and a dash of
    El Pato hot sauce)*

d. *nopalitos and ground beef (chunks of potatoes,
    onion, cilantro, tomato, and a few drops of El Pato
    hot sauce, pinto beans on the side)*

Yes, my mouth remembered! My hands responded by working even faster.

I struggled to ignore the taunting rays of the summer sun. Where was the shade that the wise old carob tree was supposed to provide to me? How could it look so strong while I was wilting? Didn't anybody care?

When I heard the sounds of laughter coming from the living room, I stabbed my kitchen knife into the picnic table and sneaked over to investigate. There he was, that ungrateful little brother of mine! He was watching a Saturday morning cartoon, without a care in the world!

Well, I would not stand for such frivolity! I stormed into the living room and pulled Payo away by his ear. Attempting to shame him, I used the strongest words I knew then: "Hey, Payo! Whose family do you belong to, anyway? Do you belong to the neighbors, or are you one of us?"

The last straw was when he volunteered to freshen up my glass of Kool-Aid a short while later. *Not only did he spill half of it on his jeans*, but he said he would promptly return after he had changed his pants. When I complained to Dad a while later that Payo hadn't returned and that I was doing all of the work in the sun, his solution was to move the picnic table into the shade of the garage and to scold me for being too harsh on my little brother. From my corner of the garage, I could see through part of the sliding glass door that Payo (and his fresh pair of pants) was sitting on my father's lap, asking him about the Lone Ranger or The Rifleman or some such show that Dad liked so much.

I felt that I had cut up a hundred nopales while he went to change pants. Of course, when you work in a hurry, things are liable to spill... onto the bench next to you, for example. I had purposely let the biggest, fattest stickers fall into the cracks of the dark wooden bench. I hoped and prayed that some laaaaazy child would sit on these spiny, fat, stickers.

Well, he had to come back to the picnic table sooner or later.

I had almost resigned myself to finishing the tedious task all by myself, when, finally, the sliding glass door to the living room began to open.

"How's it going?" he asked sweetly, closing the sliding glass door slowly behind him

"There is only one left to go, Payo. I'm leaving that one for you and then you can clean up the picnic table while I go and start my shower," I answered.

Smiling, he said, "Hey, thanks! I'll finish off that last nopal before the John Wayne movie starts. *Dad* said *I* could sit by *him* on the *sofa* to watch the movie."

"I bet he did." I frowned as I placed the broom against the table. "Don't forget to sweep the garage floor." Just as he was about to reach the bench and sit down, I asked, "When does your movie start?"

"Oh, in fifteen minutes," he smiled.

"Betcha a dime you can't finish in ten!"

With the shout of a gambler betting on a sure thing, Payo zipped around the picnic table, gleefully shouting, "Get that dime ready, 'cause I feel lucky today!" In the blink of an eye, he had plopped his fresh pair of jeans on that wooden bench.

If I was Oliver Stone or Quentin Tarantino, THAT moment of contact would have been filmed in slow motion:

Little boy in faded blue jeans... boy, face laughing, looks at sister's expressionless face... he skips around cheap wooden picnic table, eyes still looking at sister... his right leg swings over bench... close-up of little blue-jeaned booty going down, a few thick cactus stickers piercing the jeans, ... switch to boy's face ... closer ... closer...

I guessed that he was going to need another pair of pants and a set of tweezers. Dad, of course, rushed out and, surprise, surprise! He *actually* scolded Payo for not looking where he sat down first! I strolled into the kitchen and told Mom to get the tweezers, the good pair. She ran out and helped Dad pull Payo's pants down to get the biggest stickers off of his pink behind before bringing him in.

Luckily for Payo, none of the neighbors' kids were home, otherwise he would have been the star attraction, with his pincushion cheeks and his tear-stained face.

"It's Marta's fault!" he cried.

"Stop wiggling!" Dad said, in a gruff voice. "Don't you want me to take them all out?"

"But she told me to sit down!" he wailed.

Before Dad could say anything to me, Mom gave Dad a serious little look that I had rarely seen before. "The girl can't be punished every time the youngest boy sits on something that doesn't agree with his bottom."

Payo continued to turn on the tears, sobbing theatrically. He was the one who had perfected the technique of the trembling lip, and he was putting on his best performance in front of our father. Mom, having seen it before, tended to ignore the drama and focus on the task at hand.

As entertaining as the show was, I turned and headed for my shower before I got further involved.

The rest of the day was just like any another Saturday afternoon on West Connecticut Avenue. Television sets cooled down, and kids all over the neighborhood could be heard scampering about playing games like hide and go seek or baseball and eating ice cream or cold watermelon. We eventually joined in.

At almost sunset time, the sound of the approaching train made us race for the strong yet gentle branches of the guardian of our back yard. Clambering up its smooth bark, we flicked a few ants off of our favorite branch and, together, shouted and waved as the rusty train passed by.

I noticed that Payo was sitting more comfortably now, and it didn't bother me any more.

"This is kinda neat, huh?" he asked, smiling in the direction of the disappearing train.

"What?" I wondered if he was going to bring up that thing about the stickers on the picnic bench, and I was ready to help him out of the tree with my foot, if necessary. The afternoon had been really nice, and I didn't want him to ruin it.

"I mean, this is kinda fun up here. Look how the sun is turning dark orange, see? Those clouds over by the skating rink have a color like a bruise in some parts." He sighed. A moment later, he asked, "If I can get some money out of Dad, and I know that I can, I bet we can get Laly to take us to the Avo Theatre next Saturday!"

I breathed in the sweet scent of the guava trees nearby and looked at the purpling of the few clouds in the southwestern sky. "Well, Dad might get mad. I mean, it's kinda expensive to buy tickets."

"I can ask Laly if she maybe wants to take us. She will get her friend from Escondido to buy candy and popcorn for us. He is really nice. Maybe he will help pay for our tickets, too. I'll ask Dad for the money first, though. You want me to? You want to go to the show on Saturday? 'Cause I'll ask him. I can't go if you don't go. It will be my idea, okay?"

"Well, okay, but only if it's not one of those dancing and singing movies. I hate those."

"What if it's an Elvis Presley movie?"

"Hey, that's a whole different deal! Elvis is the King of Rock and Roll, and don't you forget it." I ran one hand over the bark of the carob tree, feeling the little nub left by a twig that had been broken sometime before. "Go ahead and see if you can do it. If anybody can shake a dollar out of Dad, it's you, alright." The corners of my mouth wanted to curl up, but I stifled the desire. "Look at that little cloud over there, see?" I pointed carefully in the direction where the train tracks disappeared into the little hillside.

As we balanced on the warm branches of the carob tree, we could even see the hazy edge of the field across the railroad tracks. No carob trees grew over there. I didn't think anybody over there even knew that you could eat nopales. They didn't know what they were missing.

The conversation trickled down to silence as the sun slowly dipped below the horizon. Porch lights clicked on. Time for dinner.

138

Payo in Choir Robe

Payo in His First Suit

The Needle Incident

What do you do when you're young, strong, good-looking, smart, and the only ones who really believe that are your parents?

Eddie could always be counted on to help bring in a little extra money. While Dad was gone for months at a time in the Bracero Program, my oldest brother was constantly working before or after school: selling newspapers, selling bubble gum on the international border, shining shoes, and even cutting hair in a barber shop. He was respectful to adults, he was sharp, and he could hustle. Doors would open for him.

When we moved to Vista, our oldest brother found no special classes or programs in school to welcome him. There probably weren't even any Chicano (Latino, Mexican-American, Hispanic, whatever) teachers in that part of San Diego county. Even the nicest of teachers in Vista High, like Mr. Kelly in Spanish class, didn't have enough time to really be of much help. This was the 1950's.

Yes, Eddie was the first to see that it was "sink or swim". Never having had many opportunities to swim, some of us developed a fear of deep water. So, let's just say that we learned to walk under water really, really fast.

Eddie concentrated his efforts in that area where he could achieve some immediate satisfaction and visible success: his social life. He became the James Dean of the barrio: slick hair with an Elvis curl in front, white T-shirt with the sleeves rolled up, blue jeans cuffed and creased, and the whole rebel look. At the A&W Root Beer Stand on South Santa Fe Avenue or the hamburger stand near Vista High, he was respected by the tough guys and swooned over by the females. Once or twice, angry English-speaking fathers came to our house wanting to speak to my parents, sometimes with their pony-tailed teenage daughter sobbing right next to them. Before too long, he began telling everybody that his name was "Eddie". To his peer group, he was IT.

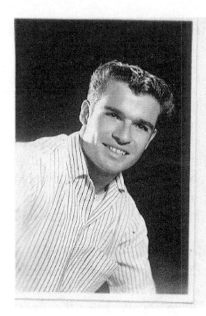

Top: Pancho, Cuco, and Chuy
Left: Eddie, Our Big Brother

He may have been a debonair Latin lover to the freckle-faced, poodle skirt wearing girls in Vista High School, and, in his own way, a good son to my parents, but he was "de buen aire" to us. We knew that his socks smelled as much as anybody else's, and we really hated his enthusiasm in helping Dad get the belt whenever one of us had committed some minor sin. You can't be popular with your siblings when your wrath is feared as much as a father's anger. He was a sight to behold, and we usually preferred to behold him from a distance… out of arm's reach, in other words.

***

Laly, my sister, tiptoed into the living room and whispered, "Marta! Payo! Just because Mom and Dad are going to be late, doesn't mean that you two can stay up late watching television!"

Our little brother, Payo, patted the sofa. "Laly, come on! Turn the light off and join us. It's an Elvis Presley movie!"

"Oooh!" She clapped her hands together in excitement. "Maybe just for a little while. Is this the one where he sings?"

"He sings in all of his movies!" we answered, more than a little bit annoyed.

Laly sometimes had a knack for stating the obvious.

"Blanket?" offered Payo, as he stretched the blanket to cover her lap as well.

A while later, she had fallen asleep on the sofa with her legs on top of ours, and we were still trying to stay awake for the next song in the movie. Payo loved the heroic parts in the movie, and I looked forward to the romantic parts.

"Laly, get off. Our legs are falling asleep and we're trying to stay awake."

"Huh?" she yawned. "Well, okay. I'm going to bed, but you two better turn off this TV before Eddie gets home. He might be home before Mom and Dad."

I was a little bit worried about something, and I had to ask, "Laly, are you gonna tell on us for staying up late to watch TV? Huh?"

She stretched and yawned, one of those long, streched-out yawns that expose all of the teeth and give a good view of the tonsils and the back of the throat. Even in the dim light of the black and white television set, I could count almost every tooth in her mouth.

"Good Lord!" I thought to myself. "Good thing we don't have to see that in broad daylight!"

With a sigh, Laly rubbed her eyes once more. "You shoulda been in bed a long time ago, but, after all, it was an Elvis Presley film. He's the King of Rock and Roll."

"We know."

"Yeah, and he's so cute!" she smiled dreamily.

Of course, I nodded. Of course, Payo glared at both of us. He liked the action: punching it out, fast cars, the wheeling and dealing, and the fact that the good guy always won. We just liked the good guy, period.

Laly continued, "Well, you two have ten minutes to watch more of the movie. After that, I promise nothing. If you're still up watching TV after ten minutes, I might tell on you and I might not. It depends on what I feel like doing. Even if I *don't* tell on you, I'm not going to take you to the show with me next Friday or Saturday night."

"What's playin'?" I asked. I hoped it was something boring, so we wouldn't be tempted to go to sleep just because she wanted us to do so. I wanted to stay up as late as I could without our parents finding out. It seemed like a good idea at the time.

"The Thirteen Ghosts!" she answered, her eyebrows going up slightly.

Ooh, we had been hearing about that movie for some time! Ghosts!!! Thirteen of them! After paying for your ticket, they gave you a pair of 3-D glasses. Our cousins down the street, Tita and Lupe, said that it was the scariest movie that they had ever seen because the ghosts seemed to jump out at you. Both Payo and I had been hoping that somebody would take us to see the movie, even though we knew we would probably have nightmares afterwards.

"Laly, can we stay up 'till the movie is over if we're real quiet? Please?" pleaded Payo, clutching the edge of the blanket.

"No, Payo. Ten minutes."

"Ten minutes or what?" I wondered aloud. "If we don't go see the movie, you don't get to go either. You know that Pancho doesn't want to go with you, and we're the only ones that will leave you alone in the theater, so you can talk with your friends... or Nicho from Escondido."

Pancho was always Laly's first choice of brothers when it came to social engagements, but he was not always available. Now Laly glared at me. "You ungrateful brat! Even if Mom and Dad won't be home for an hour, what are you going to do when Eddie comes home? He will probably be home before they are. You know what he likes to do, right?"

Yes! Of course we knew! He always checked the television set to see if it was warm, then removed his belt to go after the ones who had dared stay up past their bedtime. Pancho, Chuy, and Cuco (our other brothers) had long ago learned not to mess with him. Being younger, we were still learning.

Chuy the Mecánico

Laly went off to bed and we stayed to watch the end of the movie. Cuco, Chuy, and Panchito were all asleep. Mom and Dad had gone to Hemet or Fallbrook or somewhere to help some cousin or something.

It was a Saturday night, and Eddie was out cruising through Vista, Oceanside, Carlsbad, and Escondido, doing his own thing. We had no real idea of what his own thing was; we were only conscious of the fact that he was not home at the moment. That was enough for us to enjoy the movie, as late as it was.

The ten minutes came and went.

Soon, we heard a car in the driveway.

"That could be Dad's jeep," yawned Payo.

"And it could be Santa Claus!" I snapped at him. "That's Eddie's car! Listen!"

We heard the telltale backfire of the engine.

"Oh! Oh! What do we do now, Marta?"

"I'll turn off the TV while you get rid of the blanket!"

"Where do I put it?" he asked, his eyes wide with fear.

I wanted to say something rude, but didn't have the time. "Under the sofa!"

I saw a tear start to form in his left eye. "I can't move! My legs are asleep!"

I was busy blowing on the TV, trying to cool it off. "I'm going to drag you into your bed by the hair if you don't help me out here! Remember, Daddy isn't here to save your little pink butt this time! This time, it's just you, me, Eddie, and his belt!"

Somehow, we managed to escape from the living room and race to bed before Eddie opened the front door. I had barely pulled the covers up to my nose when I heard him in the living room. From the direction of the footsteps, I knew that he was standing in front of the television, with his right hand on top of it, checking to see if it had been on past the usual bedtime. Mom had told us stories of the persecution of Catholic priests in Mexico's history, and I felt a twinge of empathy for them.

The footsteps approached the boys' room first. I heard the door slowly open, but just a crack. A few seconds later, the dreaded footsteps came in MY direction. They stopped at the door to our bedroom. In a hushed voice, Eddie asked, "Marta? Who was watching television?"

Without thinking, I answered, "Payo", a bit too enthusiastically.

"And you too, since you are awake to answer!" I could almost see his smirk through the darkness of the night. "You're going to get it from Mom and Dad. I'd give you the belt myself, but I don't want to deprive them of the fun. Next time, go to bed on time like you're supposed to, without anybody having to remind you. That's how we were raised, and don't you forget it!"

He could be so scary, the way he hissed the "s" sound in his words. As I struggled to fall asleep, I asked myself a zillion questions. "Why was I so stupid to answer him? Why did I say Payo's name so readily? Why was Eddie so grouchy? Why didn't our parents let us set our own rules more, like the neighbors next door or that family down the street?"

I knew that Eddie would have busted Payo anyway, because he had been listening to his breathing. Payo hadn't yet figured out that people who are pretending to be asleep are supposed to breathe verrry, verry slowly. Because Payo was spoiled by my father, I forgave myself for having given his name up so quickly.

The last two questions, about Eddie's temper and about the strict discipline in our house, were too hard to answer at the moment. I finally slept, a tortured and fitful sleep.

Laly did her best to get a good night's rest, but it couldn't have been easy that night. She tried words: "Marta, stop hogging all of the blankets!" "Marta, stop talking about the devil in your sleep!" "Marta, you're drooling on my pillow!" "Marta, sleep on your own side of the bed!" When that didn't work, she kicked me once or twice. I didn't blame her; I would have kicked myself if that was possible.

The next day, sure enough, we found out that "Eddie" had turned us in. Our punishment was the usual one: no playing outside for one day, and pray a whole rosary on your knees, with your hands up in the air for forgiveness.

The day after that, Payo and I happened to be in the boys' room together, sweeping and dusting. Everybody else was somewhere else doing other chores in the house.

"You wanna do the sweeping this time?" asked Payo.

"Okay, Payo," I answered, "I like sweeping."

I noticed that Mom had been sewing up somebody's pants. "Put those pants away first."

"Oh, those are Chuy's pants. He ripped them a little bit the other day when he was picking avocados at the ranch with Dad," explained Payo. "Do they go in the clean clothes or the dirty clothes?"

"Before you answer that tough question yourself, genius, you better put away the sewing box before something slips out and pokes you."

We both looked at each other and, silently, began sorting through Mom's sewing box to see what we could see. "Oooh! Look at all of the shiny needles in this piece of plastic!" commented Payo.

"Can't use those, little brother. She would know that one was taken out on purpose."

"How about this one?" Payo held up a knitting needle.

"Too big. Nobody would think it was an accident. Besides, she wasn't knitting. She was sewing."

"Mom hardly ever drops needles by accident."

"So? Kids do. All the time."

"But we're the littlest kids in the family!"

"And we'd be the stupidest kids in the barrio if we pretended to be sewing when we were supposed to be cleaning this room! Hurry up!"

"Huh?" Payo was confused, once again.

"Let me spell it out for you. I will start with a question,: Whose fault is it that we got in trouble last time?"

"It was Eddie's fault 'cause he told on us."

"Very good, Payo. Now, question number two: Why doesn't he pick on Cuco, Chuy, or Pancho? They're his brothers, too, you know. Why doesn't he push *them* around?"

Payo smiled widely. "That's easy! They hit back and they stick together most of the times!"

I nodded, and we continued to search for a suitable needle. In a few minutes, we found it. It was at the very bottom of the sewing kit, and it was a touch longer than my thumb. It wasn't the one that Mom had used to sew up the pants, but it looked strong enough to go through a blanket! Together, we placed it in the corner of the twin bed that Cuco and Eddie shared, on the same side of the bed that Eddie usually slept in.

After we cleaned up the room, we skipped out, giggling, and went on to our next chore.

Later that day, after dinner, Eddie went to the boys' room to rest. Since we were sitting next to Dad watching the Lone Ranger, we simply smiled to each other and snuggled up next to our father.

A moment later, Cuco and Chuy had the bright idea to play baseball before it got too dark. They, too, went to the bedroom. As the Lone Ranger confronted danger on the black and white set, Cuco and Chuy faced something similar in their own bedroom.

I heard the fight begin. "Get out of the way, Eddie boy. We're looking for our baseball glove, the one that Mr. Miller gave to us."

Look somewhere else. I'm sitting here, see? I don't have to move. When you're the oldest, you can tell me what to do."

Then, I heard Chuy stumble. He must have accidentally bumped into Cuco, who accidentally bumped Eddie. That wouldn't have been worth more than one punch, but Eddie rolled over into a nasty surprise tucked into the blanket on his side of the bed.

Why, you ...you...you're dead now!" Eddie shouted.

Both Cuco and Chuy sounded surprised. "What's that?"

"Who put this needle in my bed? I'm gonna kick your ass!"

There's the *wind-up,* and the *pitch!*

As Dad jumped up to head for the boys' room, we heard the *smack* of a fist into somebody's stomach. The blankets were tossed about, something fell off of the nightstand, and quite a few punches were delivered on both sides in the short amount of time that it took for Dad to get to the door of their bedroom. We, of course, followed.

"What the @#!% is going in here? Can't a man watch television after a long day of hard work without this? What is it, the Mexican Revolution on West Connecticut Avenue?"

The fight was brief but obviously intense. A button had been torn off of Chuy's shirt, Cuco's nose had a tiny drop of blood, and even Eddie's hair was messed up. Payo and I stared at each other, and then back at the scene before us.

"Papá, these so-called brothers of mine have finally gone and stepped over the line. Look what one of them put into my bed!" accused Eddie, holding up the large, shiny needle.

Cuco and Chuy were quick to defend themselves. "We have no idea how that got into his side of the bed!"

"Then how did you know it was on my side of the bed to begin with? Why did you push me right into *that* spot?" Boy, Eddie was sure good at noticing those little details!

Cuco and Chuy looked surprised and confused.

This was enough for Dad to convict them without a fair trial. "Fine. My own sons acting like animals. Cuco and Chuy, stay in the room for the rest of the night. Eddie, you are grounded this weekend. I'm going back to what I was doing, and I don't want to hear a peep out of either of you. You have shamed me and the whole family. Eddie, stay out of that room until it is bedtime. It's over."

The house was quiet for the rest of the night. The only chatter came from the television, and the nightly parental discussion about what needed to be done the next day. That was all.

The next day, Payo told me that he heard Cuco and Chuy talking when Eddie was in the bathroom. "I heard them say that they were real mad at him and why was he blaming things on them when it wasn't even them. I think they're gonna fight him again, or let the air out of his tires maybe."

I thought about that. "What's the problem, Payo?"

He seemed shocked. "Marta! But they are our brothers! Besides, Cuco and Chuy don't pick on us very often. Sometimes, they are even kind of nice."

I frowned. He had made a point. "Well, yeah, but where are they when Eddie is getting mad at us for no reason? How come they never take the belt away from him or anything?"

"I don't know," answered Payo, licking his hand and pressing down on that Alfalfa bit of hair that wanted to salute the world. "Should we ask Laly for help?"

Furrowing my brow even more, I slowly answered, "It isn't fair, Payo. We just wanted to watch the Elvis Presley movie in peace. I never wanted for Cuco and Chuy to get beat up by Eddie."

Payo's face brightened up a bit. "Hey, they're big guys! And there's two of them!"

I started to smile a little as I said, "Well, yeah. There is that. Eddie doesn't like to be put on restriction, either."

Time is supposed to heal all wounds, and the puncture mark on Eddie's backside eventually disappeared. We tried not to think about it very much. Eddie still mistrusted those two brothers, and he occasionally pushed them around, but it never boiled over into a fight again. We tried not to think about that very much, either. For years, we lived in terror, wondering if the truth would ever become known.

I'm Sorry, Mr. Chacón

Many adults can still remember the faces, if not the names, of their teachers of so long ago. Odd bits of information refuse to be washed out by the years: who taught square dancing, who perspired a lot, who wore the most heavenly perfume, and who gave the best cookies and ice cream before Christmas. In those days, we were usually fiercely loyal to our teacher and any little treat was further proof that our teacher thought we were great.

Mr. Chacón was never my teacher, but he's still there standing next to the others. I really don't mind.

***

Every day, as I stood in line to wait for Mrs. Dimick to come for us, I would look over to my right to the drinking fountains, to see where the fifth grade classes lined up. The fifth graders, you see, were in the next to the last building. The sixth grade classes were in the last building in Santa Fe Elementary. The only classroom that was farther from the office was the Special Education trailer. Nobody knew why that was so.

There was at that time, only one male teacher in Santa Fe Elementary School. My sharp sister, Laly, had told me many stories about him. "He always wears a white shirt and a tie. His shoes are brown, and always shiny, except for when he lets us play baseball. He even pitches sometimes!"

As I got closer and closer to entering fifth grade, I would beg her to tell me more about Mr. Peter Chacón. She told me that sometimes some children would spend the whole recess making fun of her for being chubby and mixing up "chair" and "share". One day, when Mr. Chacón came early to see the class line up, he saw what was happening and told them to stop it immediately. "And they were speaking in Spanish, but he just told them to knock it off, and in Spanish, too! You should have been there. He's the greatest."

"He speaks Spanish?"

"Of course! His last name is Chacón. His full name is Mr. Peter Chacón."

"So, he really pitches? Even when he's wearing a white shirt and tie?"

"He even yells 'hurray' when you hit the ball, honest."

"Did he only speak Spanish that one time?"

"He doesn't speak it in class, if that's what you mean, but he pronounces everybody's name so much better than any other teacher. Like Mrs. Dimick, see? She puts that 'th' in your name. Mr. Chacón wouldn't do that."

"I think I'm supposed to spell it with an 'h'."

"Yes, but in Spanish you're not supposed to pronounce it. Mr. Chacón knows that. Wouldn't it be nice to have a man teacher, especially one as popular as Mr. Chacón?"

I couldn't argue with her there. It would be a refreshing change to have a teacher that smelled of Old Spice after shave instead of library paste.

So, I spent more and more time watching the fifth grade classes line up. I wanted to see if he always dressed the same way. Was his tie always straight? Were his shoes always shiny in the morning? How many pens did he carry in his shirt pocket? Was his hair always combed? Did he shave every day?

After many days of observation, I began to concentrate on spotting more serious flaws in this "man teacher". If he had any flaws, I wanted to find out before fourth grade ended. I began to ask a few of students:

Does he ever yell at you? Does he ever scare you? Does he ever burp in class or pick his nose when he thinks nobody's looking? Does he make you do square dancing?

My investigation produced mostly positive results. The worst thing that I heard about him came from a girl with a lot of freckles. She didn't like his shiny hair. "He should cut it short like Eisenhower had his or fluff it up like that new guy, President Kennedy."

I considered arguing with her and telling her that Eisenhower was bald and probably dead, too. However, not many kids even knew or cared about such important people. "She must be smart," I thought. "Best not to get smart kids angry at you."

Halloween came and went, leaving a candy wrapper here and there underneath a sofa cushion. November blew more leaves off of the trees. That year, Mrs. Miller gave us a turkey so that we could try something different for Thanksgiving. Usually, we had cheese enchiladas with nopalitos (El Pato hot sauce instead of cranberry sauce). Christmas came and went, leaving a few new things. Just as she did every Christmas, Mom gave away my old dolls "to the poor children".

That February was cool and rainy. Many times, Dad had to drive us to school because of the weather.

Pancho and Laly were busy tracing hearts onto a large brown paper bag that was cut open and flattened. While one held the paper down, the other was tracing and trying to fit as many hearts as possible onto the brown paper bag. Payo was also sitting at the kitchen table, peeling the paper off of a broken red crayon. They were so busy, what with their chatting, tracing, and peeling of crayons, that they didn't notice me even when I stood right next to them.

I cleared my throat and looked at Payo. He grinned.

"What are you guys doing? Are you helping him with his homework?"

Pancho laughed and handed me a paper bag. "Does this look like homework? Here, cut this open and throw the bottom away. It has too many folded parts on the bottom and that's no good for tracing and cutting."

Laly added, "Yeah, you should help. Payo's going to give out Valentine cards in class this year. It's his first time. You can write 'Happy Valentine's Day' on them, and then he can color them."

"Why don't you write that yourself, kid?"

Payo grinned. "I can't write so good, but I can color them. You wanna help? You can make some for Mrs. Dimick."

"Nah. ... Well, maybe, but only one. She keeps getting mad when I have to leave early on Tuesdays for catechism class."

Laly commented, "That's not all of the truth. She got mad at you last time because you didn't finish cleaning up your watercolors or whatever it was that you were supposed to do."

I objected to her version. "But I had to go and she knew it!"

"You should have paid more attention to the time. It's not Mrs. Dimick's fault if you can't tell time."

"I can tell time just fine."

They all chuckled and Laly said that recess time and lunch time didn't count.

Then, she added, "You like to draw and color things. Help Payo fix up these Valentine cards real nice. Come on; think of what it was like when you were as little as him."

Payo proceeded to hand over the red crayon, which was now naked and scarred by little fingernails. I could see bits of red wax under his nails and pointed that out to everyone there, much to his annoyance.

There were many brown paper bags to cut open, flatten out, and trim. There were pencils to be sharpened, hearts to be traced, and hearts to be cut out. By the time we had traced one for each of Payo's classmates, Laly and Pancho had gone off to other corners of the house to finish their homework.

I didn't mind much. Payo was pleasant enough company when he was actually doing something constructive. "Hey, Payo, why do you want to give out cards this Valentine's Day? Do you have a special little friend?"

"Why?"

"Because I can decorate them for you real special. I can do this, see?" I deftly twirled the scissors in my hand and cut one heart out. Then, holding it up for greater effect, I slowly turned it as I cut a scalloped border on one side, and a fringed border on the other. "Isn't that neat?"

"Now, can you write a kid's name on it? No, better write my teacher's name first. Yeah!"

"No problem, little brother. Watch this!" I pressed hard with a black crayon on the scalloped edges, taking care to not wrinkle the paper more than necessary. Then, I took the sorry looking red crayon and colored the middle area energetically, leaving the right edge uncolored. This I touched up with a bold yellow, creating the illusion of sunlight on that side. Finally, I took my fingernail and scratched 'Mrs. Norwood Happy Valentine's Day 2-U' in the middle.

We worked on the cards with as great attention to detail as two children can. I did the cutting, fancy trimming, and writing. He focused on the coloring and occasional tracing of favorite words in black crayon.

By the time we were finished making cards for Payo's schoolmates, the sun was setting and we could hear Mom and Dad in the driveway, closing the doors to Mr. Miller's truck. From the backyard came the sound of a passing train, going off into the sunset again. On our west side, I could hear Lilly and her husband calling her children to come and eat fried potatoes with chopped hot dogs... again. On the east side, I thought heard Doña Lola calling her cat.

Dad entered the kitchen carrying his sombrero in his hands. "Whew! Thank God for sombreros! They sure help keep the head warm. What a day, I tell you! What's for dinner, Lupe?"

Mom was walking right behind him and she didn't miss a beat. "What are you cooking, my darling husband? I was working at the ranch, too, remember?"

Dad playfully pretended to swat her head with his sombrero. "Alright, alright. You go wash your hands while I get the big kids to warm up the leftovers from yesterday. That'll be good enough."

He then saw what we had been doing. "What is all this love stuff? Who put you up to this?"

Seeing that his question was directed to the both of us, I quickly answered. "It's for Saint Valentine's Day, when you can give cards to your friends. It's not really love stuff."

Laly had just entered the kitchen. "She's right, Dad. Those are for Payo's friends. He even made one for his teacher. Marta, Pancho, and I all helped."

"I never heard of that saint, but I'm glad they're teaching you about him, anyway. What are you doing with the extra ones, those that are over there on edge of the table?" He pointed to a corner where a few had gotten jammed into the paper napkin holder.

"We'll throw them away."

"Oh, no you don't! If they're teaching you about this Saint Valentine, then you better learn and learn good. If Payo doesn't need any more, then you use them, Marta. Be sure to make one for your teacher. It would show respect."

The kitchen was getting crowded now. Mom squeezed by Dad at that particular moment and added her voice to the discussion. "Your father has a point. Even if we have to do without a trash bag tonight, I think you should make one of those Saint What's-his-name cards for each of your classmates, and each teacher that you've had. Oh, and one for the teacher that you want for next year. That would only be right."

I was first going to whine about the amount of time it would take me, since I had a bit of homework to take care of that night. Then, I thought of Mr. Chacón standing in front of his line, with his brown striped tie, short sleeved white shirt, polished shoes, and shiny black hair. I imagined him saying something like, "Welcome to the first day of fifth grade, children. My name is Mr. Peter Chacón. You are here because you gave me a Valentine's card last February. Thank you. Now, you may come into the classroom and choose any seat that you want. Ah, Esperanza's little sister! Wonderful to have you here!"

That being Wednesday the twelfth, I had to wait two days before handing out my cards. Those for my classmates, I was able to hand out in class that Friday after lunch. Those that were for teachers other than Mrs. Dimick, I handed out after the school day was over. Since I felt it would only be proper to start with kindergarten, it took a while to get to Mr. Chacón's room. When I finally got there, he was getting ready to lock his door.

"Mr. Chacón, are you leaving already?"

"Oh, you must be Esperanza's little sister. I can see the resemblance. How is she? Such a nice girl."

"She's okay. She's in Lincoln Junior High now, and she is taking a lot of classes."

"Well, they do give them more work up there. Oh, darn it! I forgot something in the classroom and I need it for the meeting." He then opened the door wide, propping it open with his black leather briefcase.

I placed the handmade card under his briefcase and disappeared before he found whatever it was that he was looking for.

On the morning of the very last day of school, after a hearty breakfast of fried eggs, refried beans, and hot corn tortillas, Mom gave all of us the traditional "last day of school speech". "Remember, kids. Be sure to go up to your teacher after the dismissal bell rings. You hold out your right hand, like so." Mom pretended to shake Dad's hand. "See? Your right hand goes across to their right hand. Make it a firm handshake, like an educated person. Then you tell them thank you for teaching you this year. Got that?"

Payo protested. "Do I have to do that? It's embarrassing."

He was right about that. Every year, my heart would pound as I walked toward my teacher's desk for the last time. Every year, my hands would get sweaty, my throat would begin to hurt, and the words struggled to get past my lips. The teacher usually made a big fuss over the goodbye, and I ended up staring at my shoes, twisting my braid with my hands, trying not to cry over all of the attention. This would be his first time, so it would be particularly agonizing.

"Be a man," growled our father. "This means a lot to your mother, so…"

"To both of us, Jesús," said Mom, gently correcting him.

"Yeah, so, you just go and do it. And don't you dare think that we won't find out if you forget to say goodbye to your teacher! It is a sin to disobey your parents."

"Your father's right," added Mom. "Just think of how special it will make your teacher feel, too. She will remember you for this. Remember, right hand goes to the other person's side like this, okay?"

Moments later, we were being pushed out through the front door. "Watch your step, kids. Remember what happened before, Marta. You don't want to get stitches again, do you?"

How could I forget that one time I tripped on that brick step? I was seven and had been warned to stop digging holes in the neighborhood. Chuy and Cuco would say, "You want some old lady like Doña Lola or Mrs. Sánchez to trip? Huh? You want that on your conscience?" Eddie swore that he would tell Dad if he ever saw me even pretending to dig a tiny hole. Mom warned me, "You may be little, but you're old enough to understand that everything that you do reflects on all of us. You weren't raised by wolves. We're not lowlife, you know. You dig any more holes, and you're going to get it from me. Understand? And if your father wants to make you sleep in the garage, alone, I'm not going to save you!"

Dad was off somewhere that day, Mom was in the kitchen making tortillas, and Laly was in the back yard hanging up the clothes to dry. The boys were cleaning up their room, supposedly. I was bored and I had an old rusty spoon in the pocket of my Bermuda shorts. The patch of grass that was growing by the mailbox was beckoning me. "Come on, dig here! It's soft. This isn't the neighborhood; this is your family's property. It's okay. Go ahead. Give it a poke. How deep can you dig?"

In a few minutes, I had a hole deep enough for a shoe to fit in. Being only a day or two after a decent rain, the ground was still soft. I began to carve away at the sides and scatter the dirt into West Connecticut Avenue. Scrape, dig, dig, fling …plop into the street! I was totally absorbed. It was a Zen thing.

Then I heard a sound that almost made my heart stop. Mom was calling from the kitchen. "Where are you? Come and taste what I made for you! Why are you so quiet? What are you doing?"

My only hope of being saved on that day was to get inside before she came outside. "I can always go back and fill up the hole later," I thought. Like lightning, I sped for the front door, my little heart pounding and pounding like a hammer trying to get out of my chest. Right foot, left foot, right foot, left foot, leap onto the brick step, and... I didn't quite make that leap, thanks to an unruly shoelace. My chin ended up on the edge of the brick step with a sick thud, leaving a bloody mark on the worn brick step. Because of my trembling arms and shaky legs, getting up was harder than I thought it would be. I remember thinking, "I'm not going to cry. If they don't hear me, all I have to do is clean this up and put a Band-Aid on the scratch. I'm not going to cry. I'm not going to let one tear drop fall."

Then Laly opened the screen door and screamed. "Oh, my God! Look at your blouse! Eww! Mamá, there's been an accident and I can see the bone!"

Mom ran over from the kitchen, wiping her hands on her apron. The boys were, by now, also gathered around Mom and Laly. Mom took a deep breath, straightened her back, and gave a flurry of orders. As I was helped inside, the last thing that she said to Laly and the boys was this: "Whatever you kids do, don't step on human blood. It is a sign of great disrespect and will bring bad luck to you."

Mrs. Quintanilla, the owner of the little convenience store next to the school, had to be called to give us a ride to Dr. Jantzen's office. When we got there, the doctor let everybody crowd into the examining room for a little while. Laly's eyes were red and moist, and she was squeezing my hand with a grip worthy of a wrestler. As the doctor dabbed the wound with a green antiseptic solution, Laly promised me a dollar if I didn't cry. Pancho almost fainted as three stitches were made to close the wound, but I didn't cry a single tear. I wanted that dollar.

For the next two weeks, the kids at school teased me mercilessly for the white bandage on my chin, calling me names like Santa Claus, Boris Karloff, or "The Mummy". It wasn't fun. No fun at all.

Isn't it odd that, sometimes, the people that you love the most are the ones who persist in bringing up the most embarrassing and painful memories?

Mom added, "Marta, I want you to do one more thing. After you say thank you to Mrs. Dimick, go to the next building and find that man teacher. Introduce yourself. Maybe he will remember your name and you can be in his class next year. Wouldn't that be nice? Be sure to shake his hand like I taught you. Act civilized. You're a city girl."

The day went by so quickly, that I was actually surprised to hear the final bell ring. As it did every year at that moment, a feeling of euphoria swept over the multitude of children. The air smelled sweeter. The patches of lawn seemed to turn from a beaten down yellow green to a bright, hopeful, luxurious green. The geraniums growing near the windowsills seemed to stand up straighter, waving their pretty pink petals at the students as they streamed out of the school. Here and there, you could hear clusters of children singing, "Hey, hey! What do you say? Summer's here and we can play all day!" The more rebellious ones were singing short anti-authoritarian songs, much like this classic: "Glory, glory, hallelujah! Teacher hit me with a rule-a! So I hit her on the bean with a rotten tangerine, and her teeth came marching out, out, out! And her teeth came marching out!"

I was caught up in the moment, and almost ran out of the door singing until that voice sounded the alarm in my head. "Shake your teacher's hand and say thank you for teaching you. Act civilized. Remember, it's a sin to disobey your parents."

Maybe hell wouldn't be so bad. Maybe I would only spend a day or two in purgatory, since I was a little kid.

Again, that nagging voice in my head said, more sternly this time, "You weren't raised by wolves. Don't take the chance that your parents will find out! Just do it and get it over with. Don't cry."

Fortunately, Mrs. Dimick was in a hurry to go somewhere and the handshake was quick and brief. She simply patted me on the head and smiled a quick, "Why, thank you for the compliment. Have a good summer, dear. Hope you get a good teacher next year. Bye!"

I breathed a little sigh of relief and skipped over to the fifth grade building.

Children were still walking towards the school gates, some skipping, some running, others twirling in the hallways in glorious anticipation of the summer fun to come.

When I came into Mr. Chacón's room, I was pleased to see that he had not taken down all of his bulletin boards yet. "This shows that he means business, teaching the kids right up to the last minute." He let me look around and touch some of the bulletin board displays. I thought, confidently, "I can do most of this stuff!"

I wanted more than ever to be assigned to his room and I told him so. He said that he would do what he could and, as usual, asked how my family was. When our conversation was about over, he stood up and extended his right hand to me. I was flattered that he was treating me with such respect. Shaking hands is easy when the other person starts it.

He even said "adiós" when I skipped out of the room! No teacher had ever said that to me before.

When the first day of school rolled around again, the first thing that I did was run to the fifth grade building. As Mr. Chacón's room was in the middle, I had the chance to check one or two doors to see if my name was on those class lists. It was hard to get through the crowds of kids milling around in the corridors, with their shiny new shoes and neatly combed hair, but I finally made it.

Since I hadn't seen my name on any other class list, I cheerfully walked into Mr. Chacón's class, sat down in the front row, and began to look around. I felt great and I thought I looked great, too. Mom had braided my hair into two long braids, using new white satin ribbons bought from the Five and Dime Store. My sweater top was soft and fuzzy. Having a blue and white checkered design, it matched my blue skirt and the white ribbons on my braids perfectly.

Somebody's parents were talking to Mr. Chacón, and he was quite busy with them for quite a while. Right after the bell rang, he picked up a clipboard from his desk and started to check names.

"Hmm. I see that we have a full house today. James Appleby. Jane Brown." I waited for the exciting moment when he got to my part of the alphabet. "Martha Chávez." Oops! False alarm. I was glad that I didn't make a squeak that time. "...John King. Alice Long..."

I was confused, but didn't dare correct his oversight. "He'll be grateful that I didn't make a fuss. So he skips my name, so what? Maybe he accidentally put my name at the end."

At first, I didn't hear the soft tapping near his door. Neither did Mr. Chacón. "Oh, Mrs. Stevens! I was just checking the list. What may I help you with?"

I looked over to the open door and saw a lady with a clipboard. She had sort of golden brown hair with pretty silver highlights. The sprinkling of tiny brown freckles on her kindly face reminded me of a doll that I had gotten for Christmas. Her glasses had a golden color to them, and her sweater was clipped on over her shoulders just like my old kindergarten teacher.

She smiled and answered, "Well, Mr. Chacón, I'm just a few doors down the hallway from you. I'm new to this school, and, well, I have a few empty seats. If you don't mind, why don't we compare notes to see if I have a few of yours or if you have a few of mine? I've already checked with the other teachers, and we did find a couple of duplications. Would it be okay?"

Mr. Chacón introduced her to us and they spent a minute comparing the lists. When they finished with that, they asked us all to stand. We were then instructed to sit down when our name was called.

At the end, guess who was left standing? I must have looked embarrassed. I felt my face turning red. The walls of the room seemed to expand, becoming blurry around the edges. I couldn't hear what people were saying. I became totally focused on my new shoes. At least the laces were tied on perfectly.

Mrs. Stevens walked over to me. "Thank goodness! I've found you. I knew I was missing somebody. Mr. Chacón, were you trying to steal this prize pupil from me?" She put her arm over my shoulder and handed the clipboard to me.

"Oh, Mrs. Stevens! I was looking forward to getting this one, that's a fact, but I guess the principal didn't want to spoil me again. I had her sister before, you know."

I was worried all day. Even the fresh breeze and the fluffy clouds could not tempt me to bounce a ball or skip a rope during recess time. I felt that, if I gave in too soon, I would never return to Mr. Chacón's room, and that would change the rest of my life.

After school, Mrs. Stevens took me aside and handed me a new reading book. "I heard that you like to read. I was going to hand these reading books out tomorrow, but you can look it over tonight, if you like."

Of course I liked! Those were the days of black and white television, and ours only got three or four channels: 6, sometimes 8 and 10, and always 12 (the Spanish station). A good book to me meant free entertainment. I could turn the pages any time I wanted. A television, on the other hand, had to be shared with others, and there were so many others in the house. I thanked her for the book and promised to take good care of it.

In the hallway, moments later, I began to feel guilty, as if I had betrayed someone. Darn that Mrs. Stevens! Why did she have to go and be nice to me?

After leaving her room, I walked over to Mr. Chacón's room. He was alone, sitting at his desk, his black briefcase to one side. Looking up at me, he pretended to frown. "It's too bad that I didn't get to be your teacher."

I was standing in his doorway, clutching the new reading book in front of me.

He turned his head sideways. At first, I was confused, but then I realized that he was trying to read the title.

"Mr. Chacón..."

"Ah, the escapee speaks! I really meant it when I say that I wanted you in my room. It just wasn't in the cards. The office makes up the class lists, and we have to take what we get."

"It's not fair, Mr. Chacón."

He got up from his chair and walked toward me, hands behind his back. "Why do you say that?"

"What if what we got isn't what we wanted?"

"What if she is a better teacher than me?"

"That's not even funny, Mr. Chacón.

"Why?"

"You're a man teacher. I wanted a man teacher."

"I may not always be a teacher, but I will always be a man. That will never change, just like Mrs. Stevens will always be a lady, and you will grow up to become a lady, too. That's how things work."

He was twisting my words, and I wanted to make him stop. "That's not what I mean. I wanted you as my teacher in fifth grade."

"See that book you have there? It's the same book that I will be using. All teachers use the same books. Now, maybe you knew that. Would it be the same book if you put a book cover on it?"

I nodded, but failed to see what he was getting at.

He continued. "We agree on that point. Good. See my jacket over there, on the back of my wooden chair? I'm the same person with the jacket on or with the jacket off, right?"

I nodded again, and tried to smile. It was strange to have a conversation, a meaningful conversation, with a man in a shirt and tie.

This seemed deep and important. Something to be remembered and written down in a diary some day.

He crossed his arms. "You still don't get it. Let me ask you another question, then. Have you ever been told that you can't do something because of who you are?"

"Well, yeah, sometimes some kids say stuff like 'you hit like a girl' or 'boys are smarter than...'"

"Than girls?"

My mouth opened but no words came out.

"You are a girl, but you are other things, too, just like that book is the pages inside and the cover on the outside. The stories are the same, though, no matter what kind of cover it has. I am the same person with or without my jacket. My brain..." He pointed to his head, smiling. "...is the same, whether I wear that jacket or a sweater. Do you understand?"

I didn't say a thing. I was thinking. It was hard work.

"I'm sure you've been to the library before. Have you ever walked by a book that had a plain looking cover, only to find out later that it had a really great story inside, just the story that you wanted to read, the kind of story that you would probably remember for the rest of your life?"

My mind flashed back to my last trip to the Vista library. "Yeah. There wasn't a picture on the front and hardly any pictures inside, but you could still see the pictures in your mind because the story was so good."

"People can be like books, but unlike books, people have feelings. Don't give up on somebody because they don't look like what you expected. You have to be better than that."

What could I say after that? Still holding the reading book, I gave him a half hug with my other arm.

"Now, run along home."

After I had taken a step away from his doorway, I turned and asked, "Guess what I'm going to do when I get home?"

"I don't know, but I'm sure you will tell me."

"I'm going to read the first story, then I'm going to make a book cover for this book. I'm going to put my name, my grade, and Mrs. Stevens' name on it. Then my friends can sign it on the back. When that cover gets worn out, I can make another one!"

"Can I sign it, too?"

"Okay." Once again, I clutched the book to my chest. "I'm sorry, Mr. Chacón."

"You made me feel very special. Thank you for that."

Dinner tasted especially delicious that night, even though it was what we usually ate for dinner: beans, tortillas, rice, and a few spoonfuls of nopalitos seasoned with El Pato hot sauce.

After the kitchen was all cleaned and the only remnant of dinner was the lingering smell of hot sauce and a few burnt tortillas, I settled down to read at the table. As everybody else was busy getting things ready for tomorrow, I wasn't interrupted for nearly an hour.

I finished the first story and cut open an extra grocery bag, laying it flat on the green formica of the small dining table. I was nearly finished with my book cover when, from the living room, I heard Dad's voice say, "Hey, who wants to watch roller skating with me? It's the L.A. Thunderbirds again!"

"Save a place for me, Dad!" I shouted, as hurriedly wrote my name on the front of the book cover. "I'm almost done."

From the living room, I could hear Laly and a few of my brothers calling me to hurry. "You're missing the grudge match with Little Ralphie Valaderas! This is the best part!"

I quickly added the rest of the information: room number, grade level, name of teacher (Mrs. Stevens), and the title of the book.

Dad always got caught up in the excitement of his favorite sports: boxing, wrestling, and roller skating. Everything that he saw on television seemed real to him, at least in sports. I could hear him shouting at the referee now. He shouted again, "You're missing a lot of action! You'll be sorry!"

I turned the book over for the last part, the printing of the words "Names of Friends" at the top of the back cover.

My younger brother Payo, Dad's little shadow and sometimes echo, repeated my father's words. "You'll be sorry!"

There was that word again! How odd, the chaotic way that words bounced around the hours in a day. I made a mental note to finish that thought later on.

I smiled to myself and, finally, put my pencil down.

Later that night, as my head pressed down on my pillow, the scent of the jasmine flowers drifted into our darkened room. I could hear a few crickets next to the carob tree in the back yard. Somewhere in the barrio, a door slammed and soon after, a car started. Laly, already asleep, was tangled in the blanket and breathing quietly on the other side of the twin bed. I yawned, closed my eyes, and tugged the blanket one more time. The night covered me with its curious soft symphony of smells and sounds.

I thought of circles. The skating rink was like a circle. A freckle was like a circle. The pupil of an eye was a circle within a circle. When you throw a pebble into a pond, the pebble never comes back but the circular ripples do. They always reach you. Things go around in a circle. A circle has no sides.

I tried to count how many times the word "sorry" had been used today. Too many ripples in that pool of thought.

Eventually, I drifted off to sleep trying to remember the color of Mrs. Stevens' eyes.

Afternoon in Watts

Somebody once said that Chicanos are the Rainbow People because we come in all colors. In our family tree, you almost have the whole spectrum of skin colors from nearly albino with a thin, Spanish nose and feisty freckles to smooth chocolate skin with distinctly Indian features: beautifully thick black hair, dark eyebrows, and pupils as dark as the bottom of a well. There are many trees like this in the Latino forest.

Unfortunately, not all trees know they are a part of a forest.

Long time friends of the family had moved into a cozy corner of the City of Angels called Watts. Very good friends who just happened to have very light skin and blonde hair. I mean, *really really* blonde hair, like the Morton Salt girl or the Wonder Bread girl.

"Los Angeles is a big city, amigo," Dad sighed. "You sure you want to go?"

"They're going to learn a lot of English away from here! I've already found a house for less rent than we pay on this one, Don Jesús, but not in East L.A. My kids aren't going to join any Chicano gang! No, señor! We're going to a place called Somethings. Odd name, but the rents are really cheap."

The man's wife cleared her throat. "Watts, Don Jesús. Not Somethings. It's called Watts."

I had heard that word somewhere.

Our first visit to The Big City. Three hour drive. Freeways that looped and intertwined like a tangled ball of yarn. Traffic, a constant stream of fast and slow, shiny and rusty... all seeming to push you down the gray lanes as if you were all going to the same place. And other drivers would signal you with one finger.

"What does that mean?" my mother would ask.

"Nothing," my father would answer tersely.

Los Angeles, a place that I had only seen on television. The closer we got to Watts, the more my mother babbled and tapped on her window. "This is the City of Angels? Such a holy name, but look at all the garbage. I think I saw a beggar in front of a liquor store. I thought this was supposed to be the United States."

A sea of black faces. Huge afros, some with red or blue plastic combs sticking out of the soft dark hair like spikes. Restaurants with names like "Mom's Sweet Potato Pie" and beauty shops with pictures of smiling ebony models with huge hoop earrings. Music coming from open windows, music without accordions or mariachis.

"Look at the fluffy hair-dos, Jesús! Looks like lamb's wool. Hmm…. I wonder if their heads stay warmer in winter?"

The dark faces didn't smile much as we slowly navigated the maze of streets. Florence. Normandie. Crenshaw. Kalmia.

Are we there yet?

By the time we found the right street, we were all nauseous and our bladders were ready to burst. We poured out of the Jeep and into the small crowd of smiling faces that greeted us. I stepped onto the cracked sidewalk, took a deep breath, and coughed a few times.

Mary Wells was singing "My Guy" on the AM radio of a passing '56 Chevy, candy apple red. Eddie turned his head towards the bouncing car as it rounded the corner. "Fat chance," I thought. "He can only dream of such a car!"

After the hellos and the mandatory big lunch of *sopa de arroz*, pinto beans, and *nopalitos*, the adults settled onto the old sofa in the living room and the kids clustered here and there by age. The three youngest boys took Payo, my younger brother, into their room to play with their collection of little green army men and see who could fart the loudest. The two oldest boys took my older brothers into the back yard to knock down aluminum cans with pebbles and see who could tell the tallest tales of their adventures in Gringolandia (USA). Laly helped the two oldest girls in the kitchen, where they whispered about the cute boys in church as their hands wrinkled from absorbing the soapy water. I was left with María and Nati, my old playmates.

"I got my allowance today. We saw a few corner stores on the way over here."

Nati twirled a strand of her blonde hair with the fingers of her right hand. "Well, we got our allowance, too, but … Well, if you're sure you want to, uh…I don't know…"

"…But first, you better know something," interrupted María.

I looked first at one and then the other. "Mm?" I crossed my arms. "It took a long time for us to drive up here. I didn't have to bring my allowance but I did. So, what's the big deal about going to a corner store?"

Nati and María glanced at each other and back at me. "We don't have a lot of friends in this place."

"So?" They had so many kids in their family that they could make their own baseball team and have players left over. I wondered if their blond hair made them more whiney. Perhaps they couldn't help it, after all.

"We could get beat up 'cause of the gangs."

"You're in a gang?" This I had to see. "I thought you weren't allowed to be in a gang." Should I tell their parents, or shouldn't I?? It might be best to wait until after I had some fun. Something. It was a long drive up here, anyway.

María sighed. "The only gang we're in is this family! But we're new kids here, and it's not like México, it's more like…"

"…Like they call you white girl and spit on you…" interrupted Nati.

"But you're not gringos! All they have to do is listen to you!" I managed to stifle a chuckle by covering my mouth. This was hilarious. "Even the gangsters can spell better English than you two."

Nati furrowed her brow. "Well, it's… yeah, but I don't want to talk to kids when they come at me in a group and they're not smiling."

That made me pause, but not for long. "Well, we came all the way here, girls. So, will it be stay here and wait for them to yell at us to help clean the kitchen and change the baby's diaper? Maybe you want to wait until the boys get bored and start in on us? No, wait! I know what!" I was on a roll now. "Let's go into the living room and listen to your father and my father brag about how good they are at killing a pig for making carnitas or hear your mom and my mom share their secrets for removing corns from their tired feet! Maybe we can talk them into having all of us pray a whole rosary in the living room! Wowee!"

A minute later, we were on the sidewalk, heading towards the closest convenience store. There weren't many birds singing, and the air was hazy and smelled of cheap gasoline, but it was a new place to me. Out of my barrio. Something to do. Something to talk about to my friends when I got back home. It was somewhere else. That's all that mattered. Somewhere else.

Halfway down the block, a tall boy dressed in khaki pants began to cross the street to catch up to us. I briefly considered running, but he looked like he might be

Mexican. Maybe. He had that kind of Mayan nose on him.

"Hey, rucas, where you goin'?"

Nati grabbed my elbow before I had a chance to say something clever.

"Pay no attention to him."

"Who is he? What's a 'ruca'?"

"That's Jimmy. He's a loser. We're the rucas."

María waved him away. "Our cousin from San Diego is visiting and we can't talk to any boys and especially you so see ya later, Jimmy Mack. Bye."

Jimmy ran his fingers through his slick dark hair and returned to his front porch. We continued our little adventure.

I remember thinking, "There's sure to be more than this."

The store was a tiny establishment, the windows nearly covered with advertisements: malt liquor, Johnny Walker Red, wine, cigarettes, and the interesting faces of glamorous dark-skinned models smoking those cigarettes and drinking that liquor.

Where were the movie stars? Wasn't Hollywood part of Los Angeles?

"Hey, they got Snow Balls here! And Three Musketeers bars!" I gleefully poked a package of pink snow balls, the junk food of the gods. Something familiar.

María was disgusted by my comment. "Of course, dummy! Los Angeles isn't another country."

Even Nati was amused. "I thought you would be more sophisticated. Really, Marta. You haven't changed."

María tugged on my sleeve and pointed towards the cigarette rack. "If you want to buy a pack, we can hide it in our room. I won't tell." I glanced at Nati. She shrugged her shoulders like she didn't mind if I did or not, but she half-smiled anyway.

Hmm. Back home, Mrs. Nava was always peeking through her hand-made flower print curtains that had that stupid lacey thing on the hem that reminded me of those circus poodles. And Doña Lola, of course. Watering her roses every time a bunch of us wanted to play in the street. "Stop rolling your brother down the street in that tire! You might crack his head open!" Well, I wasn't in Vista now, was I? If I wanted to buy a pack of Chesterfields, or even a pack of Marlboros or Winstons, then it was my own darn business. I wasn't a child!

The burly clerk took our money and gave the change without smiling once. Where ya from?"

"Near San Diego. Just visiting."

"You Spanish?"

"No, Mexican."

He laughed. "Well, well. Y'all have a very nice day. Yeah. Very nice day."

A minute later, we were strolling down the sidewalk, each lighting up a cigarette, walking as slowly and nonchalantly as we could.

I kept blowing out tiny, carefree clouds. "This is easy!" I thought to myself.

We chatted about this and that and even attempted to inhale just as we had seen our parents do. That left us hacking and spitting out yellow saliva, so we just stuck to blowing out hazy, gray dust balls of smoke and practicing our cigarette-holding technique. That seemed to be cool enough for the moment.

"So, why do they call this place Watts?"

"We don't know."

"Don't they tell you in school? Jeez, you girls need to ask more questions. Why, if it was me..."

Nati lifted her nose up slightly and blew smoke in my face as she responded, "We don't care. We're just taking a little walk, that's all."

María spit on the sidewalk. Yellow.

We decided to go around one more block, just one more block, slowly, to revel in the anonymity of this City of Angels. We needed the time to practice making those smoky O's. Might as well learn something new.

We almost didn't notice the girl who was standing on the corner alone, down the block, leaning against the chain link fence, staring at us. She wore bell bottomed pants and had long jet-black hair, teased on top, with bangs that almost covered her face. She didn't look much older than us, but she had lipstick on. Dark red. And three golden bracelets on each wrist.

Nati started to cross the street, motioning for us to follow her lead. Since María didn't say anything, I followed silently as well. "Nati?"

"Wait until we get on the other sidewalk. Don't look at her."

A moment later, I was able to ask. "She wasn't doing anything. There are three of us, anyway. Why can't you just be cool?"

She didn't get a chance to answer me right away, because the red-lipsticked girl was saying something like "hey what's your name rucas". It wasn't so much the question, but the nosey way she asked it, like she thought that we had crossed an invisible line over to her side of the tracks. Like she owned the train. The whole train station.

"Hey, who does she think she is? Does she want to take our cigarettes from us? Can't she count? There are three of us. What's her problem?" I had to smile. Living in a big city, far away from the known, must surely make some people insane. Really. Such delusions!

Nati wasn't sure, but María had no interest in any theory at the moment. "I say we maybe get rid of the cigarettes we're smoking and we can get home faster 'cause we'll have less to make us walk slow."

I snickered at her panicky words. Yeah, that must be it. Crowded cities must affect the delicate mental balance of the weaker ones.

In spite of my protests, the three lit cigarettes were soon tossed into the gutter. Somebody must have been washing their car earlier somewhere on that side of the street, because there was a rivulet of grimy water, ready to float away all evidence of our trip to the store.

The cigarettes let out a ssss of disapproval as they landed in the soapy stream.

The tall-haired, red-lipsticked girl on the corner shouted, "Hey, I'm talkin' to you! Where ya from?"

I had no patience for such rudeness. "*Que te importa?*" It was none of her business, and I wanted her to know that. Nobody ruins a visit for me. No, sirree.

The girl scowled and disappeared into the nearby alley.

"What's her problem?" I wondered aloud. I was glad she had gone.

Nati scolded me. "You shouldn't have made her mad! We're not supposed to talk to anybody around here."

"Why? Besides, she's probably hiding in the alley by now. Case closed."

"We should have given her the pack of cigarettes," answered María, frowning. "I think she wanted them."

"But we spent our money on this pack!" I groaned. "All we have left is that and one Big Hunk bar, and we have the whole afternoon to kill! You know that our parents will be hogging the TV. What are we going to do now?"

"We could never smoke in the house, anyway," Nati pointed out. "We have to share a room with our big sisters, and there's no place to hide things."

I knew what they meant. They had to share a twin bed, too. One careless toss of a leg in deep sleep and you would be kicked awake by an unforgiving sister. Forget about long showers or special phone calls. The worst part was, if you made one mistake, you had almost a dozen people laughing at you one at a time, a Twilight Zone gauntlet of guilt. Catholic guilt. No mercy.

The sound of approaching footsteps turned our heads around. The girl on the corner was now accompanied by two more girls who were chewing gum with their mouths open, walked with an exaggerated swagger, and wore gold rings on all fingers. At least, it looked like it from where we stood.

I asked why they needed so many rings.

"To beat the crap out of us."

Not the answer I wanted! "But we didn't do anything!" I argued in disbelief.

María tossed the pack of cigarettes and our last candy bar on the ground. "Walk faster. One more block and we'll be at our house."

"But we didn't do anything!" I repeated. "Say something to them in Spanish so they'll know that you're not gringas." That always worked in Mexico. It might work here.

"Big deal. You think those girls care?"

"Is it because I said 'none of your business' to her?"

María sighed in exasperation as she continued her brisk pace. "No, it's because you said it in Spanish, stupid!"

"And you speak it better than them," Nati nodded.

The trio of girls with the teased hair was calling us. "Hey! Little gavachas! You pick up those things up and hand them to us! You hear us? Hand them to us!"

I had no idea that the people in Watts felt so strongly about littering. "Maybe you shouldn't have thrown the pack on the ground like that. Maybe they live in that house and they don't want trash on the sidewalk in front of their house." Yeah, that could be it! It could all be a misunderstanding! I was grasping at straws and I knew it.

Nati picked up the pace even more. "You can walk faster if you shut up."

We made it to the front porch in time and had the rest of the afternoon to stare out of the windows of their bedroom, watching those three girls walk up and down the sidewalk across the street, occasionally giving us that middle finger sign. That's about all that we did. Watch and hide behind the ratty curtains and relive the experience in hushed tones.

"You girls are being so good!" their mother said more than once as she walked to the kitchen for more pan dulce and Nescafe. "See, Doña Lupita? We both have good girls!"

A few hours later, my family piled back into the Jeep and we waved our good-byes.

I was the only one who noticed the three strange girls by the telephone pole. There they were, chewing gum with their mouths open, on the edge of the shadows on the corner. As we drove away, they retreated into the darkness of another alley. I thought I heard them laugh.

I wondered if they had to be home by a certain time. I wondered if they had eaten the candy and smoked the cigarettes.

Our cigarettes. Our candy. Stupid girls! I could forget the loss of the silly cigarettes, since I had no intention of becoming a smoker anyway, but I sure wanted to eat that Big Hunk bar.

Mom leaned her head onto Dad's shoulder and sighed. "They miss us and everybody else on West Connecticut Avenue, you know. The farther north you go, the harder it is to find people who speak Spanish."

One of my brothers mentioned a dark-skinned boy with a Mayan nose. "That one boy didn't answer when I asked him to play soccer in the street with us, but I think he understood Spanish."

Dad chuckled. "One? That's nothing."

I dozed off and on, but when we finally pulled into our driveway in West Connecticut Avenue, I was awake... yawning, but awake. It wasn't too late after all. Doña Lola's light was still on. I could see Mrs. Nava peeking from behind her curtains. They still looked too frilly, but the light from her kitchen was a soft yellow. She waved at us.

Maybe I was more tired than I thought. I even waved back.

Everybody has those moments when they need just a little dose of amistad (friendship) to get by. It could be a little bit of whispered advice, such as "Your slip is showing" or "Oh, I think that's not legal in this country." It could be something as mundane as being able to borrow a cup of masa harina for a fresh batch of tortillas or a bit of cilantro for that pot of menudo boiling on the stove.

One. That's nothing. Doesn't count.

When It Rains, It Pours

Parents … are sometimes a bit of a disappointment to their children. They don't fulfill the promise of their early years.

from *A Buyer's Market* by Anthony Powell, (b. 1905),
British novelist

Dad never got drunk and he never yelled at Mom. He yelled at us now and then, but never at Mom. He had held the same job ever since I could remember, unlike some other dads. He said that a real man took care of his family first.

Dad was tall. Dad was strong. Dad went to work. Dad came home. Dad sat at the head of the green formica kitchen table, with its four matching vinyl and chrome chairs, in the only chair that didn't have a cigarette burn or a tear in it. At work, Dad was Mr. Miller's right-hand man, able to do anything that didn't require English or reading: expert pruning, fertilizing, weeding, planting exotic seedlings, caring for the horses and homing pigeons, … No, not just able to do anything. Able to do it well, and without supervision. He wasn't a coffee break kind of guy.

Before I became a teenager, I remember looking up at him and smiling inside. My dad doesn't have any gray hairs! Curses only when necessary, and usually far away from my mom. Only one beer… maybe two in one afternoon, not like some other fathers in the barrio, who guzzle beer like Kool-Aid. He was still the hero in our family and the father that some other kids in the barrio wished that they had.

When I entered Lincoln Junior High, he changed almost overnight. The slight wrinkle between his bushy eyebrows furrowed into a deep crease. Gray hairs appeared on his head, but I was reasonably sure that I had nothing to do with their sudden appearance.

The roof over their bedroom developed a leak one day. Drip. First, a towel on the linoleum floor was enough. Drip. Drip. Then came the serving bowl from the kitchen. Drip. Drippety-Drop. On the third day, when one of us had to haul out a bucket, it was obvious that stronger measures would be taken.

Mom and Dad sat down at the kitchen table to see which luxuries could be trimmed from the family budget. Most of us milled around in the kitchen, wanting to hear how this miracle of modern financing would be accomplished.

I was there, of course. I wanted to put my two cents in, just in case cream rinse wound up on the endangered list. When you have the longest hair in the family, such things are not trivial. I wasn't going to return to the bad old days when I had to wash my hair with a bar of generic label soap and nothing else. No, señor.

"Well, Lupe," Dad sighed, looking at Mom as he played with his mustache. "This must be done. Now, it remains to be decided how."

"Most people think patching the hole in a leaky roof would be a solution. I say we do that."

"Very funny, Lupita. Where the devil will the money come from? Prayer?"

The spoon in Mom's café con leche clinked on the mug. "Well, viejo, how much money do we have in the bank? It will cost more than what we have. I think. Probably, anyway."

Dad reached for a pan dulce and nibbled on its crunchy edge. He liked those that curled into the middle, crunchy golden brown, sprinkled with white sugar and sometimes cinnamon. "Hmm. You're right. We should find out how much it will cost. If it is more than we have in the bank, perhaps the carpenter or roofer will accept half now and... and the other half I don't know when. No more calls to Mexico until this is all paid off! No more trips! And don't you go buying new things for the kids without checking with me first, okay?"

"No more Seven Up when we buy groceries. No more inviting people to stay with us. And, while we're at it, no more going out to play pool with Alfredo or any other of your compadres."

"Well, see... that's just it. If a man works hard, and nobody is going hungry at home, a wife who really understands will, you know... encourage him to go out for a breath of fresh air."

"I couldn't agree with you more! Would you like to get some fresh air going to the church recreation hall on Saturday evenings? That new priest, the young gringo who speaks Spanish, he wants more men to help with the fund raising. It'll be fun, viejito. I would love for both of us to go. You know, we'll even save money on gas if we're both going in the same direction."

Clink. Stir. Storm clouds in the kitchen.

"Well, that's another subject. We're supposed to be solving the problem of the leaky roof. All we've done so far is talk about my free-spending ways. I never get drunk, I never yell at you, I don't even like hitting the kids, and…"

"And good fathers and good husbands don't do those things anyway, Jesús. You don't throw money away and I don't fritter away our money, either. We have both been very reasonable when buying clothes for the children. It may be true that, once in a while, I might buy a book for one of the kids, but such things help them so much in their schoolwork. An occasional call to one of my sisters is just that, an occasional call.

Special occasions or family emergencies. I promise."

He looked into her eyes, then flicked a few crumbs from his pan dulce at her hand. "I suppose the occasional long distance call is much more economical than a train ticket to Jalisco. Maybe a book bought for one child will help the others, too. These things are allowed in moderation."

"Whatever." She brushed the crumb off her hand and onto the formica table. "The roof? You want to ask Mr. Miller if he knows a carpenter that can do a good job at a fair price? I'm afraid of getting swindled. You know the stories about things that have happened here, and we don't know English. I would die if I had to appear in court. I wouldn't know what to do."

"I suppose that I could slowly work it into a conversation. I just have to say it in a way that he doesn't feel obligated to loan us the money. I don't want to be tacky. A Lomelí must always show some class."

Sip. "Time is of the essence."

They nodded, as if the words had come out of both of them at once.

The very next day, a man came to inspect the roof and recommended a completely new roof. The cost seemed astronomical, so my father suggested a patch.

"Only one part is leaky. We can worry about the rest later."

The man protested the logic of that, pointing out that later might well involve a visit to the emergency room when the roof caved in on the whole family some soggy night at three in the morning. "Mister Lomelí, it will cost money, but good work is never done for free."

Mom cleared her throat at that moment.

Dad hooked his thumbs on his belt and frowned. "I value hard work and I like to see it in action. If you are willing to accept partial payment now, you can start as soon as I gather the supplies that will be necessary."

So began my father's frenzied trips to the lumber yard. Stay clear of your father, children! He has big things on his mind! There were boards to be cut. Nails to be pounded. Where's that hammer? Saws. More nails. Tar paper. Roofing shingles. Two by fours. Four by fours. He was the no-starred general planning a solid defense against the elements. He was the unlicensed heart surgeon gathering the medical supplies for the life-saving operation. He was the man with the white sombrero.

"You should see all of the wonderful things that they have at that lumber yard, Lupita. Why, if they only had this back in our homeland! A man could build a house in less than a day with all of those fine hand saws and nails of different lengths and thickness. None of the nails were used, like in those hardware stores in Tijuana. The wood? All freshly cut. No tell-tale chips of paint. I have a good eye for these things. I could tell that they were all new."

Mom listened to his lumber yard adventures and kept right on chopping onions and tomatoes for the next meal. Occasionally, she would add an "Ah!" and "You don't say!".

That Saturday, the carpenter arrived and, just as he was leaning his ladder against the outside west wall, my father appeared, bucket of nails in one hand and the usual work sombrero on his head.

I couldn't see very well through the kitchen window, but I did hear words like,

"What?" and possibly, "No, really, Mister Lomelí" and "You really don't have to. Really."

Moments later, we heard the two men on the rooftop. Oh, how I wished that I could see what they were doing! As I dried dishes and put them away, I could only catch snatches of sentences. "…Wood rot… tear out and… hammer with … nails…"

Mom elbowed me once. "Why don't you go out and see if you need to translate?"

After drying and putting away the clean soup bowl in my hands, I wandered outside. I returned much more quickly than I expected. The crease between Dad's eyebrows and the glare in his eyes had said it all. When I picked up the dish towel and resumed my daily chore,

Mom uttered a sigh and briefly looked up to heaven, shaking her head ever so slightly.

The crusty sounds of old roof slowly being removed continued steadily for a long while, interrupted by words and phrases in broken English: "Oh, yeah!" "Yeah, mister." "How much dollars?"

Then, as my dish towel slowly circled around the edge of a plastic coffee mug, I heard the carpenter say, "I can get the saw myself, Mr. Lomelí, but thank you." The dry, creaking sound on the rungs of the ladder told me that only one man was descending.

I was now drying a dinner plate, Melmac plastic I believe, when I walked over to the doorway of their bedroom and saw a blue sliver of sky appear on the ceiling. Then, the groaning sound of a wooden beam giving way to the brown work boot of my father's right foot. Then his left foot. The khaki pants. Chunks of rotted wood, chipped paint, and ancient rusty nails were dropping onto the floor of my parents' bedroom and some even bounced off of the bed. The surprised look on his face. Then the white sombrero, like a confused feather, landing on his head just as he landed on his bottom, BOOM on the linoleum floor of his own bedroom, narrowly missing the bedpost. Just like in the movies!

I burst out laughing. It was an instinctive reaction, like blinking your eye when something is coming towards you. It felt natural.

The shaken look on my father's face, the dust in his gray hair, the frantic running of my mother's tired little feet and she never ran, not ever… then her moist eyes, little salty diamonds in the corner of her eyes, snuffed the laughter right out of me and left a heavy feeling in the pit of my stomach.

A few ice packs and a cold beer or two later, Dad was watching television while the carpenter whistled, alone, on the rooftop.

Neither one of them talked to me for the rest of the day, except to request more ice or to give me orders, and even then, they did not look at me.

Just as well. I didn't even want to see my own reflection in the mirror.

Stand By Your Man
Dad is wearing the vest
that Mom knitted for him.

It Just Is

Wisdom lies neither in fixity nor in change, but in the dialectic between the two.

Octavio Paz, Mexican poet
Times (London, 6-8-89)

I heard a rumor that, in some cultures, the passage of girl to young woman is celebrated with elaborate ceremony. The elder females of the tribe sing special songs for her and present her with a crown of eagle feathers. The young female views the physical change as desirable, not just inevitable. Other cultures are at the other extreme, with much wailing and moaning sadly about "the curse", hiding her in a darkened room until it passes, making a young lady feel ashamed. Some segments of society seem to cling to a middle road, where it is ignored as long as possible.

In the last few decades, public schools have gone through all sorts of spasms in dealing with the topic of adolescent changes. Vista has been no stranger to these problems. No school really wants to take over all parental duties; most just want to do their best to fill in the gaps. It is an imperfect balancing act at times, but where would we be without the attempt?

***

"Aha!" announced Mr. Cooper. "It was in this drawer. Girls, please line up here by my desk. Each of you take one of these and get both of your parents to sign it."

As soon as I got my pink paper, I walked back quickly——- but not too quickly——- to my desk. It said: *Please sign below if you would like for your daughter to receive information regarding health on Wednesday and Thursday of this week. The signatures of both mother and father will be required.*

Brenda gave my desk a little kick. "See? What did I tell ya?"

Laura was tapping on her front teeth, a sure sign that she was thinking. "I guess you were right. It's about the change."

"What change?" I asked innocently.

Slyly, Laura looked at me and at Brenda, who was smiling. "The change. From girl to woman. We will finally be told the secrets."

"What about the boys?" I whispered to them.

"They don't have any real secrets," stated Brenda. Laura's freckled face nodded in solemn agreement.

While we were discussing the importance of those pink papers, Mr. Cooper was busy sending a couple of boys to the principal's office. Evidently, they had tried to wrestle one away from Carmen, one of the girls that lived a block away from my house. She was wiping a tear away from her eye.

Usually, I was very shy at school. However, she was from my neighborhood. I was going to express my sympathy but Mr. Cooper cut in. "Next time, Carmen, don't wave it in their noses saying 'nanny nanny'. Boys don't like to be teased."

As I walked along Avenida Benito Juárez after school, I heard a girl's voice behind me. "Hey, Marta! Wait for me!"

It was Carmen. Her short black hair was dressed up with a pink ribbon, slightly askew. Today, she wore a yellow dress that looked even prettier on her dark brown skin.

"Hi, Carmen. That's a pretty dress."

"Thanks. My mom got it for me, from the lady she works for. That lady's daughter gets tired of her clothes all the time. I get her clothes for free."

"It looks brand new."

"Kind of. She only wore it once and spilled champagne on it. See at the hem, here in the back? That's a champagne stain."

It looked more like Tang or Kool-Aid, but I didn't dare question her about it. Instead, I simply commented, "You look like you were running. You get in trouble if you come home late?"

"Nah. Nobody cares if I come home or not. I wanted to, you know, talk with those two guys that got me mad this morning." She made a fist with her right hand and began smacking it into her open left hand. "Just a little talk."

I smiled. "So? What did you do?" Carmen always had so many adventures!

Carmen looked over her shoulder and then looked back at me. "Well, first I just wanted them to say 'sorry', but then I punched them in the nose when they called me names like 'black Messican'. Both of them. I told them that if they got me mad again, that my big brother would come looking for them. You should have seen their white faces turn red!"

We laughed together and continued walking on, occasionally kicking a rock into the street.

Carmen's big brother was blind, but those boys didn't know that. They also didn't know that she was the kind of girl that could form a posse at a moment's notice, if necessary. Those boys weren't from our side of the railroad tracks. How could they know?

"Were you scared, just a little?"

"Not really." She pointed to her chest, smiling. "Not this girl."

"You're just like Supergirl, Carmen."

She brightened at the compliment. "Yeah. The Supergirl of Avenida Juárez!"

It was in moments such as those that I felt a little tweak of jealousy stir within me. I knew full well that her father had left long ago, that she lived in an upstairs apartment with her blind brother, two little sisters, and a mother that was continually wringing her hands. In the summer, that upstairs apartment was a real oven. In the winter, she hated to come home because her mom was always trying to "save money on heat". Still, there was the fact that her mother did not monitor her activities. "Oh, Doña Lupe," her mother would say to mine at the store, "the school takes care of her during the day. That's the way things work in this country."

Carmen had freedom.

After the dinner dishes had been washed and the table had been cleared, Mom handed the pink paper back to me. "Here it is. Your father signed it."

"He doesn't know what it's about, Mom."

Our mother simply walked away, smiling, "Never you mind, young lady. He signed it and that's what's important."

Before I had a chance to open my mouth again, Laly whisked me away, reminding me that it was my turn to take a shower. "Make it fast. When you get to junior high, you're going to have to shower in five minutes."

Laly, my only sister, was usually a very pleasant person. She often spoke up for me and for my younger brother, Payo, but she was also the one who tried to poison the neighbor's annoying tabby cat, Minino, with an assortment of pills from the medicine cabinet. "Cats are useless creatures, Marta. They carry fleas, too. And they cry like a baby at night, like a dying baby! It's not natural."

So, when she gave me a gentle shove towards the shower, I stifled my urge to question.

Wednesday afternoon came. At the appointed time, each girl in each sixth grade classroom got up quietly and walked into the hallway, where the school nurse was waiting for us. We formed a long line behind her and marched over to the school cafeteria, where the curtains were closed.

The voice on the movie was not the usual male voice that we heard on every film that we ever saw in class. It was a lady's voice, like the voice that advertised washing machines on television. The disembodied voice began, "Today, you will learn what it means to become a young lady. You will learn that it is natural to put away the playthings of ..."

The voice droned on and on about the wonders of being a girl. "You get to use perfume and lipstick." "You will wear grown-up dresses and curl your hair." "You will limit your physical activity during your special days every month." "You will be growing up, preparing to become a perfect woman."

The more the woman's monotone voice extolled the virtues of what she called femininity, the more depressed I became. The only lipstick and perfume in our house belonged to my mother and, as much as I loved my mom, I didn't want to look or smell like her. I didn't want to wear her dresses, either. The worst part of the whole deal was that bit about limiting my physical activity for one week out of every month. "This is a rotten deal," I thought to myself. "This can't be all there is!"

In the last five minutes, they actually showed a very simple animated illustration of the female cycle. Each girl was leaning forward during this part, hands gripping the edges of the tables.

"So *that's* what they've been talking about!" I whispered to Carmen.

She was twisting part of her hair with her fingers, "Yeah, that's it. That's what's going to happen to us. Wish I knew when."

"Me, too."

I ran all the way home that day. "Mamá! Laly! Guess what? I learned all about a woman's ——-"

Laly shushed me quickly. "Get inside and stop shouting! The boys will be home any minute." She grabbed me by the elbow and directed me over to where Mom was ironing in her bedroom.

The AM radio was on Radio Ranchito, her favorite station. "What's all the fuss? You're acting like one of Lilly's kids. Calm down."

I began to ask her about the new words that I had heard in the movie. Laly helped me translate some of them into Spanish, but after a minute or so, Mom put one hand up. "I understand your enthusiasm at learning, but you must lower your voice. A young lady doesn't shout."

"I'm a little girl."

"But you will become a young lady soon enough, God willing."

"Then I can't ever shout again?" The situation was back to grim and I did not like it.

Laly started to giggle as she hung up a pair of our father's pants. "You sure like to exaggerate."

"Mom, how did you feel when you went through your change?" I was hoping to jog her memory of what it was like to be a young girl, a little girl, a playful young female person who found no harm in showing enthusiasm now and then.

She looked at me briefly through her glasses but continued to spray starch onto yet another shirt for one of my older brothers. "You don't know how good you have it."

Oh, great. Another one of those "I walked through the snow to get to school" stories. I was already in a foul mood. My enthusiasm had been squashed by the "ladies don't shout" rule. The depressing mood of the early part of the "health" film was returning to me, and it wanted to linger like a bad smell that won't go away no matter how many windows you open. I swore to myself that, if I ever had a daughter, I would let her shout now and then. Not always, but just now and then.

My mother continued ironing a perfect crease onto the back of the cotton shirt. The iron hissed as it made contact with the dampness of the cloth. "I was thirteen. Since it was a hot day, Toña wanted to go to the river. She persuaded her mother to let me go with her. So, as soon as I had finished cleaning the whole house, my madrina let us both go."

"Why didn't Toña help you clean the house?" I asked.

"Toña dusted, I think. Of all of my nina's kids, she was the one who did the most. The others were okay, but cleaning the house was my job. Remember, my madrina had adopted me rather reluctantly when I became an orphan. She was my godmother, and she was obligated to take me in." The hot iron hissed again as she ironed the cuff of the sleeve. "As I was saying, we went to the river and found a spot that provided enough privacy so we could get into the river with only a slip on. The water was so cool and so beautiful. It was dark green and swirling blue, with a gentle force that went in one direction. The trees near the edge had a few overhanging branches, like strong arms that would let you dip your toes in. Toña liked to jump in from one branch. It was such a beautiful day. You can forget who you are on days such as that."

"And then what happened?"

"We enjoyed the river for...how long? Time just cannot be used to describe such beautiful moments. It is the contrast that allows us to appreciate such times. One moment, Toña and I were splashing each other with the coolness of the river, and the next moment, Toña began to scream and point to the water behind me. When I turned around to look, I saw a red cloud. It looked purple because of the water, but I knew it was red. I had cut myself plenty of times as I washed those big skillets and pots that my madrina had in her kitchen. I ran out of the river and quickly squeezed the water out of my braids. We both got dressed very quickly."

Mom handed the shirt to Laly and pointed to a hanger nearby. "I told Toña to run and get her mother. Neither of us knew what it was. I thought that I was dying. I really thought that this was it. I remember being very frightened, and then, right before Toña got back with my madrina, I stopped crying and shaking. A strange sense of calm took over me. I thought, 'If I die today, then I may go to heaven and see my parents again.' That thought comforted me."

A pair of dress pants was now on the *burro*, our creaky ironing board, being sprayed with starch.

"You wanted to die?" Somehow, I wasn't feeling better.

"Not really. I just wanted to see my parents. Besides, if you're going to suffer and die, why not ignore the suffering and just accept the fact that you're facing death? Anyway, my madrina told me that I was now a young lady. She took me back to the house, assured me that I was not going to die, and also made a point of saying that I should continue with my regular chores. She said that I would bleed for seven days of every month for most of the rest of my life. She called it the curse of being female."

Now, there's a cheerful thought! "Mom, is this supposed to make me feel good?"

"Try and listen beyond my words. I did not have a mother to tell me the truth. It is not the curse of being female. It just is. That's all. It just is. Get it?"

"Okay."

Her words echoed around inside my head for a long time: 'It just is. That's all. It just is.'

The next day, we saw another short film in the darkened cafeteria. Again, all of the curtains were drawn and voices were hushed during the viewing. This movie repeated the vague points made yesterday. Carmen and I were shaking our heads during most of it. Some of the suggestions were a little bit out of our world:

"The joy of being a young lady returns to you every month."

(Why so often?)

"A young woman should not ride a horse during this special time of the month."

(Oh, yes! That would limit participation in the Equestrian Club of West Connecticut Avenue)

"Young ladies should stay away from the beach or swimming pool at those times."

(Most of us couldn't swim anyway)

"Talk with your mother if you have further questions."

(Talk to your own *mom*? What were they thinking???)

The female teachers in the cafeteria confined their teaching to controlling the light switch and the film projector. After the second movie and that little talk with my mother, I had more questions than ever. Where did babies come from? Why don't boys go through this monthly change? Neither of these two topics had even been approached yet!

I was much too shy to ask my teacher and it just didn't seem right to talk to my friends. What if they told my parents that I had asked about that? I was even too embarrassed to ask Laly about much. She might become annoyed. I hoped that my anxiety would go away.

In seventh grade, there were many new things to adjust to, and it was not easy! The two that were the most stressful were the scant five minutes between classes and the mandatory gym class. That class required a uniform that was fondly referred to as a "monkey suit" by the boys. It was a one-piece blue jumpsuit: shorts (mid- thigh length), elastic at the waist, two pockets on the sides, short sleeves, one breast pocket on the right side, standard collar, and about a dozen metal snaps down the front. Not only were you required to change into the p.e. suit for exercising, but you only had five minutes to do it in. Five minutes to shower. Five minutes between classes. Five minutes. Five minutes. Sometimes, I felt like a lab rat running through the cold cement hallways, trying to avoid the electric shock of the bell that would sound when my five minutes were up.

I found some comfort in my classes, because, even though some of them were difficult, most of them were interesting. The amount of homework was considerably more than in elementary school. There were more books to carry home, and my arms would ache from carrying them back and forth to school. The knowledge within them gave me other things to think of; the sheer weight of their pages caused me pain. I didn't know how to separate the two.

There were so many new things that I almost forgot about "the change". My mother, however, did not. When I began eighth grade, she pulled me aside and told me that she was taking me to see Dr. Jantzen to see if there was anything wrong with me. As Laly translated to our mother, he looked at my throat, checked my ears, checked my heart rate and temperature, asked a few questions about my diet, and scribbled something on a prescription pad.

The days and months disappeared, pages drifting from a calendar like leaves falling from a tree. I felt as shy as ever, maybe more so, and so many things pressed upon me. I couldn't stand the looks that some girls gave me. "You only have two outfits, don't you?" "Man, those shoes went out of style last year." "When are you going to shave your legs? Don't you think that boys notice that?"

Sometimes, the only peaceful time of the day was when I would walk home along the railroad tracks, usually with Carmen. We would balance our steps on the rails and gossip about school. While my arms usually struggled to balance a heavy load of books, Carmen (book-less) would often fling rocks at stray cats and the occasional crow that would be perched on a telephone pole. She would say things like, "That rock is for that pig, Suzy, for asking me to find Mexico on the map!" and, "That rock is for little Mary Joe and her little skinny white butt for sitting next to Joey during lunchtime!"

Easter vacation finally came. After working every day at the Miller Ranch with my parents, I felt that I deserved an afternoon of baseball on the new field at the corner of Calle Chapultepec and West Connecticut Avenue. Rumor had it that there would soon be a Vista Boys Club built there, and we all wanted to get the most use out of it before the chain link fences came up.

On the baseball field, the only things that you care about are hitting, pitching, catching, and running. No mention of what side of town you are from. What for? We were all from the same barrio! Besides, it felt nice to be one of the biggest kids on the team, for a change.

We had played a few innings in the warm sunshine and everything was Norman Rockwell picture perfect. Most of us were a bit sweaty, but nobody cared. Then, I began to feel a small stomach ache, nothing big, just a tiny bit of discomfort. I excused myself and went to the restroom.

A minute or so later, I came right out and looked for my mother. I found her ironing again. The homemade curtains, yellow cotton with tiny white flower designs, were waving gently in the breeze. She liked to iron in her bedroom, listening to *corridos* and Agustín Lara on Radio Ranchito, with the smell of the orange blossoms coming through the open window. I guess there's always something to iron when you have seven kids. "Mamá, it's happened!"

She made me close the door behind me, gave me a hug, and fifty cents. "You know what you have to buy at the store, right? You remember that the box is blue and you won't forget to have them put it into a paper bag, right? Okay, now go. Hurry."

Laly had been allowed to remain in the room during the conversation. She was smiling, big time. As I walked past her, she put her hand on my shoulder. "My little sister is a young lady now!"

I was glad that the inevitable had come. I felt that I would never hear the words "little girl" applied to me!

As I closed the screen door and stepped outside, I saw my brother, Pancho coming toward me, punching his baseball glove. "Hey, where do you think you're going?"

I put the coins in my pocket and continued walking. "To the store."

"But my team was winning! You come back here and finish the inning, you big cheater."

Not wanting to draw more attention to my mission, I skipped away and didn't turn back. I was sure that, if I did, he would begin shaking his fist at me.

As I approached Redlands Street, I slowed down to be able to notice things. This would be the first time in my life that I bought feminine supplies. This was the day. This was it. What would it feel like to come home with that box? Would the world ever be the same?

There was the Vista Irrigation District office to my right, on the corner of Redlands and West Connecticut Avenue. It had a great parking lot, perfect for bike riding on weekends. On the next corner, the small auto repair shop. Each man working there wore a blue and white striped shirt, with his name embroidered on the left side. They dressed more nicely than my father did, and I'm sure they were paid more, but their hands got just as dirty as my father's hands. Past that was the slaughterhouse. I could hear the suffering sounds of sheep, crammed into small pens, unable to stretch their wooly legs or drink water. No shade for them, until they were dragged, bleating, into the shadows of the warehouse, where the cement floor was slippery with blood.

On the corner, To the left, between Redlands and Santa Fe, there was that block which was half covered with small wooden apartments, all gray, with many rusty nails holding them together. That's where my cousin Rita lived, with her many brothers and sisters and their father who drank way too much. I saw her sitting on her rickety porch, and waved, but immediately regretted it. She stepped back inside, slamming the door behind her. She was still mad that I had told everybody she was born in Tijuana, just like me, and not in Guadalajara. She was like that sometimes.

I knew which aisle to go to in the store. Waiting for the checkout counter to empty of customers, I walked up and put the box down on the counter. I was biting my lip while she pressed the keys on the cash register and counted my change. Finally, she smiled and said, "That's it, honey. Here you go!" She brought out the biggest paper bag, put the box of supplies inside, and folded it once at the top. "Have a nice day!"

I felt rather foolish, carrying a small box inside such a big paper bag!

I didn't see Rita on the way home, and I ignored the smell of the slaughterhouse as I walked quickly up West Connecticut Avenue. When I got to our front yard, Pancho was leaning against the mailbox, tossing the baseball up lazily into the air and catching it in the worn leather glove that one of Mr. Miller's boys had given to him. "So, you're finally back. How was the store?"

I tried to ignore him, but he threw the ball at my legs. Luckily, he missed.

"Stop it, *tonto,* or I'll tell Mom on you."

His eyes narrowed. "Say, where did you get the money to go to the store, anyway?"

"From Mom. She gave me fifty cents."

"I knew it! I knew it! When Dad isn't around, you get away with murder." I kept making my way toward the front door, but he put his hands on his hips and stood right in front of me to continue his petty interrogation. "Well, what's in the bag?"

I didn't have time for this. I sighed, still clutching the big paper bag, and said, "Nothing for you."

My heart skipped a beat as he lunged toward the bag.

"You've got candy!" he hissed accusingly.

Thank goodness that Mom came to the door at that moment! "What's this all about?"

Pancho straightened up and tried to comb his hair with his fingers. It never worked, of course, because his thick brown curls had a mind of their own. "How come she gets to go to the store? If she gets an extra candy bar, she should share. It's not fair, Mom."

"You think she has candy?" She was trying not to grin.

He was sulking now. "Well, yeah. She's hiding it from me. If I went to get something from the store and you let me buy candy with some of the change, I'd share with her. Besides, I wouldn't walk out on a good baseball game in the first place. Make her give me some of that candy!"

Whenever Mom laughed, her stomach would jiggle and she'd have to adjust her glasses to keep them from falling off. "No, you don't want any of that candy!"

Pancho scowled. Mom continued, "Oh, don't make such a fuss. It's not candy, anyway, just something that I wanted her to buy… for me, okay? For me. Come on inside and have a Seven Up."

That was a treat! The Seven Ups were usually reserved for our father. As I went about my business, Pancho got a tall glass of Seven Up, complete with three ice cubes. From behind the door of my bedroom, I could hear him going "aaah" as he drank the delicious, sparkling beverage.

When he had left the kitchen, I came out and began to help Mom in the kitchen. I just loved the sound of the masa as it was placed flat on the hot comal. You had to do it quickly, or your fingers would get burned. A minute on one side, then flip the tortilla. A minute later, and it was done, all hot and steamy and ready for salt and butter. Today, there was a fresh pot of nopalitos cooking on one of the burners. It would be my job to rinse them out, place them in a large bowl, and add the goodies: finely chopped white onion, small chunks of tomato, a dash of salt, and lots of chopped cilantro, followed by a sprinkling of freshly squeezed lime.

"Mamá, I was thinking."

"About what?" Her hands were forming the masa into little round balls. First, a small chunk was placed in the palm of one hand. Then, both hands would press gently with a circular motion. When the ball was perfect, it would be set aside and slightly drizzled with melted butter. She was quite an artist in the kitchen.

Smiling, I continued, "If I hurry up and help in here, can I go out and finish just one more inning of baseball? We were almost finished with the game."

I watched her chubby hands move gracefully, as she placed the pan full of the little round balls of tortilla dough next to the tortilla press. "You are right where you should be."

"In this kitchen?"

"For now, yes."

"Why can't I go back out and play after my work is done?"

"It wouldn't be appropriate."

"Mom, that's not fair!"

"It isn't fair and it isn't unfair. It just is, that's all."

I watched the handle of the wooden tortilla press come down, flattening the masa into a perfectly round and even circle.

I continued chopping the onion, but the smell was getting into my eyes.

After dinner, Mom made the whole family kneel to say the rosary. After that much fun, I was tired. When the others drifted over to the living room, I curled up in bed with a nice, thick book. I knew that I would be left alone.

When Laly came to bed an hour later, I was more than ready to go to sleep. Before I knew it, I began to drift off to another world. I was standing on the roof of our house. An unknown voice told me to go ahead and jump, that it was okay, that I wouldn't hurt myself.

"You can fly if you really, really want to!" said the voice, which now resembled my godmother's voice.

"Nina Chayo? Is that you?"

I looked down at the lawn. The blades of grass were thick and green and spongy. They seemed to be so very far away.

Was it day or night?

Now, I was on top of the pine tree of our front yard.

I hesitated. The lawn was so distant, and I seemed to be so very high up. I spoke aloud, "What if I just curl up against this cluster of pine cones for a minute?"

For a little while, I became one of the branches, swaying with each breeze. Other branches would rustle up next to me. It was nice. Then, other pine needles began to stab and scratch my sides as the wind kicked up a bit. A gust of wind blew a few pine needles out of my head. I felt like I was going bald and couldn't do a thing about it. It was getting colder. The pigeons that usually lived in the neighbor's palm tree decided to roost on me long enough to leave a few decorations. The sky grew dark gray. A lightning bolt singed me, leaving a dark, crusty spot on my bark. Sap was painfully oozing out of the edges.

What could I do? I wanted to cry, but I had no voice. I was connected, but could not move. I was a branch in a tree.

My body jerked in fear. I sat up quickly and blinked. My heart spoke to me, "Thump, thump—- thump, thump—- thump, thump."

The whole house was in a deep sleep. I tiptoed out of the bedroom, and, blending into the warm shadows of the sleepy little house, I made my way to the living room window. Once there, I pulled aside the delicate pattern of tiny flowers on the homemade curtain, to see what I could see.

Dimly lit by a lone yellow light bulb above the front door, I could see our white picket fence, Mr. Miller's Jeep in the dirt driveway, and the powerful outline of the pine tree in our front yard. Nothing unexpected so far.

I twisted my head in an attempt to look at the top of the pine tree. The branches seemed to be whispering gently in the deep purple breeze, in a language that I did not understand. A falling pine cone startled me, and I quickly closed the curtain.

On my way back to my warm bed, I again passed through the empty kitchen.

There, on the formica counter next to the sink, delicately outlined in the silver moonlight coming through the window, was the tortilla press. Somebody had been playing with it and left the handle pointing up. I opened the cupboard and moved a few chipped plates over. I ran my fingers up and down the smooth wooden handle that still smelled of tortillas.

I didn't know where the empty sadness came from, but it was there in the still air as I pushed the handle down and, oh so very quietly, placed it in the cupboard and closed the door on it.

Señor Hernández

And he smiled a kind of sickly smile, and curled
up on the floor,
And the subsequent proceedings interested him
no more.

The Society Upon the Stanislaus
Francis Bret Harte (1836- 1902),
U.S. author, journalist, and poet

West Connecticut Avenue and the surrounding streets contained almost the same characters as any other barrio. We had, for example, the widows in permanent mourning, the church ladies, some pachucos (now called cholos or gangsters), the blind, the crippled, the laborers with permanent grass stains on the knees of their khaki pants, the auto mechanics, the beauticians with bleached blonde hair and beehive hairdos, and two types of the unemployed: those unemployed by chance and those unemployed by choice.

Having had little formal education, and thus more vulnerable to the whims of employers, my parents sympathized with those unemployed by chance. "Not everybody finds a fine boss like Mr. Miller," my mother would say. "See how he teaches your father how to do so many things? He welcomed our whole family and sends my little Pancho to Camp Marston in the summer. He lets us drive his truck, which is such a convenience on shopping day. Remember my words, children. If you ever become someone's boss, always show respect to your workers. That's how you earn their loyalty."

There were few unemployed by choice. The most visible one was the groggy wino who would stagger harmlessly about the barrio, nodding respectfully to the ladies and always saying "Buenos dias" to the men as they went to and from work. It seemed that he never would or never wanted to justify his existence by work.

His name was Señor Hernández, and the good Lord had blessed him with a hard working wife and two beautiful daughters.

The younger daughter, Leticia, was maybe one year ahead of me, and always said hello, but we didn't play together often. The older daughter, Patricia, was my sister Laly's best friend. Whenever they could get together, they would go on and on about which town had the cutest guys.

"Vista, of course!"

"No, Escondido."

"Carlsbad?"

"Fallbrook?" Hysterical laughter. "Farmboys! Rancheritos!"

"Oceanside?"

They would let Laly win the argument every time. "Okay, girl. Escondido guys are cutest. Why you insist is beyond me, though. The guys from Carlsbad are really the coolest."

Both of the girls in that family were very neat. Their makeup was always on just right, false eyelashes and all. Their dresses always seemed to be of the latest fashion to me.

The older one, Patricia, teased her hair a lot more than Laly, but not enough to be mistaken for a pachuca. No, no, no. Those girls made it very clear that they wanted to get out of the barrio by marrying a guy with money, even if he was a white guy.

Their yard was enclosed by a wrought iron fence. Tidy little flowerpots were tastefully arranged under the windowsill and formed a colorful margin to the small but well-kept yard. When the girls were home, the curtains were tied open with a gold velvet rope. If you were at the front door, you could lean over to one side and peek through the window. If you did, you would see the crushed red velvet sofa, covered in plastic. On the opposite side, you would see a mirror with a French style frame. Many photographs were displayed in the living room, and all frames had been spray painted a dignified golden yellow.

Their mother was always off somewhere, cleaning some rich person's house. I didn't see her very often, but nobody did, really. The one we saw the most was the dad, and we called him Señor Hernández. Sometimes my dad called him other names, but that's besides the point.

"Mom, there's somebody at the door."

"Ay, who could it be? It is so early in the morning. Marta, answer the door."

I yawned and put my spoon in the bowl of corn flakes. "Me?"

"Yes, my sweet daughter. Hurry."

When I got to the front door, I could see that there was indeed a man. His corduroy pants were too clean to belong to a bum. He leaned against the door frame, just like my dad did when he was exhausted from an extra hard day of work.

"Hello. Who are you, señor?"

"Ay, does Don Jesús Lomelí live here?"

From the kitchen, my mother's voice replied, "Oh, it must be you, Señor Hernández! I know your wife and our older daughter gets along so well with your two beautiful daughters. Come on in and have some coffee with us!"

Since we often spent Saturdays working on the ranch, picking avocados or macadamia nuts, Señor Hernández was lucky to find us at home that day.

"Hey, are you sure it's okay? I was accidentally locked out of my house, and my wife and kids went somewhere. You know, trying to make a little extra money on a Saturday, and…" His voice trailed off as he stared at the pan of chorizo con huevos on the stove.

"Señor Hernández, I insist that you have breakfast with us. Look, the children prefer corn flakes. Have a fresh burrito. Coffee?"

I was confused now. Why would Mom let him believe that we would rather eat corn flakes instead of chorizo con huevos? It was never our first choice. It was, however, often the only choice for kids because our mother loved the way it lasted so long. Mom liked to save the chorizo con huevo for the oldest ones in the family: her, Dad, and Eddie.

He thanked her profusely as she served him a complete breakfast. I watched him as he ate with gusto, smacking his lips after each of the four (count 'em!) burritos and two cups of coffee. "Oh, Doña Lupita, what a wonderful breakfast! I will repay you for such kindness. Ah, well, except that money has been so very tight. I lost my job a while back, you know."

"Oh, I'm so sorry to hear that. When I spoke to your wife at church last Sunday, I didn't see you there and she didn't say anything about that."

"She is a proud woman, my wife. Yes, yes indeed. She's got the car. I know that she doesn't get paid today, so… I don't know. This is so embarrassing."

His eyes were getting redder. For a moment, he held one hand to his throat and stared down at his empty plate. Then his droopy eyes looked up at my mother and he mumbled, "Could you loan me a few dollars? At least one dollar? I'll pay you back in a couple of days. I don't want my family to be without milk and tortillas for the whole weekend."

Mom shooed Payo and me away from the breakfast table and into the living room, quickly turning the television on for us. As Wimpie convinced Popeye that he would be paid back Tuesday for a hamburger today, Señor Hernández sat in our little kitchen and borrowed a dollar from Mom.

They stayed in the kitchen for quite a while, chatting over coffee and pan dulce. Eventually, Mom started to get restless and finally said, "Señor Hernández, thank you for stopping by. I really must get back to my housework now. Please say hello to your lovely wife. Don't you worry about a thing. Everything will turn out all right."

Shortly after noon, I heard the jeep drive up. "Dad's home, everybody!"

Just as Dad's boot stepped out of the jeep and into the dirt driveway, Payo and I rushed up to him. "Papá! Did you bring us something?"

Slamming the door to Mr. Miller's jeep, he adjusted his sombrero and growled, "Crazy kids! Leave me alone. I'm your father, not a 'Santo Clós.'"

I nudged Payo and he quickly put his left hand into Dad's left jacket pocket, fishing around for anything edible.

Now smiling slightly, our father gruffly added, "I said get your paws off of me, you two!" Dad grabbed his sombrero and swatted Payo on his behind.

"Hey, can we have that gum?" grinned Payo. "Can we have that gum in your jacket pocket, dear father?"

A similar scene was repeated every time that our father came home. The only details that sometimes changed were simple, trivial things. Sometimes Dad swatted me with his sombrero, sometimes he had butterscotch candy in his pocket, and sometimes he had a few pennies. Occasionally, he had a screwdriver or wrench and then, of course, all we could get out of him was his pocket lint.

He always let us follow him into the kitchen. Mom would say something like, "Hello, dear." Then, before asking her about her day, he would ask, "So, what's to eat?" That family scene was one of many that seemed to be locked in an eternal loop.

Always the same thing. Always the same sounds, the same sights: grass stains and work boots for my father, tortilla dough on the hands of my mother. The only time it changed was when Mom worked with Dad, and when all of us went to work together to pick avocados or macadamia nuts. Then we all had grass stains and smelled of perspiration.

This day, the usual chatter was about Señor Hernández.

"You did what?" asked Dad as he pulled out his chair from the green formica kitchen table.

"A dollar. You heard me clearly, Jesús. I…"

"A dollar? Do you know what a dollar could buy in Mexico?" His head being bare, we could now see the tan line across his forehead, proof that he was a man who loved his sombrero.

"Here. Eat." Mom sighed as she served him a full plate of sopa, pinto beans, and ground beef and green beans seasoned with El Pato hot sauce.

"Is this all the meat I get?" he complained, as his fork poked at the small mound of ground beef with a sprinkling of green vegetable. "What in the name of God is this?"

"Green beans. They're fresh from our neighbor's garden. Don't they brighten up the ground beef?"

"They're vegetables. Feed them to the kids."

"Okay. Then I'll feed the beans and the rice to them, too. You won't even have tortillas to eat because they come from vegetables, too."

Dad gave her one of those "Stop while you're ahead" stares. Then, he got back to the first matter. "You say that he said he was desperate for money?"

"I thought you heard me the first time. Yes, I did. I thought it was the kind and neighborly thing to do. I wanted to set a good example for the children. We need to teach them to be compassionate."

Then, Dad did a curious thing. He began to smile, which perplexed us all. He clapped his hands together as he chuckled. "Damn that guy! He is the best actor in the barrio!" A few chuckles later, he looked across the table to Mom and added, "Lupe, I thought you were smarter than that. Do you know what he needs the money for?"

Mom quietly sprinkled some salsa on her pinto beans. "Go ahead and tell me, Jesús. I suppose you're going to tell me your opinion, anyway."

"He's a borrachito, Lupita, a plain old wino. He's not going to spend it on his family. He would rather spend money on Jack Daniels and Johnny Walker than do something for his girls. His wife works even harder than you do, and that's not easy."

"Jesús, what if you're wrong? What if you maybe saw him have a drink once, like you do sometimes, and that's all? Maybe he had two. Maybe he lost his job, which is what he told me."

"He told you that he lost his job?" His eyebrows went up slightly.

"Yes. Now, don't you feel foolish?"

"Do you know if he was laid off or fired? Do you know how long it has been since he worked? Do you?"

"Jesús, do you really want to get into this in front of the kids? Shall I ask you about any money orders you have sent recently to Mexico?"

Dad just grunted and changed the subject.

I sat down to feast. Putting the tortilla on my left hand, I used the fingertips of my right hand to roll it tightly. Before I bit into each fresh tortilla, I always smelled it. It made the food taste better.

The following Saturday, our parents packed us into Mr. Miller's jeep. "The Millers are going to have some people over this evening, and I told Mr. Miller that we would pitch in to get their yard ready."

"A party?" asked Payo, as he tried to roll up the sleeves of his T-shirt. He liked to imitate our older brothers sometimes. "Are we invited? Cake?"

"Don't be so dumb. Maybe you can't help it," grumbled Panchito. "They won't invite us 'cause…"

"Well, maybe this time they will," I interrupted. "Mr. Miller sent you to Camp Marston last summer. Maybe they will invite us."

"No, you got me wrong," sighed Pancho. "Why should they invite us when we don't invite them to any parties at our house, over here?"

"What parties?" I wondered aloud.

"Exactly. So, shut up and move over. I get the window seat."

I moved over, but not because he had told us to do so. I moved because, all things said and done, he was a very hard worker. If Mom told Payo and me to work with him today, I knew that my work load would be light. Cuco, on the other hand, was likely to supervise us, the way the pharaohs supervised the building of the pyramids. Eddie and Chuy had already chosen to work with each other in one corner of Mr. Miller's property, trimming trees.

Dad put the key in the engine. "Mr. Miller is paying us for half a day, but I won't leave a job undone. We're staying until all the weeds on the hillside are gone. If you kids do a good job, I'll remember that tomorrow when you ask for your domingo. That's one thing you are very consistent on. I know that for sure. Asking for your allowance every Sunday after church, that's the kind of thing you kids always remember. Every Sunday, alright."

We worked fast enough to be done by 11:30. As we drove home, our parents complimented us.

"Kids, we're really proud of you," smiled Dad.

Mom still had her scarf and apron on. "Oh, yes, children. You know I've said it before, 'There's always room in heaven for a hard worker.' Well done, well done. This is how we want our children to behave."

"Hey, Marta," whispered Payo. "Do you think Mr. Miller is really paying Dad and Mom today, or did we all just work for free?"

What a good question! "Why don't you ask Dad?"

"Are you kidding? Are you nuts?" His eyes always looked so round when he was bewildered. "Take a chance on Dad losing the good mood he is in?"

"Yeah, I guess. Let's just enjoy it while it lasts." It felt strange to agree with him so early in the day.

"Right again. One point for me."

As we got closer and closer to West Connecticut Avenue, Mom began discussing the possibility of making a few dozen enchiladas for the Millers. "You know, Jesús, they won't be expecting it, but they do like my enchiladas. Mrs. Miller doesn't know a thing about Mexican cooking, and Mr. Miller loves my enchiladas. I'll even make extra for us."

I only half heard what Dad was saying to her because the jeep was turning onto our street. I was focusing my attention on the parking lot at the corner of West Connecticut and Santa Fe. "Payo, look at that guy sitting on the sidewalk near the side door of the store. Is that who I think it is?"

He wrinkled his nose as he leaned toward me. "It looks like Señor Hernández drinking a soda, but why does he cover the soda with a paper bag?"

"I dunno. Wish we had that soda in here, though. Look at the wet circles under my arms, see?" I sighed. "Mom, do we have any soda in the refrigerator?"

The next Saturday, Dad asked if any of us wanted to go with him to feed the horses on the Miller ranch. "If you come with me, I might let you give the horses an apple from that tree at the bottom of the hill. Those big green apples smell so nice. The horses love them."

Laly nudged me before I could say yes. She reminded me, "He might be gone all day. After you help me clean the house and after lunch, we can watch the scary movie on channel six in the afternoon. If I bake a cake, I'll let you lick the bowl."

So, I stayed.

Shortly after Dad and the boys drove away in Mr. Miller's jeep, Mom went into the back yard to hang up the latest load of clothes that had come out of the washing machine. Laly began ironing in one bedroom, and I was busy scrubbing the only toilet bowl in the house.

I was just about to pour in some more soap into the toilet bowl when, all of a sudden, I heard footsteps not far from me. When had the screen door opened? I didn't hear it screech. I didn't hear a knock. Those footsteps had a sort of shuffle to them, similar to a hunchback in a Vincent Price movie. A cough joined the shuffling footsteps. Then, the mystery person cleared his throat in a most uncivilized manner. Hack. Gag. Gargle. Spit. Hey, wait a minute! That was all happening in our living room!

"Tío Miguel, is that you?" I knew it wasn't him. He never did anything so uncouth. He was eccentric at times, but never gross. Never scary.

I saw the shuffling feet and droopy eyes of Señor Hernández "Hey, you got anything to eat? I'm really hungry. I lost my job, you know. Where's your mom? Where's Don Jesús?"

He tried to smile, but his mouth couldn't finish the job. At first, I thought he had been crying because his nose was red and his droopy eyes couldn't seem to twinkle like my father's eyes often did. "My dad never cries," I thought to myself. "My daddy is strong."

Then, I noticed how his hands kept wiping one side of his face, like he was trying to wake up. I had seen the very same thing before in a Cantinflas comedy movie, only Cantinflas was much funnier. Mr. Hernández just looked like his batteries had run out.

Being that nobody else was there at the moment, I felt bold enough to scold him.

Gently, I said, "Señor Hernández, why didn't you knock? It's good manners to knock."

"Huh? Oh, I thought I did. Didn't I?" His left hand was trying to find his lower lip to wipe what appeared to be a drop of spittle slowly going down to his chin. It was slimy, with specks of white foam.

"No. No, you didn't. I'll go get Mom. You sit down, okay?"

He was an obedient man. The trouble was… he only imagined that a chair was nearby. He fell flat on his behind and slumped there. This time, he really did look embarrassed.

I remember feeling grateful that he was not my father. "Dad never did anything stupid like that. At least, I don't think so." I made a mental note to talk to Mom about that later.

"I'm …ah… really sorry. Don Jesús, your father, he is such… so nice a man. I … ah… wish…"

Before he could finish his sentence, I had brought Mom over. As Laly and I continued our chores, Mom sat and chatted with Señor Hernández.

As we were mopping the floor in the boys' bedroom, I expressed my concerns with Laly. "Laly, is he ever going to leave?"

"Of course, tonta. He has a home."

"Well, then, why is he here now?"

Laly handed a bucket of dirty water to me. "Dump this in the toilet. Fill it up half ways, to about there, and bring it back. These little piggies we have for brothers never wipe their shoes when they put them under the bed." As I carefully took the bucket from her, she added, "You'd better not tell any of the other kids on the block."

"You mean…?"

"Yeah. His daughters are my best friends." She hesitated before continuing. "I like to go over to their house when he's not there and we play records and stuff. They got a big collection of 45's and it's so much fun closing the curtains so the guys won't walk by and see us. We put on Elvis, The Big Bopper, and Mary Wells. *Nothin' you can do, 'cause I'm stuck like glue, to my guy!* I just learned to dance the mashed potato. I'll show you later on today, if you like. Sometimes, we call people on the phone. I can't do it here, you know. The girls are the only ones who aren't related to us that I can talk with. They're not so bad. Not so bad at all."

"But, still, don't you think…?"

"Weren't you listening to me?" She sighed. "Stop expecting the world to be so perfect."

Well, Señor Hernández did eventually go away that day, but he did not head straight home. In the next few weeks, I began to hear about his wanderings from my playmates in the barrio:

Hey, guess whom we found snoozing on our doorstep

Guess who borrowed money from my grandma again?

Guess who tripped and fell in the street?

Guess who was checking the pay phone again for spare change?

I didn't think that last one was a particularly bad sin, having done that myself quite often. However, I had never heard of a grown man, let alone somebody's father, stooping to such lows.

One night, I had a little trouble falling asleep and I had the chance to hear part of the late evening conversation between Mom and Dad. Everyone else was off in la-la land.

In whispers, I could hear my father trying to convince my mother about something. At first, I was worried that I might be hearing things that a little girl shouldn't hear. Then, I caught a few words and their mumbling began to make sense.

"No, Lupita. Of course I trust you."

"Good. Then stop criticizing me, Jesús. We will be paid back, I give you my word."

"Ay, why do you keep saying that? That guy hasn't had a job in years. Years! All the men in the barrio know this. He stopped borrowing from us a long, long time ago. First, it was cigarettes, then a beer, then a whole six pack or a bottle of wine. His wife, I'm sure, knows it, too. I can't blame her for trying to keep it a secret. It's such a shame that she has to work so hard, you know."

"I work hard. Seven kids. How often do I go to work with you on Mr. Miller's ranch? Sometimes every day. Sometimes only twice a week, and do you think…"

"I'm sorry, Lupita." I heard the light click off in their bedroom. "I know that you work hard. I work to support the family, and I do my best. You know that. I'm sorry that I have to ask for your help."

By this time, my eyelids were feeling very, very heavy. I lost interest and fell into a deep slumber.

Mom awakened us in the usual way: "Everybody up, muchachos and muchachas! The sun is up, and you should be, too!"

Seconds later, our father's voice would say something like, "Either you get up now, or your mother starts singing. Your choice." We would hear him fumbling with the AM radio, and then the sounds of Radio Ranchito, his favorite Mexican radio station.

That day, Dad took all five of the boys with him to work before I had a chance to ask him if Laly and I had to go, too. I didn't mind, really. That was as close as I could get to having peace and quiet in the house.

Mom, Laly, and I quietly went about cleaning the house. We fell into a rhythm of movement: sweep, dust, mop, scrub, straighten that up, put that away, wash your hands.

Occasionally, Laly would beg Mom for permission to tune the radio to an English radio station. Sometimes she got her wish. When that happened, she would wait for Mom to begin ironing in the other room, then she would hold the broom like it was her dancing partner. "Look. This is something that Patty showed me. She saw it in a movie with Frankie Avalon, I think."

"Isn't her name Patricia?"

Her feet would shuffle as she held the broom with one hand and snapped her fingers with the other hand. "Yeah, but she likes to be called Patty."

"Isn't that a gringo name?"

"Who cares? She's my friend. She's nice. So, shut up and learn what I'm trying to teach you. Someday, you're going to dance with a boy, and you just know that Mom won't prepare you for that."

"Yeah, but…"

"Right now you don't know any boys that you want to dance with. You will. Someday. You're pretty and you're smart. Guys will be fighting over you. You gotta be willing to dance with the one that wins."

I pondered that for a moment. Would I be able to choose who fought over me? Did Dad ever fight over Mom? What if he had lost the fight?

Our little conversation was interrupted by the sound of the front screen door opening. A masculine cough was heard.

"It might be Tío Miguel, Laly." Our uncle, Miguel, often came in unannounced.

She frowned. "Hmm, I don't think so."

We stepped into the small hallway next to the living room. In the living room, there was Mr. Hernández, standing and grinning. "Hey, girls! Your father home? No? I got somethin' for you, then."

Where had Mom gone? Had she gone to Doña Lola's house to borrow some starch for the ironing?

Mr. Hernández began to search his shirt pocket. In his eagerness to find whatever it was, his thumb snagged on the pocket and tore the pocket slightly.

"Oops. I guess it's not in my shirt pocket."

Laly pulled me behind her. "Our father isn't here, Señor Hernández. Our mother is ironing in the next room."

His droopy eyes looked at both of us, back and forth. "So, the old man isn't here. My old lady doesn't know where I am. She doesn't need to know everything I do. You'll understand when you're older."

"What are you looking for? If it's not in your pocket, then where is it?" I interrupted.

He grinned foolishly and began to search the two back pockets of his corduroy pants. "Doña Lupe? You here? You there? You anywhere?" Then, he giggled.

I started to say something, but Laly jabbed her elbow into my stomach, hissing, "Let me handle this."

I hoped that somebody would. He was starting to make me uneasy. I remembered my mother's words: "If a man makes you feel strange, run away. Run fast. Run very fast. Then, come and tell me. Always tell your mother everything. Your mother is your best friend." Mom was famous for laying it on kind of thick, but still... Mr. Hernández was trying too hard to be friendly. Is this what a *robachicos* was like? Did child kidnappers first pretend to search for the candy before they showed you something that you didn't want to see?

He took a couple of steps toward us, still smiling. "Ah, if your parents aren't here, that's okay. I won't be long. Anything to eat in the kitchen? Your mother sure is a good cook. She won't mind if I look around, would she? You and my two girls are always hanging out in my house. It would be okay if I had a bite to eat, wouldn't it?"

Would he still be acting weird if Eddie or my daddy was here? Would he still be acting strangely if Mom was in the room?

Laly cleared her throat. "Don't you take another step. This is our house."

Clutching her arm from behind, I added, "Yeah. Our house."

Despite our protests, he walked right past us into the kitchen and began to gobble the leftovers on the table.

"Laly," I whispered, "He smells funny. What should we do?"

"Run out the front door and go see if Mom is at Doña Lola's house. That's probably where she is. Go."

"I better not leave you alone."

He devoured a small pot of leftovers and, licking his fingers, turned in the chair to look at us. "You girls have been real nice. Real nice. I was hungry, but you let me eat. Just like your mother, so pretty and so nice. Don Jesús is a lucky man to have such a wonderful family. Do you know that my Patricia and my Lety never fix breakfast for me? Do you know that my wife makes me sleep outside sometimes, on the porch? She did last night. Really".

Just like in a bad movie, the scene continued. His droopy eyes got misty. His torn shirt pocket just dangled there on the left side of his chest, a few threads pointing to nowhere. "Nobody wants to talk to me at home. That's why I walk around the neighborhood sometimes, just to hear somebody say something to me."

Laly tried to be respectful, but I could tell that she was uncomfortable. "Why don't you just leave whatever it was you were going to leave for our parents?" she said sternly. "Hurry up and do that or I'll tell your wife."

We were surprised to see tears begin to form in his eyes. "Okay. I guess I just better stick to business. I guess that your parents raised you to be rude to adults, but then, my wife taught my daughters to treat me like that, too. What could I expect from strangers? I will never darken your step again. I just want to give you somethin' that I got here, but don't tell your parents."

As he stood up from the chair to take a step toward us, he began to search his front pant pockets. He then tried to take a step toward us as he continued his search, but one foot stepped on an untied shoelace and …well, he kissed the floor, so to speak.

That was when we heard the back door creak open. "Girls! I'm back! Doña Lola sends you some…"

There was Señor Hernández, droopy eyes all misty around the edges, writhing on the floor, both hands caught in his pockets, desperately trying to regain his dignity.

"Señor Hernández!" Mom gasped.

"He ate our food, Mamá!" I shouted.

"He was talking about giving us something and to not tell you or Papá!"

Mom instinctively took one step over to the stove, grabbed the rolling pin, and stood over him. "The devil would be easier for you to handle than an angry mother, Señor Hernández. Get the picture? Get your sorry self off of my kitchen floor. My girls just mopped it twenty minutes ago! Go! Scoot!"

By now, he was on his knees; hands still in his pockets. His bushy black eyebrows, combined with the dark circles under his eyes, made him look like a sad clown. With a sniffle, he took his hands out of his pockets, withdrew a wrinkled up five-dollar bill, and placed the money on the table. Then, holding onto the edge of the nearby chair, he stood up and wobbled ever so slightly.

Staring down at his shoes, he said, "I beg your forgiveness. I like to drink. I do. I never hit anybody, though I can't say the same thing for my wife. But, bless that woman, she works and spends the money on our two beautiful daughters and on our house. I can't do those things, because, like I told you, I like to drink. So there."

Mom lowered the rolling pin and glanced at the five-dollar bill on the table. "Where did that money come from?"

He continued to look down at his shoes, especially the one that was untied. "I promised you that I would pay you back. So, that's that."

"You only borrowed one dollar. With five dollars, you can fill up a grocery bag!"

His hands covered his eyes as he began to cry quietly. "I…(sob) took the money out of my wife's purse when she wasn't looking. I wanted… wanted to (sob)…let your girls spend the money to go to the movies, maybe with Patricia and Lety. You see, I could have spent it on whiskey."

His head hanging low, he began to shuffle towards the front door, mumbling to himself.

"What did you drink on the way over here?" Mom asked. "You drink whisky again?"

He kept mumbling as he left. "I told you no." When he had closed the screen door behind him, he kept muttering. "A couple of beers, just a couple of beers. They weren't even that cold."

In the *Leave it to Beaver* sitcom, Ward worked as an engineer and June worked at home. In *Ozzie and Harriet*, Ozzie didn't seem to ever leave the home, but he was often busy about the house, helping Harriet and giving advice to Ricky or Dave. In *Father Knows Best*, the audience was always being entertained by the mild pranks of the teenagers and the precocious younger daughter. Nobody spoke Spanish and the only people with dark brown skin were foreign exchange students, but the parents always made everything work out. No matter what the story line, there was always a happy ending thirty minutes later.

I wondered if "Patty" and Lety were waiting for their thirty minutes to be over.

The Green American

When a seed feels secure, it takes root and presents the world with a bit of greenery. Maybe a flower, maybe a weed, but a contribution to the cycle of life any way you look at it.

West Connecticut Avenue had what I needed in my early years: my family, my friends, a corner store, and Santa Fe Elementary School. We kept the street clean in front of our house because it was our house and our barrio. To neglect to do so would have been shameful. You're supposed to take care of the people and the things that you love.

I knew that, eventually, I would have to attend seventh grade … across town. *Way* across town. I hoped that I could maintain enough of my root system to keep the winds of change from blowing me away.

***

It was a long walk from West Connecticut Avenue to Lincoln Junior High. Most of my homegirls like Carmen and Marilú preferred to walk both ways, to and from. But, then again, they didn't have as many books to carry as I did. So, I endured the humiliation of riding with my father in a truck that smelled of lawn mowers and tar. If I got up early enough, I would be dropped off in front of Vista High and be able to cross the street to Lincoln before the popular kids could see me.

In ninth grade, I decided to try participating in some school-wide activities. I thought it would be fun, and maybe, just maybe, help me deal with those snide remarks and disapproving looks that I often got from my wealthier classmates. I knew that I could only afford maybe two new outfits per school year, and my clothes were always clean, but they didn't care. I was from the other side of the tracks.

Since I didn't have permission to stay after school to join any clubs, I tried journalism class. The teacher was an old fossil who loved the printed word but barely tolerated teenagers. If you approached her with an original idea and were willing to do the extra work yourself without causing her too much stress, she would usually give you a green light. That's how I became the cartoonist, drawing cartoons such as "Avocado Al", and the advice columnist called "Dear Morticia".

Getting involved with something outside of the four walls of that little house on West Connecticut Avenue gave me something else to look at, something else to focus on, something else to think about. My complexion still wasn't perfect because my body was still that of a young girl, but every time that somebody picked up the school paper and looked at something that I had drawn or written, I felt a little bit taller.

It was a wonderful feeling, even when people didn't agree with what I had written. To everybody except my immediate circle of acquaintances, I was just a name on a paper. I wasn't getting invited to any parties or dances outside of my barrio, but, still, everybody read the school newspaper. It was free!

That was more than I had been before. I was beginning to get the hang of junior high life.

One day, a new student arrived from Mexico. Consuelo was placed right next to me in almost every class, and for a couple of months, we were the best of buddies. She struggled to learn English and I tried to do my best to translate the assignments. She was a quick student, at first. Because she lived in a ranch in the outskirts of Vista, we could not walk home with Carmen and Marilú and the other girls of my neighborhood. Still, we were the best of buddies for a short time.

The more English she could grasp, the more she changed. First, it was her name. "Don't call me Consuelo anymore. Call me Connie." Then, she began wearing eye shadow and putting white powder on her face. I tried to point out to her that her skin was a dark chocolate brown, and the powder was actually light beige but she would only laugh and say, "This is how boys notice you. How long have you been living in *el norte,* anyway?" As her skirts got shorter and tighter, she seemed less interested in our friendship and more curious about who was who in school.

Poor Consuelo. I knew that none of the football players would ever go out with her. Her teeth had permanent brown stains on them, the kind you get from drinking unfluoridated water in some parts of the world. She could cut her hair and curl it like a cheerleader, and she didn't exactly live in the barrio, but her skin was dark and her father's fingernails got the same kind of grass stains that my father's often did. The higher she hiked her skirts, the more the boys looked at her legs, but it was the kind of look that my mother had warned me about. I wondered if "Connie" had a mother to warn her what she was headed for.

I knew that I had lost a friend when she came to school with a purple mark on her neck. "Consuelo, what is that?" I whispered as I sat down next to her in science class.

"Connie. I told you to say Connie."

I stared at her eye makeup. "Wow, you look like Cleopatra or something."

She took that as a compliment. "Oh, thank you."

Then, she winked at Brad, the muscular boy in the corner. He pointed to her with his pencil and winked back.

I hesitated, but finally had to put my two cents in. "Connie, what have you done?"

"Jealous?" she snapped. "You've been in this country for years. I don't see your boyfriend anywhere. Maybe that's because you don't have one, huh? You'll be fifteen next year. You're just going to wait until the last minute, aren't you?"

"Consuelo, just because you're fifteen now doesn't mean you have to throw yourself on the first guy that talks to you. Look at that thing on your neck! You want them to think that all Mexicans are like that?"

Her Cleopatra eyes stared at me furiously. Her eyebrows, or what was left of them, were arching up like the bride of Frankenstein. "Stop it. We're not in Mexico and my name is Connie. You got that? Connie, Connie, Connie! And what I do with my time is my own business! You're just jealous. You may be fourteen, but you still look like you're eleven and you still dress like it. You're jealous and you're never going to get married."

My face felt warm and my heart began to beat a little bit faster. I looked down at my pink dress. It was clean and I had ironed and starched it with care. It had been brand new in September, and so pretty with its tiny white polka dots. Now, the hem was slightly faded and the polka dots were a bit on the fuzzy side.

I clenched my teeth together and hissed, "He can't speak Spanish, but I guess you know that by now."

"Get out of my face."

For the next two weeks, that Brad would follow her to the nearby park after school. I never saw him carry her books, but then again, I wasn't really looking. I had other problems of my own.

My homegirls were distancing themselves from me. I was beginning to hear things like, "Why do you carry so many books? You gonna start a library?" and "Girls don't need to study so much. Spend some time learning how to put on some makeup, instead. Grow up." Sometimes, even my cousins would tease me in the same way.

I was angry and offended. It is one thing to hear it from kids who live on the other side of the railroad tracks, kids who had never tasted menudo before, kids whose mothers didn't know how to make tortillas or a good pot of pinto beans. It was almost as bad to hear it from "Connie". It was much, much more confusing when the voices came from my neighborhood.

Were they trying to be helpful? Maybe they didn't want me to end up picking lemons or avocados like my parents. Maybe they hoped that there was a knight in shining armor for each of us, if we just played the game right.

I was holding all of these feelings in my throat and it hurt. I felt as if I had bitten into a fresh orange with my eyes closed and been surprised by an unknown flavor, not quite sweet and not quite sour. I couldn't pinpoint what it was about that game just then, but I wasn't ready to swallow on faith alone. I wasn't so sure I even wanted to play any stupid game. I had my doubts, and it was eating me from the inside out.

Another problem that was on my mind had to do with the small circle of my new friends, girls who, while not in the top social class, still lived far from West Connecticut Avenue. In their part of town, the velvet painting in the living room was one of dogs playing cards or pool. In my part of town, the velvet painting was of the first Catholic president, John F. Kennedy. In their part of town, children ran barefoot by choice. In our house, if we went barefoot, my mother would scream in horror. "Put those huaraches back on! Do you want people to think that we can't afford shoes?"

These girls were in most of my core classes. We would sometimes share class notes and be on the same science group. It felt good to be working together on projects instead of focusing on what we did or did not have. Mom had always told me that school was my number one job, anyway.

Unfortunately, everybody's hormones started kicking in just about then. Two of the girls, Kim and Wanita, had their eyes on the same guy. It was fascinating to see the little schemes that each would invent to get his attention and discredit each other. I hoped to remain an innocent bystander for as long as possible. I enjoyed their friendship separately, and that would have been okay. Not as good as all three of us being friends, but almost as good.

Mr. Wonderful was enjoying the attention, and he took advantage of every opportunity to flirt with them. The little weasel would start talking to one, and as soon as the other could be seen coming toward them, he would excuse himself and scamper off to class, with a "see ya later". This gave each girl the feeling that he was a classy guy who wouldn't dream of breaking up two good friends.

The soap opera continued to unfold. Wanita would confide in me about stress at home, and, during another class, Kim would do the same. Wanita would come to school depressed about her problems at home, and Kim would feign concern and ask me if she was all right.

"Wanita looks depressed. I think her eye makeup is smudged. Is the poor girl okay?"

"I don't know what you're talking about." That was the answer I always gave her. I wanted to play it safe.

The trouble with standing on the fence is that it is so easy to fall off. You're not on one side and you're not on the other and you're not even on your own side. You just can't have your cake and eat it, too. It is a lesson that some of us have to learn more than once.

One day, Carmen and Marilú entered the restroom after me. They then approached me with some disturbing gossip. "We hate to tell you this, but it's about one of those gavachas that you're friends with."

I looked up at both of them as I finished washing my hands. "Well, they're just friends, you know. It's not a big deal."

Marilú had one hand on her hip. "Well, not that we care, but that gringa Kim and I were talking about p.e. and she said something really bad about that Wanita. She said that Wanita was maybe putting on a little weight, like getting a little fat, if you know what I mean, because she was doing it with that guy so he would like her more."

Carmen nodded, her jet-black bangs swishing back and forth over her big silver hoop earrings. "Yeah. I was getting dressed next to my p.e. locker, and I heard it."

Marilú took a step toward me. "That's a low down dirty thing to say about somebody, even if it is true."

Carmen put one hand on my shoulder. "Nobody else knows. We don't care if it is true or not. They're gavachas. They don't like us and we don't like them. Besides, we think that guy is ugly!"

The three of us laughed. I thanked them for not blabbing it to anybody else.

Later on, I got a chance to talk with Wanita. Once again, the girls' restroom was the location of choice. All of the best meetings in junior high happen in the restroom. "You been seeing much of that guy?"

"Well, he plays basketball with my brother now and then. I try to be around and pretend like I'm not watching, but you know." She giggled and looked up at the ceiling, sighing.

"That's all?"

"I wish it was more, but my brother calls me lard butt if I hang around for more than two seconds. He did it once in front of him, and I turned red. I almost cried. I was really mad, and I would have killed him but then he smiled at me."

"Your brother?"

"No, dummy. HIM. He smiled at me like he was defending me. He even told my brother that I was no bother at all. Can you believe that? It was so ...ooh la la!"

Afterwards, I managed to get a hold of the other girl, Kim, in the hallway. I began by stating the obvious fact that we were friends. She nodded in agreement. Then, I stated that I was also Wanita's friend. She pretended to be bored and rolled her eyes, saying that it was fine with her. Going on to the main point, I asked her directly, "If you don't want to be Wanita's friend, that's okay, but does that make you two enemies? Huh?"

It seemed like the right thing to do. Those two had been close friends before they knew me. They weren't perfect, but I didn't care. I just wanted for the three of us to hang out like we used to.

Kim got suspicious. "What? Did you talk to Wanita? Who told her? I was just joking when I said ...oh, my God! You better not have told her anything!"

"No, I didn't, but you should. You two are still friends even if you don't realize it."

Kim glared at me. "I'm going to straighten this out right now."

I didn't like the edge to her voice, and I couldn't stop her as she stomped away.

"Oh, well," I thought, "some good will come out of this. I just have a feeling."

That evening, I finished my homework early and was already sitting next to my father when the L. A. Thunderbirds came on the television. Even Laly sat with us on that worn old couch. She had heard that there would be a grudge match before the roller skating game began.

The announcer was always the same man that announced the wrestling and boxing matches. He was an old guy who always wore a black suit and tie, which added a touch of class to each event that he announced. He just had a way of making you want to pay attention without getting too hysterical. His voice, posture, and mannerisms made him the Walter Cronkite of televised sports.

To my father, all he needed to be the very picture of masculine authority was a sombrero. "For a gringo, he's not bad!"

The two female skaters glared at each other as the announcer briefly introduced the grudge match. "Ladieeeees and gentlemennn! We will begin the evening with a special treat for you. On my left, Raquel "Rocky" Sánchez of the visiting team. On the right, proudly wearing the uniform of the league champions, the one and only Darlene "Killer" Martin. Ladies, remember the rules! Get ready, get set, GO!"

We cheered for little Raquel and booed every time that the other woman elbowed her or tried to trip her. The people watching the event live were cheering loudly for her, too. "Watch that," our father would say, pointing every time the cameras swung over to the audience. "You can always tell who is going to win by listening to the cheers."

The next day, between first and second period, Wanita and Kim both got a hold of me in the restroom. "I guess you two are talking to each other now. That's good, isn't it?" Seeing that they weren't smiling at me, I put my books down next to the wall. "What's going on?"

First, Wanita started to point her finger at me and babble hysterically. "How could you? I thought you were my friend!" She wanted to say more than that, but the angry tears were making her mascara run, so she reached for the paper towel dispenser.

Then, Kim approached me, shaking one fist in front of my face. "I should have known you would do something like this. You took an innocent joke and turned it into nasty rumors. You... you're nothing but a... Well, you didn't act like Wanita's friend and you certainly aren't acting like mine, either! You were trying to turn her against me!"

Wanita was hugging her notebook to her chest and glaring angrily at me. "How could you? This is going to get back to him, and then he'll... well, then he'll never like me!"

Kim threw a book at me and missed. "You like to get people into trouble, don't you? Don't you? Why can't you people learn to just let people be themselves? Huh?"

You people?

I was frozen in the corner. They were two. I was one. No cheering section for me. I started to talk fast, letting the words in my throat come out, hoping that something would make sense to them. They were my friends! Why would they turn on me like this? How many times had we eaten lunch in the cafeteria together?

You people?

I thought I heard some voices outside, but I was too busy trying to talk my way out of the corner. Wanita was beginning to head for the door, but Kim seemed to be high on adrenaline. Besides, I was in the corner and she wasn't. She kept tossing books at me, and I kept ducking.

A moment later, Wanita had run out of the restroom and Kim was right in front of me. I didn't want to fight, and I didn't want to turn the other cheek, but I had to do something. My heart began to beat faster and faster. What could I do without getting suspended? What could I do that wouldn't make me suffer any more than I was suffering right now?

I couldn't have been that wrong about our friendship. I was positive that it had really happened. It couldn't have been my imagination. Deep down, they must still be my friends, but still...

You people?

What would Carmen or Marilú or one of the Figueroa girls do in my situation? I longed for the comforting blanket of friendship, the sense that there was going to be someone on the other end of the telephone line, that there would be somebody saving me a place at the lunch table, that there would always be someone to pat me on the back for helping them. No cheering in my corner today!

When Kim swung at my face to slap me, I grabbed her wrist and squeezed with all of my might. Surprised, she gasped in pain. "People like you are so stupid. Let go of me!"

I smiled sarcastically. "People like me? You're nothing but a … a gringa!"

She seemed caught between confusion and rage. "You call me a green American? What's that supposed to mean? Is that what you said? Did you call me a green American? You better not be talking Spanish to me!"

She wasn't supposed to get confused. She was supposed to make me feel triumphant by recognizing the insult. She was supposed to stop saying "you people" and start being my friend once more. My brief smile of victory withered.

Gringo this, gringo that. Mom used it to refer to people who would dress their toddler in nothing but a disposable diaper on hot days or those who only went to church on Christmas and Easter Sunday. Dad used it to describe anybody who believed in coffee breaks and could not speak God's language, Spanish. Tío Basilio who lived two blocks away on Avenida Benito Juárez, well, he used it as a cuss word, and so did many other relatives for various reasons. In our house, however, gringo meant someone who was not fortunate enough to have been born into our culture.

My dad's boss, Mr. Miller, had learned a lot about people as a colonel in World War II. He believed in my dad and trusted us 100%. Because the trust was mutual, Mom and Dad would *never* allow us to actually address people in that manner. The word *gringo* was forbidden outside of our four walls. I had broken a taboo.

Shortly thereafter, I was in the principal's office, sitting in a dark brown chair that was covered with little scratch marks. Some of them were names that had been carved into the arms. "Johnny Rincón was here" and "I love Franky Archuleta" were the first ones that I noticed. Some marks seemed to have been made as the convict du jour dug his/her nails into the wooden arms. What had ever happened to those that sat there before me?

I couldn't help staring at his phone and nervously fidgeting with the papers in my notebook. In my head, I was chanting the same words over and over: "Please don't call my parents. Please don't call my parents."

Because I was desperately trying to avoid tears, I didn't have the energy to ask why the other two girls weren't there as well. I was more than curious. Would their parents scold them for getting into a fight? Would it even be a topic of discussion over whatever meatloaf and potatoes they had for dinner? Somehow, I doubted that. They got to run barefoot in the summertime.

I could only hear my own breathing and the slight squeek whenever I moved in the chair. The whole world was turning without me. Kids were walking down the corridors to so many other destinations, but I heard no other footsteps. I was in the principal's office, and I couldn't even hear any typing or stapling or phones ringing. I was alone in that black hole.

What would happen to me? I took a deep breath and examined my options. There would almost surely be a rosary prayed that night. Buzz, buzz, buzz, our father forgive us our trespasses, amen. I would most likely be put on restriction for the rest of the month. That meant staying indoors, no television, no radio, and getting up early on weekends. Buzz, buzz, buzz, hail Mary, full of grace, amen. I knew that I could forget about any allowance or any pan dulce, too. Buzz, buzz, buzz, give us this day our daily bread, amen.

There were many things that I wanted to be first at, and being suspended was not one of them.

I became even more depressed. It was taking all of my self control to hold my notebook in my lap and keep from groveling hysterically.

About twenty minutes later, I noticed that the principal had entered his office and was now standing in front of me, leaning against his desk, his arms crossed in front of his chest. "Look at me, young lady."

I looked up, my lips a thin line of nervous energy and fear.

"I hear that you were scuffling with two other girls."

There was a knot in my throat. I couldn't get the words out.

He cleared his throat and frowned. "Now, you've got to tell me why you were fighting, unless you want to see a lot more of me this year. I have a way of giving certain people a lot of attention, if you know what I mean."

I gasped. "No! I mean, I wasn't fighting. Not really."

"Well, witnesses say that you had grabbed one girl by the arm."

Digging a nail into the arm of the dark brown chair, I swallowed the saliva that had accumulated in my mouth and got up the nerve to speak more. "She was going to hit me."

There we were, the two of us. The principal with his long legs and shiny brown Stacey Adams shoes, leaning against the desk like a district attorney, and little old me, trying not to cringe in the dark brown chair that whispered "Johnny Rincón was here". I wondered where Johnny was now.

"Tell me more."

A couple of minutes later, the ordeal was over. The principal was running a big hand through his thinning blonde hair and leading me out of his office with the other one as he recited the words he must have used on countless other students: "I will pretend that this never happened as long as you never end up here again because yadda yadda yadda, and remember, no name calling yadda yadda yadda..."

So that was it. First offense. No consequences.

How can that be? Everything has a consequence. Even doing nothing has consequences. I wanted a little blood to be spilled! Not mine, of course.

It had felt so good to just let go. I had felt tall and powerful, like I could snap a pine cone off of the tallest branch of our tree, but the high disappeared like smoke on a windy day. I had stooped to using a disgusting word. Me! I had always considered myself above cheap theatrics.

I had received my lecture, but why just me? Because I had stooped to vulgar name calling? What about ... what if...

No punishment. Just don't do it again.

I walked by the railroad tracks, kicking stones and occasionally balancing myself on the rails. They were rusty on the sides, but smooth in the middle, where the weight of the trains would press down and rub against the metal. That was the job of a railroad track. It was to lead the train in the chosen direction and provide a reliable surface for iron wheels to roll on.

What kind of people really rode the train? People like me or "green Americans"? I was too emotionally drained to care. My eyes were getting blurry and I wished to the Virgen de Guadalupe that they be dry before I got home.

My footsteps quickened the closer I got to the house. I could see the guava bushes and cactus plants in the back yard and the wavy outline of the carob tree, rustling a "hello" to me with the help of the afternoon breeze. I could even see the pointy top of the pine tree. The distant sound of Radio Ranchito reached my ears. I didn't snap my fingers to it like I did when listening to Motown on KCBQ, but it seemed like just the right kind of music to come home to, especially on a day like today.

Did the people who rode the train even know what cilantro and homemade salsa tasted like on a fresh, hot tortilla? Maybe someday the train would stop and the people would all get down and come into our kitchen. Maybe they would turn up their noses at our menudo. "Oh, is this what you people eat? The part of a cow that we throw away?" I would be tempted to say something clever like, "Well, it's not gourmet food like a hot dog or bologna. Which part of the pig does that meat come from?" Then I would tilt my head and laugh confidently, like Ida Lupino or Rita Moreno in the movies.

Back in the nooks and crannies of my brain, tucked neatly below the instinct for food and shelter, was the craving for normal friends who would eat lunch with me and laugh at my jokes and appreciate me, even if only a little bit. I wanted my greatness to be recognized by people outside of my family and my barrio, but I didn't feel so great right now. Not at all. I was torn between wanting perfect friends and admitting that I could not say the same about myself.

Where was my guardian angel when I needed her? Probably in Saint Francis church, lighting another candle for me. A lot that helped today! I wanted to rewind the day back to the moment before I was tricked into falling from grace. I could at least have saved some of my self-respect if only I hadn't gotten in the gutter with that Wanita. Woulda, coulda, shoulda. It made my eyeballs sting just to think of it.

I didn't want any of these people, those people, or little green Americans to keep me in that black hole forever. I knew there must be a way out.

Left, right, left, right… I was almost there.

Last Thoughts:

If you visit Vista today, you won't see the footsteps of the children that grew up and moved on; some grew up to make some very bad decisions, and they are no longer with us. You won't hear the old taunts and jumping rope rhymes; each generation invents new ones. You will, however, see the carob tree and the guava bushes in the back yard of that little house. You will also see the railroad tracks. If you look to where the sun also rises, you will see the same far-away palm trees and hills that I would often stare at, wondering who lived over there and what they were like.

Over thirty years ago, the local elementary school was called Santa Fe Elementary School. Now, it is called the Vista Academy for Creative and Performing Arts. Vista High School, where my best friend Rosa and I gossiped and plotted in the hallways between classes, was rebuilt at a different location in the early seventies.

Mom used to tell us our family history in story form as she ironed Dad's shirts. My little brother, Payo, and I would listen attentively as we folded and put away the clothes we had just harvested from the clothesline. We would beg her for more and more stories as we did our chores. I suppose that Mom sometimes had ulterior motives for keeping us within her reach and busy, but I don't care about that.

Stories of our past give us perspective. Something came before and there will always be something coming after. If you choose to remember where you've been, it's easier to point yourself in the direction that you want to go.

Until we meet again, I bid you, "Hasta la vista." Thank you, dear reader.

Payo, Laly, and Friends

Cousin Tita and Me

Pancho and Payo

About the Author

Marta A. Lomelí has over twenty-five years of teaching experience, over ten years in the martial arts, and years of community involvement: youth mentoring programs, police community relations support, and precinct walking.

Beginning with her college years, she was well-known for her original cartoons, many of which were published in college newspapers. She has had poetry published, as well as many articles on personal safety and self-defense for women and children.

A few years ago, she achieved the rank of second degree black belt in Chinese Shao-lin Kempo, an ancient form of martial arts. She managed to reach this goal even though she was a single mother for a number of years.

She has discovered other wild ways to enjoy life, such as skydiving, public speaking, and painting.

Made in the USA
Las Vegas, NV
01 February 2022

42819449R00135